Dedication

To the community leaders in Albany
who took the time to mentor students
for my course on social and community informatics.
And to family,
for ongoing interest and support.

–Tom Mackey

To the UNL instructors at the University at Albany
for their camaraderie, innovation, and commitment.
And to John,
husband and teacher extraordinaire.

–Trudi Jacobson

Contents

List of Figures and Appendices

FIGURES

APPENDICES

Foreword

Librarians and technology—as *Using Technology to Teach Information Literacy* illustrates so well—are inextricably linked. We buy or license online research tools and materials along with printed books and periodicals, microform, videos, CDs, manuscripts, and much more, and we reach out to meet our users where they are, utilizing an ever-growing array of technologies. We list and categorize all of our research tools and materials in online catalogs, which themselves are freely available remotely to anyone with an Internet connection. We help our users discover that there is an "invisible Web" that includes both research tools and items they may not be able to find, nor fully access for free through the "visible Web." Then we help them learn how to evaluate and select appropriate research tools for their information needs, how to use them effectively, how to select and access useful items they identify through these tools, and how to use information responsibly.

Although we provide free access to library catalogs, and pay for licenses and access to many other valuable research tools, librarians have little control or influence over the look, the feel, the operation, and the political decision making regarding these resources (Wilder, 2005; Grassian, 2005). Instead, librarians struggle to keep abreast of a vast array of interfaces, often changed at will by vendors and frequently with help that does not meet the needs of many users. As a result, in order to help their users who struggle with selecting among and utilizing these research resources, librarians teach effective use in myriad ways, including through synchronous group instruction, online tutorials and point-of-use help guides, and through reference increasingly embedded or available where the users are, in Facebook, in virtual worlds like Second Life, and through text messaging. Added to this are new technologies—visual search engines, blogs, wikis, and other social networking tools. These rapidly evolving and proliferating forms of technology empower individuals and lead to a common perception that all information is free and available to all, instantaneously. Participatory social networking tools provide powerful and empowering opportunities for individuals to make their voices heard and also to band together, to share, to create, and to tag and mine data collectively and collaboratively (Weinberger, 2007). The open source movement, too, rightly or wrongly, has contributed to the notion of the goodness and correctness of mass opinion and mass collaboration (Tapscott and Williams, 2006).

As we see in *Using Technology to Teach Information Literacy*, many librarians enjoy learning new technologies like these and utilizing them to help their learners become more powerful information researchers. These teams of librarians, faculty, and technologists are enthusiastic risk-takers and yet judicious about technology use, recognizing its potential for engaging learners and furthering pedagogical aims. For instance, Mackey and McLaughlin assign a holistic service learning/information literacy project, grounding students in the real world and the need to be information literate for a lifetime. Clobridge and Del Testa require students to create virtual World War II posters and a digital library and provide support for doing so. Briggs and Skidmore require three-student teams to take "virtual field trips" and report on them using a variety of media.

Threaded throughout this edited collection are lessons we can take away and apply to our own educational situations and circumstances. These include:

- Pretest, if at all possible, before developing expected learning outcomes, rather than making assumptions about what students do and do not know, especially regarding technology (Clobridge and Del Testa).
- Be aware of the fact that pretesting also raises consciousness among students who take the test as to what they do and do not already know. As a result they pay more attention to instruction (Clobridge and Del Testa).
- Use the technology and tools that are familiar to learners in order to help them become more powerful information researchers. Many of our learners already apply metadata—they just call it "tagging." We can point to tag "clustering" as an illustration of the need for both controlled vocabulary and tags. A typical Flickr tag cluster—nature, birds, animal, wildlife, animals, blue, specanimal—offers a useful example.
- Librarians and their collaborators/partners need lots of time to learn, to prepare for, and to teach using new technologies.
- As long as they are supported, guided, and helped to fill in the gaps, students will benefit from learning that research takes time and that they do not know as much as they thought they did about information researching (Briggs and Skidmore).
- Finding your way in the physical library is still important and needed, as illustrated by student requests for library tours and how to find books in the library. Walking tours can do both (Hillyer, Maring, and Richards).

- Some technologies can be used effectively on a small scale, but may be too expensive and time-consuming to implement on a large scale—for example, videotaping all students in a single course throughout the semester.

Finally, although this valuable book focuses on technology and teaching, we must remember and emphasize to others that librarians are much more than technology experts. We are information researching and research tool experts who use technology and collaborate with others in order to help our users learn to learn and to question—on their own. *Using Technology to Teach Information Literacy* provides ample and excellent examples of collaborative efforts among librarians, faculty, and technologists. Librarians bring much to these team efforts, including their knowledge of a wide range of information resources in many formats along with practiced skills in helping people learn to think critically about information tools and materials. Faculty bring their subject expertise, and technologists provide invaluable help by working with faculty and librarians to make technology meet pedagogical needs. These collaborations seem so natural, yet they take an incredible amount of work, including diplomatic negotiation and team effort.

We need to support and applaud these risk-takers for their daring, their enthusiasm, and their outreach efforts. They are watching and listening to their users, and they are working together to help their students and each other. Each chapter in Mackey's and Jacobson's collection documents effective and engaging collaborative uses of technology in support of pedagogy. *Using Technology to Teach Information Literacy* educates and inspires, and I commend the editors and the authors highly for their excellent contribution to the literature of information literacy instruction.

Esther Grassian
Information Literacy Librarian
UCLA College Library

REFERENCES

Grassian, Esther. 2005. "Information Literacy: Wilder Makes (Some Right, But) Many Wrong Assumptions." Available: www.ucop.edu/lauc/opinions/literacy.html. Accessed March 23, 2008.

Tapscott, Don and Anthony D. Williams. 2006. *Wikinomics: How Mass Collaboration Changes Everything.* New York: Penguin Group.

Weinberger, David. 2007. *Everything Is Miscellaneous: The Power of the New Digital Disorder.* New York: Henry Holt and Co.

Wilder, Stanley. 2005. "Information Literacy Makes All the Wrong Assumptions." *The Chronicle of Higher Education* (January): 13.

Preface

Technology is an ever-changing and integral part of higher education that faculty and librarians continue to explore in their teaching. *Using Technology to Teach Information Literacy* introduces eight distinct collaborative models for teaching information literacy with technology. As with our first book, *Information Literacy Collaborations That Work* (2007), this new volume brings theory and practice together. The models included can be applied in a range of disciplinary and interdisciplinary settings. In *Using Technology to Teach Information Literacy* we show-case the innovative work of faculty-librarian teams in Canada and the United States who use technology to support, create, assess, and redesign information literacy courses and programs. These chapters offer much more than the "uses" of technology and provide meaningful contexts for collaboration that involve pedagogical and disciplinary perspectives. Whether you are a novice or an expert, an early adopter or late bloomer, you will learn a great deal from the approaches to teaching information literacy discussed in this book.

This is a timely volume because technology has evolved from wired machines in designated rooms to a portable social network of laptops, cell phones, and personal digital assistants (PDAs). Many of our students bring these mobile devices into the classroom and demonstrate a confident familiarity with not only surfing the Web but TXTing (text messaging) and IMing (instant messaging). They know the Web as a social medium for making friends, sharing information, writing journals, creating digital images, producing videos, and exploring virtual worlds. Our students are constantly connected and have a great deal of practical experience with online culture. Some instructors, however, may feel that they are behind the learning curve rather than in front of it, which makes it difficult to know how to teach with these resources, especially for an audience of experts. But it is essential to understand our role in all of this. While our students may use these technologies every day, they may not automatically examine the deeper academic issues related to these devices, such as copyright, intellectual property, online ethics, and peer review. In addition, our students may not have fully developed the critical thinking needed to effectively question and challenge the latest technology trends. As we observe the rapid changes in technology, the need for information literacy is stronger now than it ever was.

Faculty and librarians may be faced with challenges in teaching with technology. For example, information literacy instructors may have difficulty responding to the technology needs of our students if classrooms are not fully equipped to handle this form of instruction. At the same time, schools that do provide easy access to up-to-date computing may lack the human support for learning how to use these tools. Some instructors may consider information technology a specialization that does not apply to them, or they may not have the necessary institutional support to merge information literacy with technology. In addition, information literacy efforts may be focused extensively on learning how to search library databases and Web-based catalogs, not necessarily how to produce information with podcasts, blogs, or wikis. Of course this picture continues to change, and it is the library that is often at the forefront of innovation, integrating technology into instruction and using it effectively to transform the institution. This is one of the many lessons we learned through editing this book. Faculty and librarians are finding ways to overcome institutional and infrastructure limits and are taking the lead in implementing original approaches to enhancing information literacy instruction with technology. They are also responding to the evolution of the Web as an open and interactive medium to deliver freely available resources for instruction.

INFORMATION LITERACY INSTRUCTION AND STANDARDS

The relationship between information literacy and technology is critical to life-long learning because it has become increasingly difficult to develop one set of skills without the other. This point is supported by the work of these authors and has been promoted in different ways by the associations and organizations that first articulated the need for information literacy in higher education.

The American Library Association's (ALA) *Presidential Committee on Information Literacy: Final Report* (1989) argued for the development of lifelong learning skills to address "the complexities of life in today's information and technology dependent society." This report defined an integral role for collaboration that often involved technology in which "teachers would work consistently with librarians, media resource people, and instructional designers . . . to ensure that student projects and explorations are challenging, interesting, and productive learning experiences. . . ." In a follow-up document titled *A Progress Report on Information Literacy: An Update on the American Library Association Presidential Committee on Information Literacy: Final Report* (1998) ALA committee members argued that "quality education requires not only investments in technology, but also in programs that empower people to find, evaluate, and use all information effectively" (1998). ALA recognizes that as a practice of lifelong learning, information literacy must prepare students to understand information in a variety of media contexts, which requires the meaningful use of technology to access and produce information.

The Association of College and Research Libraries' (ACRL) *Information Literacy Competency Standards for Higher Education* addresses information literacy and technology by stating that "Information literate individuals necessarily develop some technology skills" (2000, p. 3). This assertion does not go far in enough to support the use of technology for information literacy instruction and seems to diminish it as a secondary or peripheral concern. But many of the complementary skills associated with technology use are evident in the actual standards. For example, according to one of the learning outcomes defined in Standard Four of the ACRL's competency standards, an information-literate student "uses a range of information technology applications in creating the product or performance" (13). This supports a student-centered problem-solving activity that must involve the use of current technologies. According to Standard Five, "the information literate student understands many of the ethical, legal and socio-economic issues surrounding information and information technology" (14). In this example, ACRL addresses the use of information technology within a larger context that focuses on critical thinking, the ethics of information, and ultimately the production of new information. As such, these skills are situated within a complex framework that extends beyond basic computing skills.

The relationship between information literacy and technology is further addressed by the Middle States Commission on Higher Education (MSCHE) in *Characteristics of Excellence in Higher Education* (2002). MSCHE closely aligns the two skill areas in *Standard 12 for General Education* by arguing for an approach to curricular design in general education that includes "oral and written communication, scientific and quantitative reasoning, critical analysis and reasoning, technological competency, and information literacy" (37). This statement reflects a comprehensive approach to general education that promotes the key skill areas for student learning and success. In a guidebook for information literacy titled *Developing Research & Communication Skills: Guidelines for Information Literacy in the Curriculum* (2003) MSCHE emphasizes the importance of "producing new information" in writing, oral presentations, and student-centered Web, hypertext, and multimedia projects (35–36). These are just some of the examples of new media tools that provide students with the opportunity to put theory into practice through the design of their own projects and presentations.

Information literacy emerged with a necessary focus on critical thinking and lifelong learning regardless of any particular technology format. Practitioners in the field continue to apply technology in creative and innovative ways to capture the imagination of our students and to support information literacy learning objectives. This book is an effort to locate the connections between information literacy and technology through collaborative teaching among faculty and librarians. We believe the examples provided in this text will generate new ideas and encourage instructors to apply technology in appropriate ways to further advance student learning. This work extends far beyond the use of any particular software or device and explores thoughtful pedagogical models for teaching information literacy in faculty-librarian teams.

BOOK ORGANIZATION

The book is divided into three sections, Part I: The Collaborative Web, Part II: Course Management Systems, and Part III: Online Assessment. This organizing strategy is defined by three major forms of technology, but each part offers additional insights about related technologies, approaches to pedagogy, and disciplinary perspectives. We wrote section introductions for each part, describing core themes, summarizing each chapter, and providing recommendations to readers based on the lessons learned. In Part I: The Collaborative Web, the chapter authors examine the use of blogs, wikis, RSS feeds, video streaming, digital imaging, and "clicker" devices to encourage student-centered production of digital materials, promote interactivity, and personalize education. In Part II: Course Management Systems, the emphasis shifts to a specific form of Web-based technology, using standardized course management tools or designing new ones to support information literacy instruction within disciplines. In Part III: Online Assessment, two author teams close out the book with a focus on the use of technology to measure student learning outcomes through online assessment initiatives.

Part I: The Collaborative Web

The first section of the book examines the use of the Web to enhance collaboration between instructors and among students with a particular emphasis on the creation of projects and presentations with new media. Faculty-librarian teams discuss their partnerships at three different institutions, including The State University of New York (SUNY) at Albany, Carleton University in Ottawa, Ontario, and Bucknell University in Lewisburg, Pennsylvania. The authors explain how information literacy instruction is designed for discipline-specific courses in the fields of information science, psychology, and history. The chapters also address how these courses relate to general education and honors programs.

The book's first author team examines the influence of social and community informatics and Web 2.0 on the design of a new honors course at The University at Albany, SUNY. A faculty member from the Department of Information Studies collaborated with the Honors College librarian to teach students an introduction to academic research, the relevance of government documents, and the critical analysis of Web 2.0 technologies such as blogs, wikis, RSS feeds, and podcasts. Students were challenged to write collaboratively in blog and wiki environments as a way to discuss their work in the community through semester-length service learning projects. Information literacy and oral discourse were combined with service learning to advance student writing, presentation, and technology proficiencies.

In the second chapter of this section, the faculty and librarian team from Carleton University discuss their approach to teaching collaboratively as a dialogue among instructors. They address what they describe as the "systemic obstacles" to developing a collaborative pedagogy at research universities especially and how to overcome such barriers. Part of their solution was to use the collaborative Web as a medium for creating a series of information literacy streaming videos that were available to students anytime online. The Web-based tools supported the research assignment in a large psychology course and helped to personalize instruction by featuring the faculty and librarians in speaking roles.

The third chapter features a faculty-librarian team from Bucknell University who describe their project in a history course that immersed students in both analog and digital worlds. Students worked in "learning teams" to develop a digital library based on original World War II posters in the special collections of the university library. They combined information literacy and technology skills to write research papers and to create digital images of the posters. The collaborative Web provided a means to share the results of this process, which included partnerships between the instructors, among the students, and with technology and archival specialists at the institution. Through this digital project students gained a real-world experience that required them to use the same techniques of a contemporary historian.

Part II: Course Management Systems

The second section of the book examines the development and use of course management systems (CMS) to support information literacy efforts. Three faculty-librarian teams write about their teaching at the University of Waterloo–Ontario, the University of Calgary, and California State University–San Marcos. The authors describe their collaboration in support of courses in German, science, nursing, and business. They explore postmodernism, constructivism, and inquiry-based learning and present insights about integrating information literacy and technology in general education, honors courses, and senior seminar.

The first chapter in this section presents a complex look at information in a postmodern age and argues for collaborative partnerships to integrate information literacy into the curriculum. The authors describe how they redesigned an honors course in German studies at the University of Waterloo–Ontario with technology. Through this partnership the information literacy instruction was integrated into this course and enhanced by a shared interest between this faculty and librarian team to employ a new CMS. This collaboration resulted in virtual field trips, e-lectures, discussion forums, access to readings, and reader response exercises. The instructors used a "classroom flip" to shift as much material as possible to the CMS, which reframed in-class time for exercises that involved problem solving and active learning.

The "classroom flip" strategy was also used by the next faculty-librarian team to revise the information literacy curriculum at the University of Calgary. This collaboration led to a complete rethinking of information literacy instruction and of the role of librarians by transitioning from "one shot" library sessions to a blended model that featured the extensive use of a CMS. This chapter describes the design of the Workshop on the Information Search Process for Research (WISPR) by the librarians at this institution to support an inquiry-based learning approach to collaborative information literacy instruction. The constructivist methodology explored by this team created an active learning environment for students in class and online through Web-enhanced instruction that included interactive tutorials, multimedia "screencasts," and student logbooks.

The effective use of CMS is also discussed by a faculty-librarian team from California State University–San Marcos. They redesigned a preparatory course in a capstone business sequence by integrating information literacy and technology learning outcomes in a distributed format. This team developed Web-based multimedia in CMS to provide students with a cogent set of interactive learning modules. As with the other two models in this section, this faculty-librarian team also shifted much of the instruction to the CMS, using interactive features that appeal to students, such as Web-based multimedia. This approach provides students with access to materials anytime they want while supporting real-world teamwork and problem solving that prepares them for professional business settings.

Part III: Online Assessment

In the last section of the book the author teams explore the use of technology to develop information literacy assessment. Faculty and librarians discuss their partnerships at the University of Nebraska–Omaha and Suffolk County Community College in New York State. This section examines the assessment of information literacy and technology in English and English as a second language (ESL) courses. The authors demonstrate the value of information literacy assessment, as mediated by technology, in an effort to better understand student learning.

The faculty-librarian team at the University of Nebraska–Omaha determined that they needed to change their existing assessment of information literacy sessions. They wanted to shift from surveying student perceptions of the instruction to determining what students knew prior to the classes, what they knew following them, and how effective the instruction was. They decided to evaluate instruction connected to their first-year composition course, both because of the large number of students involved, but also because there was an established, faculty-supported curriculum. They developed an assessment instrument that they were able to administer using Blackboard. Faculty consultants from several departments provided guidance to librarians as the assessment was being conceptualized and developed, and collaboration with the English department was critical to the success of the project. Both the strengths and weaknesses of Blackboard as an assessment tool are considered.

The last chapter in the volume, written by a librarian and an ESL professor, examines the importance of including information literacy and technology instruction into an advanced ESL speaking and listening course. This model includes four workshops co-taught by the authors emphasizing information literacy skills, and additional technology workshops offered by the professor. The students are able to show what they have learned through a challenging final project—a demographic study of a city that each student presents orally, reinforced by a digital presentation. Students are videotaped at various stages throughout the semester, a motivational strategy that enables self-, peer, and instructor assessment. A constructivist pedagogy is used in which the professor acts as facilitator and students work in groups to complete inquiry-oriented tasks. Scaffolding is provided in this student-centered environment.

USING TECHNOLOGY AT YOUR INSTITUTION

Technology is in constant flux, so we recognize that specific software, hardware, and online tools will always change. But this book provides much more than guidance on how to use technology in your teaching. Each chapter includes a literature review, institutional background, disciplinary perspective, case study model, assessment strategies, and references. This range of information is critical to understanding how a particular model worked in its own setting and why the authors addressed a situation as they did. While your institution will certainly vary from those included in this volume, there will be approaches, strategies, technologies, assignments, and other elements included in the chapters that might meet a need of yours and that can be adapted to fit the situation at hand. You might be reading about a program instituted in a discipline different from the one that concerns you and still have one or more "aha" moments. Thus, we encourage you to read even those chapters that you think might not pertain to you. Being able to identify successful technology strategies used elsewhere might provide just the extra push you need to try something locally.

The authors have all provided their e-mail addresses in case you have questions or would like to discuss something in more detail.

REFERENCES

American Library Association. 1989. "Presidential Committee on Information Literacy: Final Report." Retrieved April 2, 2008, from www.ala.org/ala/acrl/acrlpubs/white papers/presidential.cfm

American Library Association. 1998. "A Progress Report on Information Literacy: An Update on the American Library Association Presidential Committee on Information Literacy: Final Report." Retrieved April 2, 2008, from www.ala.org/ala/acrl/acrlpubs/ whitepapers/progressreport.cfm

Association of College and Research Libraries (ACRL). 2000. "Information Literacy Competency Standards for Higher Education." American Library Association Retrieved April 2, 2008 from www.ala.org/ala/acrl/acrlstandards/informationliteracy competency.cfm

Middle States Commission on Higher Education (MSCHE). 2002. *Characteristics of Excellence in Higher Education: Eligibility Requirements and Standards for Accreditation.* Philadelphia: MSCHE.

Middle States Commission on Higher Education (MSCHE). 2003. *Developing Research & Communication Skills: Guidelines for Information Literacy in the Curriculum.* Philadelphia: MSCHE.

Acknowledgments

We acknowledge the outstanding work of our faculty and librarian author teams who present innovative models for teaching information literacy with technology. We enjoyed working with you on this project and gained new insights about information literacy and technology partnerships by reading and editing your chapters.

We are grateful to Esther Grassian for writing such an exceptional Foreword. Esther was the first external reader of our book chapters, carefully reading all of these materials before writing a foreword that provided a thoughtful context for the entire project.

Further, we appreciate the support we received from the excellent team at Neal-Schuman Publishers, including Charles Harmon, Vice President and Director of Publishing; Paul Seeman, Assistant Director of Publishing; Sandy Wood, Development Editor; and Amy L. Rentner, Production Editor.

Part I

The Collaborative Web

SECTION INTRODUCTION

The Web has become such a ubiquitous technology that it is mentioned in all of the chapters in this book, but in this first section especially it is understood as a collaborative medium for writing, communication, and instructional design. The collaborative Web supports faculty and librarians working together on information literacy initiatives with such shared resources as library tutorials, discipline-specific course Web pages, or Web-based video streaming. It supports student collaboration in writing, searching, sharing sources, and in building original projects using freely available resources such as blogs, wikis, podcasts, and RSS aggregators. While the formats continue to change, instructors work in these collaborative Web-based environments to promote the core information literacy learning outcomes. For instance, when students are encouraged to develop their own information for the Web they are challenged to research and write, evaluate source types, and to think critically about the information they locate and synthesize. The production of new knowledge also involves an understanding of the ethics of information, the attribution of source materials, and the definition of copyright and intellectual property in a digital age.

Technology is often viewed as a tool to support instruction, but the collaborative Web influences the way we work and how we understand information and knowledge. For example, the original Web was different from print because it was based on hypertext linking and relationships among and within documents that print materials did not traditionally contain (except through footnotes or bibliographies). In turn, Web 2.0 is different from the first static Web because it is based on interactivity, collaboration, and how people communicate, and not just the structure or relationship of information in linked documents. As we will see in the chapters that make up this section these characteristics influence how students locate and evaluate information, exchange information, and synthesize information. This work is articulated in dialogue with other users through text, digital images, blogs, wikis, discussion boards, and multimedia. The availability of easy-to-use production software also encourages faculty and librarians to design Web-based presentations that expand content options and personalize instruction.

The collaborative Web encourages users to build knowledge in partnership with one another. As part of this process, students may grapple with the ownership of original ideas, raising questions about the authority of authorship itself. They may have some difficulty embracing the notion that writing could be more than an individual activity, that the challenges of working together offer valuable insights about the creation of information and knowledge. The partnerships in this part of the book demonstrate that the Web provides a means to explore these ideas and to produce work in tandem, beyond the traditional restrictions of time or location. The faculty-librarian teams in this section model ways to use Web-based technology in information literacy courses while maintaining a critical perspective on lessons learned and best practices.

In this first section, Thomas P. Mackey, one of the editors, examines his collaboration with Jean McLaughlin to design an honors course on social and community informatics at the State University of New York at Albany. In "Developing Blog and Wiki Communities to Link Student Research, Community Service, and Collaborative Discourse," this faculty-librarian team discusses the development of a new course that meets a general education requirement for information literacy and oral discourse. In an effort to examine the use of technology from a social and community informatics perspective, students conducted library and Web-based research on these topic areas using a set of resources developed by the librarian for this class, with a particular emphasis on such Web 2.0 technologies as blogs, wikis, RSS feeds, and podcasts. This focus on emerging technologies also informed the development of two library sessions on introducing students to research and government documents. In this course students learned about Web 2.0 tools for conducting research but also for communicating with one another and for developing Web content in weekly blogs and team-produced wikis. This work culminated in a semester-length service learning project where students made a collaborative contribution to a community organization. Their collaborative wikis became open spaces for planning, scheduling, reflecting, and presenting on the progress of their work in the community. The wikis also challenged individual assumptions about the creation and ownership of ideas in collaborative Web 2.0 environments.

The next chapter in this section, "A Conversation about Collaboration: Using Web-based Video Streaming to Integrate Information Literacy into a Research Assignment for a Large Blended Class" by Flavia Renon, Timothy A. Pychyl, and

Christopher P. Motz, from Carleton University, Ottawa, Ontario, Canada, explores the use of technology in a large lecture class in psychology. The authors provide individual and collaborative narratives from the perspectives of a librarian and two faculty members to examine the pedagogical issues involved in teaching information literacy with technology. The central assignment in this course required students to identify an article in a popular information source about personality and then connect this issue to scholarly research examined in a peer-reviewed journal. As part of the information literacy and technology support provided by the instructors, a course Web site was developed that included instructions, assignment templates, problem-solving tips, presentations, a discussion board, and streaming videos. All of these resources were developed through instructor collaboration. The videos featured the entire faculty-librarian team providing personalized instructions for students in support of the course content and based on sound pedagogical theory. Through this experience the instructors found that "just-in-time capture and delivery of course content is more appropriate than expensively produced video segments that are only renewed periodically." The availability of video streaming technology extended the collaboration of this team to a 24/7 Web environment in support of the information literacy learning outcomes.

The third chapter, "The World War II Poster Project: Building a Digital Library through Information Literacy Partnerships" by Abby Clobridge and David Del Testa from Bucknell University in Lewisburg, Pennsylvania, describes the use of technology to support a 100-level history course that incorporates an information literacy component. This faculty-librarian team expanded on traditional methods of instruction and "incorporated a broad range of information and digital image technologies in their approaches to reach students and broaden the scope of skills the unit encompassed." While the previous chapter focused on the use of the collaborative Web by instructors to enhance course content, this chapter also involved student-centered production. In this class, students played an active role and "cataloged, digitized, analyzed, and reported on an original World War II–era poster from the library's Special Collections department." Through this process students integrated historical research methods with practical lessons on how to create digital images with digital cameras and digital imaging software. This project provided a real-world experience for students to play an active role of a contemporary historian applying some of the professional tools of the field. They gained insights about source materials through the analysis of original World War II posters in the library collection and learned how to carefully manage and document these materials for a digital library.

Based on these chapters we make the following recommendations for using the collaborative Web in information literacy courses:

- Encourage your institution to support emerging Web 2.0 technologies such as blogs, wikis, and RSS feeds, but also consider freely available resources found online.
- Research contemporary trends to select the appropriate Web technologies to meet the needs of a current course, to reinvent an existing class, or to develop a new one.
- Avoid a one-size-fits-all approach to the Web and use a range of collaborative formats to deliver instruction, such as in-class teamwork, service learning, and in-class "clicker" devices to encourage student feedback.
- Build a three-part strategy into your course planning, one that involves the use of the Web to enhance faculty-library partnerships, a second to encourage teamwork among students, and a third to maximize collaboration among students, faculty, and librarians.
- Develop assignments with the Web that challenge students to think critically about existing sources and to be creative in the design of their own materials.
- Encourage students to solve problems, to interact, and to build something new in partnership with their peers.
- Contrast experiences in virtual worlds with the real world through community service, library research, popular culture, or archival documents.

These first three chapters illustrate the creative potential of the collaborative Web, but this work was also driven by partnerships with members of the community, information technology support specialists, librarians, and archivists. While the disciplines in this section included information science, psychology, and history, these collaborative models could be applied in other fields as well.

Chapter 1

Developing Blog and Wiki Communities to Link Student Research, Community Service, and Collaborative Discourse

Thomas P. Mackey and Jean McLaughlin

INTRODUCTION

While collaboration between faculty and librarians was already embedded in the curriculum at the State University of New York (SUNY) at Albany, primarily through a general education requirement for information literacy, a new course in social and community informatics (IST250H) expanded these partnerships ("Information Literacy Courses," 2007–2008). This course was developed by a faculty member in the Department of Information Studies specifically for a recently established undergraduate Honors College at the university and focused on the social dimension of emergent technologies such as blogs, wikis, RSS, and podcasts ("Undergraduate Bulletin 2007–2008," 2008). IST250H provided a novel context for collaboration and resulted in the development of Web-based resources for the Honors College and entire university community. It also created an impetus for discussions between faculty and librarians about how to effectively support students in the critical evaluation of Web 2.0 technologies. These conversations led to newly designed in-class sessions on how to conduct research with these resources, including how to evaluate information from blogs and wikis, how to access and retrieve reliable RSS feeds and podcasts, and how to better understand online access to government information.

Since this course examined social and community informatics, collaboration extended to the local community as students completed their 30-hour service

learning requirement. This created a small network of four community organizations in Albany, New York, with committed leaders willing to attend class
sessions and supervise and mentor students as they completed their projects. In
addition, because this class used freely available Web-based tools for creating
blogs, wikis, and RSS feeds, it also helped to define the need on campus for
resources that extended beyond the traditional e-mail, UNIX, and WebCT. This
led to the first-ever university-wide pilot programs for blog and wiki resources,
developed and supported by the university's Information Technology Services
(ITS). Although this course did not benefit directly from the pilot programs that
followed, it was one of the motivators for this new level of support. The Honors
College librarian used the subsequent wiki pilot as a tool to create a supplementary
resource list for information literacy topics and as a student forum for sharing
details describing databases.

This chapter will examine these collaborations, with a particular emphasis on
the faculty and librarian partnership, which was pivotal to all other aspects of the
course, including the information literacy and technology learning outcomes.
Students were challenged in this course to develop information literacy skills for
individual and collaborative research and writing assignments that included a
research paper, reader responses, and online journals using the Web. They studied
social and community informatics and put theory into practice through their
work in the community and in their exploration of ideas in student-centered
blogs and collaborative wikis. Faculty, librarians, and our community partners
were challenged as well to provide a meaningful learning environment for
these explorations. This involved an exchange of ideas about course content and
delivery, library resources and instruction, technology infrastructure and support,
and the distinct missions and needs of community organizations.

LITERATURE REVIEW

Considering the focus of this course on social and community informatics, we
will review some of the key literature in this area that guided the conceptual
emphasis of the class as well as the pedagogy and the uses of social technology.
We will also explore Web 2.0 as an interactive and participatory technology and
discuss the 2.0 paradigm as a central theme in this course. Information literacy
and informatics are not often associated in the literature, but we believe these
are necessary connections to make in this discussion of our course collaboration.

Social and Community Informatics

According to Rob Kling (1999), social informatics is "the interdisciplinary
study of the design, uses and consequences of information technologies that
takes into account their interaction with institutional and cultural contexts."

This involves ongoing critical inquiry that considers the social aspects of information, communication, and technology (ICT). Social informatics extends far beyond a consumer-oriented approach to technology development and use. Instead, it focuses on research methodologies that raise critical questions about our experiences with these technologies. This is an important consideration when working with student authors who may be most familiar with ICTs as consumers of information in these environments. That is, students engage with social computing through such sites as MySpace and Facebook, but this does not necessarily mean that they critically evaluate these resources beyond their own experience. According to Kling, Rosenbaum, and Sawyer (2005), "ICT-oriented students need to learn Social Informatics analysis techniques in order to increase the likelihood that ICT-based systems will be used and be valued" (86). This approach envisions the student as more than a consumer of any given technology and instead prepares them to ask critical questions that consider the larger social contexts. Critical thinking from a social informatics standpoint involves "developing in students the ability to examine ICTs from perspectives that do not automatically and often implicitly adopt the goals and beliefs of the groups that commission, design, or implement specific ICTs" (Kling, Rosenbaum, and Sawyer, 2005: 96). The challenge then is to create a learning environment for students to think about technology in new ways, in relation to social considerations, while expanding their abilities as critical thinkers.

Alex Halavais (2005) argues that "social change is not merely a secondary effect, but also the reason many new technologies are developed and adopted." This point is especially relevant in an age of social computing that is driven by the speed of innovation as well as the emergence of diverse online communities that develop relationships in such Web-based environments as MySpace, Facebook, Blogger, and Second Life. Halavais (2005) argues that one of the challenges faced by social informatics as a field is that many of the researchers in this area are not actively engaged in the forms of social computing they critique. He states that "outside of a few graduate students and an even smaller number of faculty, researchers in the area do not maintain weblogs or even home pages where their work can be easily accessed." Although researchers do not need to experience a particular technology to analyze it, the collaborative potential of social computing shifts our understanding of how we produce knowledge from an individual activity to a shared practice. As such it is valuable to bridge the gap between theory and practice to gain critical insights about the impacts of social technology on learning.

Community informatics relates to the larger field of social informatics but focuses specifically on the design and use of ICTs within community settings. According to the *Journal of Community Informatics* (2008), the term is best defined as "the study and the practice of enabling communities with Information and Communications Technologies (ICTs)." Michael Gurstein (2003) argues that "a Community Informatics approach, which firmly situates the design and implementation of ICT systems in their community and social context thus most usefully provides a conceptual and methodological foundation for designing for effective use." Gurstein asserts that the "effective use" of a community informatics perspective is a necessary replacement for the "digital divide" rhetoric that he believes focuses too narrowly on "access" issues. Mark Warshauer uses a social and community informatics perspective to challenge the notion that access alone will solve the digital divide. He argues that community informatics "considers unique aspects of the particular culture into which technology is placed, so that communities can most effectively use that technology to achieve social, economic, political or cultural goals" (Warshauer, 2003: 3). This approach confirms that we must understand how and why community organizations use technology to achieve goals rather than rely on the false assumption that access to these technologies alone would automatically create change.

Web 2.0

According to Tim O'Reilly (2005), Web 2.0 is defined by many of the innovations we know from today's online environment, such as Google, Flickr, Wikipedia, RSS, and blogging. At the same time this idea extends beyond any specific technical consideration and encompasses the way people use the Web as an interactive and participatory interface. O'Reilly emphasizes the issues surrounding the role of the user and how to most effectively utilize the "collective intelligence" of Web 2.0. His focus is on collaboration and how to maximize the benefits of this approach, in business contexts especially, and through user-centered and scalable design. Prior to any discussion of Web 2.0, Ben Shneiderman (2002) argued that "Renaissance 2.0" described a new era that "would emphasize collaborations that enrich us with fresh perspectives and foster partnerships that enable us to create more freely" (2). Schneiderman's examination of a new era in social computing is based on the "personal needs" of users rather than on the technological innovation of the machines, although there is a relationship between the design of any system and user experience (58–60). His discussion of the "new computing," with its emphasis on the collaborative and empowering potential of technology, is consistent with the way we understand Web 2.0. Michael Wesch (2008) challenges old assumptions about teaching and learning in today's media rich environment. He defines learning itself as a process of creating significance and he raises questions about how we can effectively teach students to make meaningful connections with new media. With his own classroom teaching, he strives to "create a learning environment that values and leverages the learners themselves." Through the appropriate use of technology the classroom expands beyond a room and into the world at large, creating significant student engagement and effective learning outcomes.

Library 2.0 and Hypertext

A "2.0" shift is taking place in libraries through "Library 2.0," which, according to Michael E. Casey and Laura C. Savastinuk (2006), "gives library users a participatory role in the services libraries offer and the way they are used." In this new model the user is at the center of activity, not only as a patron seeking access to information, but as an active collaborator, working with librarians to build a participatory and open environment. Explorations of this flexible use of library tools include user contribution of nontypical content. Library resource or book reviews and tagging individual entries are user-generated additions to the library catalog. PennTags, which was developed by librarians at the University of Pennsylvania, is a social bookmarking tool. It enables users to locate, organize, and share favorite online resources. According to the University of Pennsylvania's library Web page, users can tag and "collect and maintain URLs, links to journal articles, and records in Franklin, our online catalog and VCat, our online video catalog" (University of Pennsylvania, 2008). Karen Coombs, Head of Libraries Web Services Department, University of Houston, notes that "because of proprietary systems, fully realizing the dream of a Web 2.0 site is daunting" (Coombs, 2007). Even so, libraries can gradually add user input features, achieving a higher level of interactivity for the library user and setting the stage for future offerings. Designing functionality such as this is one way of marketing library resources and increasing the appeal of what appears to be a static tool. It merges the capability of the Web-based library catalog more intimately with its network of users. With the user population's high interest in using free Web search tools such as Google, information literacy efforts can draw on the exchange of authority and perspective inherent to the librarian-user dialogue in Library 2.0.

Michael Stephens and Maria Collins (2007) argue that "the hyperlinked library is simply the Read/Write library, where conversations, connections, and community are born" (p. 256). They define Library 2.0 tools as blogs, wikis, RSS, and podcasting, but also argue that this approach is about more than the technology and involves *conversations, community and participation, experience,* and *sharing* (Stephens and Collins, 2007: 253–255). Their reference to hypertext is relevant in this context since so much of hypertext theory in the 1990s explored the kinds of role reversals we are seeing in collaborative Web environments. George P. Landow (1992), for example, described a set of convergences in the relationships between author and audience, self and community, as well as teacher and student. Hypertext systems allowed for a rethinking of traditional barriers because the technology enabled dual and multiple forms of creating, working, reading, and writing based on collaborative processes that were inherently different from print.

Tim Berners-Lee (2000) was aware of the collaborative and social aspects of hypertext when he envisioned the ultimate hypertext system, the World Wide Web, "as an intimate collaborative medium" (57). He was also perceptive about the challenges faced in these shared environments because "collaboration required much more of a social change in how people worked" (Berners-Lee, 2000: 57). The dual function of early browsers as both readers and editors enabled the sharing and production of information and knowledge on a vast scale. This convergence of reader/writer and viewer/producer also created a nascent framework for Web 2.0, which further extends the capability of users to participate and produce online.

2.0 PARADIGM

Within a 2.0 paradigm, which has become the version number for anything that resembles a new technology, educational initiative, or online partnership, we see the intersection of user-centered design, information, and collaboration. The potential for these technologies is clear, but a social informatics approach looks beyond the buzzwords and optimistic outlook of these formats and raises critical questions about how people work in virtual environments to achieve their goals. According to Rob Kling (1999), "social informatics researchers are specially interested in developing reliable knowledge about information technology and social change, based on systematic empirical research, to inform both public policy debates and professional practice." This is a critical perspective for understanding how information is accessed and produced within social contexts. It also supports the development of a course that raises questions about Web 2.0 and its impact on social and community settings. In an article that specifically examines information literacy from a social informatics perspective, Kimmo Tuominen, Reijo Savolainen, and Sanna Talja (2005) argue, "Information literacy is embedded in the activities of particular groups and communities; that is, information skills evolve in disciplinary and other contexts, and they are practiced by communities using appropriate technologies" (341). This approach to information and technology literacy requires a pedagogical response that goes beyond isolated skills development and instead works toward a comprehensive view of information within specific communities and social practices (Tuominen, Savolainen, and Sanna Talja, 2005: 341).

The relationships we have introduced among information literacy, informatics, and Web 2.0 have not yet been fully developed in the literature as a comprehensive area of study. We explore these connections based on common objectives for critical thinking and the effective use of emerging Web-based ICTs. These associations influenced the development of our information literacy course on social and community informatics and informed the collaborations between faculty and librarians, among student teams, and between student and community partners. Social informatics provided the conceptual framework for this course that encouraged students to be effective researchers actively engaged in critical inquiry. Community informatics allowed students to examine technology as active participants in the community and not just consumers or users of ICTs. This course challenged students to produce original digital information for their own weekly assignments and as part of their final service learning projects.

THE HONORS COLLEGE

Strategic planning in 2003, originating in the College of Arts and Sciences, prompted a focus on the recruitment, retention, and advancement of undergraduate students. The number one planning recommendation was to form an Honors College that would provide "a small college experience" for students by "fostering and encouraging the creation of closely knit cohorts of like-minded, motivated students" ("Our History," 2008). Contributing to the university's goal of attracting some especially academically talented students to university programs, the University at Albany Honors College plays a role in establishing a concrete honors path from first year to the honors program in a student's major. The students benefit from the community established within a research university by actively participating in intellectual, cultural, and social activities. These developing scholars participate in courses with demanding critical thinking, research, and writing components. Active learning techniques embrace discussions, field experiences, debates, simulations, and small group projects. Students are challenged to absorb a body of knowledge as well as contribute to the discourse of the discipline.

Housed in the Office of Undergraduate Studies and administered by the Associate Vice Provost and Director of the Honors College with the Honors College Governing Board, this new program welcomed the first students in fall 2006. Initial enrollment was 120 freshman, 35 sophomores, and 10 juniors. Forty additional students joined after completing their first or second semester.

The target enrollment is 150 students in each graduating class, with an ultimate goal of 600 students in the college. The Honors College invites Presidential Scholars and Douglass Scholars to become students in the college as they are admitted to the university. These scholars are students with distinguished high school records; Frederick Scholars, additionally, demonstrate the potential to contribute to the diversity of the university. Course offerings, available only to Honors College students, span the disciplines offered at the university and are taught by professors who have a record of excellence in undergraduate education. Courses include one of the following: in-depth study of subject matter, a research or creative component, or a service learning component. In the first two years, students explore a wide range of subjects, moving into the honors program in their major during their second two years. Students are required to take six honors courses prior to their junior year. Working with a mentor, seniors complete a research thesis or creative project that enables them to contribute to knowledge in their discipline. In addition to the resources available at the University Libraries for their course and thesis research, The New York State Library and Archives is local and provides easy access to state historical and primary source documents of great value to scholars.

Collaborating with faculty teaching Honors College courses, including those that fulfill general education information literacy requirements, the Honors College librarian provides instructional support for teaching basic research skills. Research assignments may precede the students' acquisition of appropriate information literacy skills through required coursework. It is important for the librarian to work closely with faculty to understand skill development needs and upcoming assignments. Instructional support is available, although not all Honors College courses may have a research component nor may all faculty members teaching in the program take advantage of it. In any case, rigorous research assignments demand that Honors College students quickly acquire those skills that the general student population will develop in upper division coursework.

DISCIPLINARY PERSPECTIVES

This course was taught from an information science perspective through the Department of Information Studies at the University at Albany.

Information Science

Information studies was the ideal departmental home for a new course in social and community informatics for several reasons. First, social informatics is an interdisciplinary field of study that is grounded in the information, technology, and social issues examined in the fields of information and computer science. These intersections were consistent with some of the ideas that were being explored at the time in the undergraduate major in the Department of Information Studies. Specifically, an upper-level course titled "The Information Environment" (IST301X) addressed information theory, the digital divide, social and community informatics, human-computer interaction (HCI), Web usability, Web accessibility, and copyright in a digital age. This focus on information access and production through the Web provided an effective intellectual grounding for the new Honors course on social informatics. Second, links between information literacy and technology were already established in the information studies program because students were challenged to combine research and Web literacy through the development of their own Web-based projects in IST301X (Mackey and Ho, 2005). This class as well as a graduate-level version also incorporated student-centered blogs and collaborative wiki assignments into the learning objectives (Mackey, 2007). Third, this same course provided an effective model for the Honors class because it had already established collaborative partnerships between a faculty member from Information Studies and librarians at the University Libraries (Mackey and Jacobson, 2004; Mackey, Jacobson, and Bernnard, 2007). While IST301X was a fairly large class (from 70 to 120 students per semester), IST250H was a much smaller class (13 students), which allowed for the examination of information science issues with nonmajors in a more intimate environment than the larger course provided.

The interdisciplinary nature of the Honors College and the institutional incentives for departments to get involved in this high profile initiative were also factors that encouraged the involvement of information studies. The university provided departments with funds to cover the course release for one faculty member who would teach in the Honors College. This encouraged full-time faculty to teach in the program while compensating departments for the cost of hiring instructors to cover the discipline-specific course usually taught by the faculty member. It also encouraged the contribution of multiple disciplinary perspectives throughout the campus and an ever-changing curriculum. As a result of this process, which included a university-wide call for proposals, the social informatics course was initiated by a faculty member from the Department of Information Studies within a newly formed College of Computing and Information (CCI).

General Education: Social Sciences, Information Literacy, and Oral Discourse

IST250H fulfilled three general education requirements at the University at Albany: social sciences, information literacy, and oral discourse ("Learning Objectives for Oral Discourse," 2008). The learning outcomes for social sciences were supported throughout the course in the critical examination of course readings, the exploration of social informatics research methods, and the exploration of social issues related to the design and use of Web-based ICTs. This approach provided the intellectual foundation of the course and helped to shape the information literacy and oral discourse requirements. Since this was an Honors class, but not a higher level course, the learning outcomes for information literacy were focused on both the early development of skills and a higher level of integrating these proficiencies and synthesizing results from sources. Students were challenged to find, evaluate, and integrate sources of information and to understand the ethical issues related to copyright, intellectual property, and documenting sources. They were also expected to differentiate between scholarly, trade, and popular sources, as well as primary and secondary sources, and to understand the potential resource options with regard to format and audience. They gained insights about information access, retrieval, and production through their collaborations with one another and in their service learning projects. The objectives for oral discourse were met though informal and formal student presentations that required teamwork, critical reflection and evaluation, and the use of a range of technology, such as PowerPoint, digital images, Web-based multimedia, and wikis.

LIBRARY SUPPORT FOR DISCIPLINE-SPECIFIC COURSES

The faculty and librarian collaboration for this class was based on a model established at the University at Albany to support a general education requirement for information literacy. This approach provides library support and encourages collaborative opportunities between faculty and librarians for departmental information literacy courses. Students have two key options for completing this general education requirement. They can take a one-credit class offered by the University Libraries, taught by library faculty, or they can complete a discipline-specific course that integrates information literacy into the curriculum, taught by departmental faculty. The level of support provided by the library for the discipline-specific classes depends on the needs of the course and the level of collaboration defined by the faculty-librarian team. Resources provided by the library may include Web-based tutorials on a range of topics from research methods to plagiarism prevention, in-class instruction by librarians or in partnership with departmental faculty, or direct involvement in course planning and assignments.

This model is flexible enough to promote creativity between faculty and librarians based on the disciplinary perspective of the course while providing several standardized resources that could be applied and adapted in different classes. The collaborative relationship between the library and information studies was especially strong because one of the core requirements in the undergraduate major (IST301X) was envisioned from the start as an upper-level information literacy course within the new general education program. This allowed for the development of information literacy resources, such as in-class sessions and online tutorials, in partnership with faculty from the Department of Information Studies and the University Libraries. This team-oriented approach to instructional design also informed the new Honors course in social and community informatics (IST250H).

PARTNERSHIPS IN PEDAGOGY

The design of this course was informed by conversations between a faculty member from the Department of Information Studies and the faculty librarian dedicated to the Honors College. Although this was not a comprehensive team teaching experience that involved the development of the entire course, it did entail critical collaborations at key points in the class. This partnership started with a conversation about the goals of the course including ways to explore information literacy within a social and community informatics perspective. Discussions involved a detailed review of the content of each class as well as an understanding of specific assignments and resources required to complete those assignments. We exchanged ideas about the use of student-centered course blogs, RSS feeds, and collaborative wikis. At this early stage we discussed the learning objectives for information literacy and technology instruction and explored plans to develop two Web-based resources: an Honors College Web page for research and a page for new media resources such as blogs, RSS feeds, and podcasts. At this initial meeting we mapped out two information literacy sessions, to be taught at the University Library, focusing on an introduction to research methods and government documents. This collaboration continued throughout the semester by phone, via e-mail, and during class sessions as we combined our efforts to engage students in research and writing. Through in-class observation, the librarian saw that the students were engaged in course elements related to new technology. Students expressed a high interest in the community organizations and related projects. The librarian supported the course assignments through both class instruction and development of appropriate Web resources.

Introduction to Research and Government Documents

Two classes paved the way to basic library instruction and orientation to resources at a large research university. The first part of instruction provided a broad overview for starting the research process. This was an introduction to primary and secondary resources, the library catalog, reference books, subject bibliographer resources, databases, and search techniques. More detailed instruction about academic journals and related tools followed. The librarian talked about the push technology feature of RSS feeds and its help to scholars who are just beginning research. The automatic delivery of scholarly journal tables of contents provides students with access to the latest articles. *Science*, from the American Association for the Advancement of Science, has one of many sites with this journal alert feature. Since the journal contents cover a range of topics, at least some of which are meant for more general interest, this was one link included on the Web page. With an increasing number of options, students can direct information delivery from databases to e-mail or search alerts without reexecuting searches. This assumes that searches are well developed and produce appropriate results. Although using these tools is of value with many research projects, the work on a senior thesis provides an excellent opportunity to capitalize on efficient research practices.

The Government Documents Librarian presented a class on how to research federal government information as well as demonstrating the relevance of government information by bringing documents to class on topics familiar to the Honors students. The librarian cautioned students about the fluidity of government information based on changes among elected officials. Through discussion of U.S. government podcasts, the students discovered the range of materials available to them in Web 2.0 formats, from the Census Bureau to Profile America and the weekly podcasts from the White House. Information from the government in formats other than print, even with the tremendous legacy of print materials from the Government Printing Office, demonstrates that researchers can use official and authoritative material in nontraditional formats. Through all the interactions with this class, the librarians found a highly motivated group of students who could assimilate concepts quickly and move, at a rapid pace, through the information literacy topics essential to their skills as researchers.

Honors College Web Site

The Library Web page for the Honors College supported the social and community informatics course. This page listed links to blogs, RSS feeds, podcasts, and other technologies that were key components of the course. Although the students in the social and community informatics course created digital content using blogs and wikis, there was no need to provide links to instructions for using these tools. Instead, the library page provided links to locate Web 2.0 tools related to course content. A logical progression in determining appropriate links for the library page was to look for the specific format needed. It was reasonable to look for directories in these formats with academic content so that students could find appropriate coverage in a subject area. Although logical in approach, finding directories of a more academic nature was challenging. The conflicting nature of popular technology formats with academic content, at a time when sites were just beginning to provide alternative formats, required a close look at the scholarly nature of the material available.

Resources about using these technologies were common. Lists of scholarly resources in new technology formats were not. A second challenge was in meeting the interdisciplinary nature of the course. Directory categories provided subject access. As with the creation of any resource list or subject guide, the selection of appropriate links needed to follow some standard or heuristic for inclusion. Determining the most appropriate Web sites, in addition to finding a more academic or scholarly focus related to social informatics, were criteria used in the selection of appropriate links. Sites from respected organizations complemented and expanded on resources available solely by searching directories. Enabling readers to automatically receive new content, feeds provide customized information delivery. For instance, the Library of Congress, *The Chronicle of Higher Education*, the White House, and many other resources provided news feed services for news readers or aggregators. In addition, NPR, BBC, and the *New York Times* offered resources appropriate for inclusion. BlogScholar is described as an academic blogging portal and directory, a resource for academics who blog. This was one of the blog resources included.

TECHNOLOGY TOOLS: BLOGGER, BLOGLINES, AND PEANUT BUTTER WIKIS (PBWIKI.COM)

Throughout the course, students used technology as active producers of digital information to communicate and to share knowledge. They developed several individual and collaborative course assignments using free Web-based resources, including Blogger, Bloglines, and Peanut Butter Wiki (PBwiki, 2008). Blogger was founded by a small company in 1999 and then purchased by Google in 2002. This service provides easy-to-use instructions for establishing an account and several standardized templates for developing individual and collaborative blogs. Originally established in 2003, Bloglines is an aggregator for subscribing to and sharing RSS feeds (Bloglines, 2008). Bloglines also provides tools for creating blogs, but, for this course, students used it exclusively for researching and sharing sources of information in RSS formats. Peanut Butter Wiki (PBwiki) was founded in 2005 and today it hosts more than 400,000 wikis as "the world's largest provider of hosted business and educational wikis." PBwiki provides an easy to use interface for creating wikis. It offers multiple features and variable levels of service that depend on package pricing ranging from free to yearly subscription rates. In the Honors College course these tools supported the development of a field study and service learning project that required a team wiki and presentation. Students also maintained a weekly blog that incorporated the RSS feeds they subscribed to as well as resources from the library Web pages.

The blog assignment required students to post weekly responses to course readings based on directed questions from the instructor. This engaged students in the content of the course related to social and community informatics and informed our class discussions. Course readings were challenging and included a range of sources including books, scholarly journal articles, and popular sources of information. Students were expected to synthesize course readings with additional research using the search tools and resources of the Honors College library pages (Honors College Library Page, 2008; Honors College Library Resource Page, 2008). The reader response blogs allowed us to define social and community informatics and to address such issues as ICT policy, design, and educational considerations as well as the digital divide and technological determinism. Current trends in blogging, RSS, and podcasts were examined in the weekly blogs, with a particular focus on the use of these technologies in the classroom and the motivations of users for maintaining blogs. The blog postings about wikis focused on the John Seigenthaler controversy, which raised critical questions about the authenticity of information in open-editing environments (Seigenthaler, 2005). The blog was also a space for students to journal about their service learning projects and to propose topic ideas for their research paper. The Bloglines assignment required students to subscribe to relevant RSS feeds and to synthesize these resources in their blog responses. While this assignment allowed students to experience a different flow of information, based on their subscription to information sources rather than individual searches for information, the source types identified were not always relevant to the course and often focused on popular sources of information rather than scholarly. The reader response blogs, however, were effective in supporting an intellectual foundation for the class that engaged students in major themes while providing a space for them to link to resources, upload digital images, respond to one another, prepare for class discussions and presentations, and to continually reflect on readings and the experiential component of the class.

COLLABORATIVE COURSE ASSIGNMENTS

The 2.0 paradigm influenced the design of the collaborative course assignments because students were expected to interact, create, and communicate in partnership with others. The service learning project was the culminating experience in the class that was informed by a research-oriented field study assignment. Both projects used Web-based tools to plan, document, and present the objectives and observations of each team.

Field Study

As the first Honors College course to require a service learning component, it was necessary to establish another partnership on campus to involve community organizations in this endeavor. As part of this outreach, we contacted Nancy Machold, Director of the Community & Public Service Program (CPSP) in the School of Social Welfare at the University at Albany. CPSP offers students credit bearing courses in community service at "nearly 500 not-for-profit and public agencies in the Capital Region and arrange for other placements in their home communities" (Community & Public Service Program, 2008). Through conversations with the director of the program we arrived at an initial list of 21 community organizations that was eventually narrowed down to six groups and then to four specific placements, based on feedback from students:

1. Capital City Rescue Mission
2. Food Pantries for the Capital District
3. Upper Hudson Peace Action
4. Ronald McDonald House Charities of the Capital Region (Capital City Rescue Mission, 2008; Food Pantries for the Capital District, 2008; Upper Hudson Peace Action, 2008; Ronald McDonald House Charities of the Capital Region, 2008)

In the third week of the semester we invited representatives from six organizations to attend class, present their community group to the class, respond to questions from students, and define a specific need or project that would benefit from student participation. One of the six representatives dropped out of the project due to unrelated personnel issues at the organization. The remaining five were then narrowed down to four based on student input, which was provided during a subsequent class session. Students were not automatically assigned by the instructor to specific organizations but rather they made informed choices based on their analysis of the information presented.

As part of this assignment, students were required to conduct a collaborative field study and PowerPoint presentation for the community organization they planned on working with. This project required them to conduct field research about this organization, including such primary sources as personal interviews and mission statements as well as secondary sources that included newspaper articles and Web sites. This research informed a PowerPoint presentation that addressed the background, history, and mission of their organization. They were also asked to examine the population served by this nonprofit group as well as the specific services provided and how the organization fits into the larger Albany community. Students were asked to explore such internal considerations as management, staffing, funding, and the technology infrastructure.

The purpose of the field study was to provide students with sufficient background information about their organization to inform the development of their service learning project. Through their critical analysis of the community setting they developed a specific proposal that met the needs of the organization. They blogged about their experiences by posting preliminary observations about their site visits and started to plan their projects via their collaborative wikis. Students also provided updates about their projects during class sessions and used Power-Point to organize all of this information, respond to the questions, and propose the ideas for their community service project, based on their research and conversations with their community mentor. The wiki became a collaborative portal and presentation tool that linked to their blogs, digital images, Web-based information and team reflections about their community sites, and the PowerPoint slides they created to talk about their field study observations during formal presentations in class.

Service Learning Projects

As a result of the field study assignment students proposed several ambitious project ideas, defining the contribution they would make in each community setting. They continued to work on these projects throughout the semester in a transparent manner that allowed everyone in the course to follow their progress through their blogs, wikis, and in-class discussions and presentations. Some of these projects involved technology more than others, but students were well on their way to thinking about the role of technology in these environments and making a commitment to the mission of each group with their teamwork, ideas, and time.

The Capital City Rescue Mission provides services such as food, clothing, and shelter for the homeless and individuals in need in the Albany area. This organization was especially interested in a technology solution that would allow them to completely redesign their Web site to improve the usability of the site, update content and images to accurately reflect the activities of this nonprofit, enhance Web-based fund-raising, and to incorporate a blog that would allow them to easily update content on their own. The student team in charge of this initiative worked with the Capital City Rescue Mission to develop a new site using the program Dreamweaver, incorporating templates to create consistency among pages and cascading style sheets (CSS) to control the style elements. They also updated content, graphics, and digital images, and created a blog using the same blog software they used in the course, Blogger.com (Blogger, 2008). This team did more than develop a new Web site. As part of their work on this project they also worked at the organization, interacting with staff and the people who visited this location. This allowed for a deeper understanding of the role of technology in this nonprofit and the importance of using the Web to communicate with the larger Albany community. They appreciated the value of the Web site to support the organization's role as service provider in the community, to promote practical fund-raising goals, and to accurately reflect the ways they fulfill their mission. Students also gained insights about the importance of user-centered design when developing the site because they focused extensively on how the staff at this organization would continue to maintain it and how their users and potential donors would respond to their design. This team valued the experience and was recognized with a profile story about their project, featured on the University at Albany home page (Reda, 2007).

According to its mission statement, the Ronald McDonald House Charities of the Capital Region "promotes the health, development and well-being of children and their families." This is accomplished through the Ronald McDonald House in Albany, which provides "a home away from home for families of seriously ill children, and by creating and supporting programs that directly improve the lives of children and their families." The student team responsible for this project worked at this location on several initiatives that involved improving the technology infrastructure to support the children and families who depend on this resource. This work included updating previously discarded computers with standardized software, upgrading a kids computer with appropriate software and games for the intended age groups, scanning and organizing family photographs to create an onsite digital memory resource, establishing a Gmail (Google e-mail) account and blog for the organization, and making updates to the Ronald McDonald House Web site. This team also interacted with the staff, children, and families throughout the project and made astute observations that reflected the critical questions we raised in the course about technology and its uses in social contexts. For example, they discussed the strong motivations they had for addressing the technology needs of the organization based on their familiarity with the people at this nonprofit and the knowledge that these updates and changes would provide direct benefits for the children and families they met. They were also aware that their contribution would extend to the larger community through one project in particular that required them to organize video game consoles that would be distributed to children beyond the Ronald McDonald House.

The Food Pantries for the Capital District is "a coalition of forty- three food pantries working together, in a spirit of cooperation, to do together what no one of us could do alone." According to the mission statement of this organization they have a clearly defined goal "to eliminate hunger in our neighborhoods." The student team responsible for this project worked in partnership with one another and their community mentor to accomplish several goals. This initiative was not as technology focused as some of the others, which led to valuable insights from this team about the limits of technology alone to easily resolve such a serious issue as hunger. This project also challenged their expectations about the nature of this assignment as a technology support project and instead provided them with a meaningful opportunity to experience the inner workings of a community group with a clearly defined mission. For example, this team worked closely with the director to prepare an annual fund-raising auction, which is a critical outreach program for the food pantries. They also prepared for and participated in the annual St. Patrick's Day Parade in Albany, which was a high profile event that placed this organization in the community to further promote name recognition and fund-raising opportunities. In addition to this community outreach, the students contributed insights about the use of technology for promotional purposes especially through the creation of an online presence in Facebook and MySpace. This team concluded, however, that these online formats were not as effective as actual events for college students, which led to a proposal for a basketball tournament on campus to enhance student awareness of this organization and to further extend fund-raising opportunities. Although this team was not convinced that Facebook or MySpace would help get the word out about the Food Pantries, they did use technology for the production of a newsletter for this organization that would be distributed in print and via e-mail. According to this team, the clarity and immediacy of the newsletter offered more potential than the social networking sites that required time to generate interest and membership.

The Upper Hudson Peace Action "works to end wars and prevent new wars through education and public witness." This organization also seeks "to abolish nuclear weapons" and to "support human rights, economic justice, and international cooperation." The student team in charge of this service learning project gained valuable insights about the technology infrastructure, which was much more limited than they expected, and about the importance of the real world events and advocacy in the community. Similar to the food pantries team, these students also created on online presence in Facebook and Myspace for the Upper Hudson Peace Action, and saw this as a potentially promising area to develop further. Their initial observation about these social networking sites was that Facebook was successful in promoting Upper Hudson Peace Action while MySpace may be too large of a community to promote a regional group. The students taught their community mentor how to use these tools so that each site could be further developed and maintained over time. This team worked on the Peace Action Web site, adding plug-ins, creating a link to the Google search bar, developing a Web-based survey tool, establishing a Gmail account, and making usability suggestions that led to the reorganization of the navigation bar. Beyond their work with technology at this location, perhaps the most influential and long-lasting experiences for this team included their participation in community events such as a peace march and rally in Albany and handing out flyers and talking with members of the community to promote peace during a time of war.

On the last day of class each student team presented their closing observations for a final presentation that provided an overview of their projects and how each related to the themes of the course. This session also involved the participation of the community service mentors who attended the class to show their support for the students and to provide their own thoughts and observations about the service learning projects. During final presentations, the team wikis were used to link to a range of resources developed by the students during the semester, including the community organization Web site, their PowerPoint presentations, and digital images of organization logos and pictures taken of students to document their experiences. The Peace Action team also linked to resources they created using Web-based multimedia and podcasts, which further illustrated with word, image, and sound, their participation in this project over the entire semester.

Overall, the service learning project was a culminating experience for each team that provided connections among information literacy, oral discourse, technology, and the social science perspective of social and community informatics ("Social Science Courses," 2007–2008). Students were active producers of information working in collaboration with one another and their community partners to conduct research, project plan, and solve problems. The field study provided students with experiential knowledge to understand the specific social contexts of their community organization and to make an informed contribution with an understanding of the needs of their nonprofit group. The technology tools supported collaboration among students at any time and, most importantly, offered a way to think about achieving common goals through interaction, experience, and documentation (with text, image, sound, and multimedia). The wiki created a common area to share observations and insights among the teams while synthesizing this information for an audience that primarily included the instructor and class. This course did not include instruction on Web page design or any of the other technology-related contributions students made in the community. Students brought their own expertise to each setting while building on this experience by sharing knowledge with one another and by learning new technical skills based on the needs of the organization. While the results of this work were impressive, as the brief description of each project here demonstrates, we needed to gain insights from assessment about the ways students actually perceived these activities within a context of research and writing in online environments.

ASSESSMENT STRATEGIES

The institutional assessment of this course included standardized surveys from the Department of Information Studies, the Honors College, and the University at Albany. The departmental survey included both multiple-choice and open-ended questions while the university-wide student instructional rating form (SIRF) was entirely multiple choice. The Honors College survey included questions with seven-point Likert Scale responses and short answer, addressing such categories as course challenge, time management, how the course compared to high school and other University at Albany classes, the professor's teaching style, teaching strategies, and assignments. This survey also included an open-ended question about the overall evaluation of the course. These instruments did offer some useful feedback to the instructor in anonymous formats but the emphasis was more about student perception of the instruction rather than a reflection of their learning. The instructor also designed open-ended survey questions in WebCT at the midsemester and end of the semester, which offered similar evaluative feedback.

Beyond the institutional assessments, students were asked to reflect on their learning as part of their final wiki project and presentation. Students were also invited to participate in an end of semester survey that focused specifically on student writing in collaborative wiki environments. These approaches offered more substantive feedback about how students perceived collaboration and learning in this course than the course evaluation formats of the mandated assessments. For example, a review of student comments in the final presentation section of their wikis suggested that overall they:

- Identified connections between their service learning projects and course content
- Learned about the role of technology in community environments
- Gained insights about usability through a better understanding of the community context
- Confirmed the value of personal interactions in community settings
- Valued the dedication of community volunteers and understood the impact this had on the larger community
- Overcame initial resistance to a required service learning project
- Gained a sense of accomplishment by completing community service
- Improved technical skills by working on technology projects in the community
- Learned how to develop and communicate information in wiki environments

Generally student discussion of the service learning and technology components of the course were favorable although some students believed that the wiki requirement was overemphasized. One student argued that while the wiki supports collaborative writing and editing, the students actually wrote their individual parts for their assignments without much online interaction with one another. This issue was raised in class as well by some students who questioned the value of collaborative writing, suggesting that students should be able to maintain control over their individual contributions.

The end-of-semester survey instrument that focused specifically on writing in wiki environments also revealed some resistance to Web-based collaborative writing. For example, one student argued that the editing process does not "efficiently eliminate overlap between individual's ideas" suggesting that it is difficult to differentiate between individual contributions, but that "the wiki is a good system to present our group findings." This comment suggested that the student valued the wiki as a space to prepare for presentations but may have had some reservations about losing the distinction of individual contributions. Another student wrote: "we don't usually edit each other's work." Instead, this team communicated primarily during in-person meetings, via e-mail and with cell phones. This student described the process for developing a wiki entry: "we get together outside of class and write on paper what we want our group entry to be. Then we post that as well as our own thoughts. We find this system to be the most effective in terms of getting a group entry as well as individual ones." This shows that students did collaborate on their project, through meetings, e-mail, and phone conversations, but not necessarily by combining their writing in a wiki format.

Another student argued that "the Wiki is good for displaying one's thoughts, but not for scheduling appointments." These mixed responses to the process of working together in the wiki suggest that students were reluctant to fully engage with an open editing environment as a process of collaborative writing. This was apparent throughout the semester as students insisted on simply posting individual responses in a common wiki page, even when encouraged to develop a cohesive team response. Many students even labeled their contributions with their names to identify their individual contributions.

Even with this resistance to writing collaboratively, the students did use this technology to share information about their service learning experiences and to prepare for their in-class presentations. Although students were provided a basic framework for this assignment, they were not given strict guidelines on how to use the wiki. This may have led to the separation in writing contributions and the apparent need to identify their individual work, but it also may have encouraged students to use the wiki in novel ways. For example, students used the wikis to draft ideas, plan projects, share Web-based resources (including multimedia), upload original digital images and podcasts, link to original PowerPoint presentations (in various drafts), create schedules, reports, and document their hours for community service. Interestingly the wikis themselves did not follow a particular visual or organizational format such as Wikipedia but developed over time to meet the goals of each group. Ultimately students created and shared resources in ways that were closer to a digital bulletin board and hypertext outline or collage than an encyclopedia. This was perhaps unexpected because of their familiarity with Wikipedia, but they were not asked to re-create what was already known and instead demonstrated an openness to explore and to build something new.

CONCLUSION

Web 2.0 technologies such as wikis offer easy-to-use and interactive resources that facilitate collaboration, although not necessarily for writing only. The resistance to shared writing in this course demonstrates the need to further explore the social dimension of wiki production and to identify areas of difficulty in online communication. Tim Berners-Lee (2000) was correct when he suggested that collaboration on the Web may be inherent but requires us to take a close look at the challenges of how people actually work in these spaces (57). It also demonstrates a need for social and community informatics to gain a critical understanding of the relationship between ICTs and people in social environments. The 2.0 paradigm offers an effective means to evaluate business, government, academia, and society's application of technologies in various stages of development. For instance, we found that teaching and learning with Web 2.0 is a collaborative practice and not just an individual activity based on disciplinary expertise. As part of this process we must engage students in Web-based authorship as active producers of information and knowledge and not just searchers, readers, or viewers of information sources. This approach provides students with insights about such issues as the validity, authenticity, and ethics of information when mediated by technology.

As with all information literacy efforts, the effective evaluation of available resource materials is vital. Not only do students need to determine if what they found is truly relevant to their research, they also need to determine the authority and quality of this information. These are critical components of information literacy and influence the development of responsible scholars in a digital age. Michael Jensen (2007) designates future shifts in scholarly authority as Authority 2.0. He contrasts information abundance and ease of participation with mechanisms that make the most of scarce resources such as validation of scholarship. The ubiquitous subject-specific categorization of resources on library Web pages is supplemented by federated and discovery search tools that are similar to the kind of functionality already known to future scholars in their regular use of Google. In addition, the classroom is increasingly mediated by technologies of practice that provide students with instant, open access to information and to freely available online communication and production tools. In a Web 2.0 world, authority itself is challenged as the traditional barriers between teacher and student, author and reader, novice and expert, public and private, individual and team, technician and user continue to converge.

Tim O'Reilly (2005) argues that Web 2.0 is the "end of the software release cycle" because the Web is more of a service platform than it is a product in a box. Ironically, this suggests that the "2.0" terminology may already be obsolete. Rather than define a 2.0 nomenclature to describe the various uses of technology for teaching information literacy, we may want to acknowledge the confluence of emerging technologies with creativity and critical thinking as enduring processes of lifelong learning. As we found in the progress of this course, it is the continual development and expression of ideas through collaboration that enriches the information environment. Learning takes place when making new knowledge, driven by individual and shared practices online and in person.

REFERENCES

Berners-Lee, Tim. 2000. *Weaving the Web: The Original Design and Ultimate Destiny of the World Wide Web*. New York: HarperCollins.

Blogger. "The Story of Blogger" Available: www.blogger.com/about/. Retrieved March 9, 2008.

Bloglines. "About Bloglines." Available: www.bloglines.com/about/. Accessed March 9, 2008.

Capital City Rescue Mission. "Capital City Rescue Mission." Available: www.capitalcityrescue mission.com. Retrieved March 8, 2008.

Casey, Michael E., and Laura C. Savastinuk. 2006. "Library 2.0: Service for the Next-Generation Library." *Library Journal*, September 1. Available: www.libraryjournal .com/article/CA6365200.html/. Accessed February 19, 2008.

Community & Public Service Program. School of Social Welfare. University at Albany, State University of New York. Available: www.albany.edu/cpsp/. Accessed March 2, 2008.

Coombs, Karen A. 2007. "Building a Library Web Site on the Pillars of Web 2.0." *Computers in Libraries* 27, no. 1 (January). Available: www.infotoday.com/cilmag/jan07/Coombs .shtml/. Accessed February 26, 2008.

Food Pantries for the Capital District. "Food Pantries for the Capital District." Available http://foodpantries.net/. Accessed March 8, 2008.

Gurstein, Michael. 2003. "Effective Use: A Community Informatics Strategy Beyond the Digital Divide." *First Monday* 8, no. 12 (December). Available: www.firstmonday.org/ ISSUES/issue8_12/gurstein/. Accessed February 4, 2008.

Halavais, Alex. 2005. "Social Informatics: Beyond Emergence." *Bulletin of the American Society for Information Science and Technology* 31, no. 5 (June/July). Available: www.asis.org/ Bulletin/Jun-05/helavais.html/. Accessed February 3, 2008.

"Honors College Library Page." Honors College, SUNY Albany. Available: http://library .albany.edu/honorscoll/. Accessed March 11, 2008.

"Honors College Library Resource Page." Honors College, SUNY Albany. Available: http://library.albany.edu/honorscoll/socialinformatics.html/. Accessed March 11, 2008.

"Information Literacy Courses." 2007–2008. Available: http://www.albany.edu/gened/ cr_infolit.shtml/. Accessed March 1, 2008.

Jensen, Michael. 2007. "The New Metrics of Scholarly Authority." *The Chronicle Review* 53, no. 4 (June): B6. Available: http://chronicle.com/free/v53/i41/41b00601.htm/. Accessed March 3, 2008.

Journal of Community Informatics. "Editorial Policies." Available: http://ci-journal.net/ index.php/ciej/about/editorialPolicies#focusAndScope/. Accessed February 3, 2008.

Kling, Rob. 1999. "What Is Social Informatics and Why Does It Matter?" *D-Lib Magazine* 5, no. 1 (January). Available: www.dlib.org/dlib/january99/kling/01kling.html/. Accessed February 3, 2008.

Kling, Rob, Howard Rosenbaum, and Steve Sawyer. 2005. *Understanding and Communicating Social Informatics: A Framework for Studying and Teaching the Human Contexts of Information and Communication Technologies*. Medford, NJ: Information Today.

Landow, George P. 1992. *Hypertext: The Convergence of Contemporary Critical Theory and Technology*. Baltimore: The Johns Hopkins University Press.

"Learning Objectives for Oral Discourse." Available: www.albany.edu/gened/cr_oraldiscourse .shtml/. Accessed March 1, 2008.

Mackey, Thomas P. 2007. "The Social Informatics of Blog and Wiki Communities: Authoring Communities of Practice (CoPs)." Canadian Association for Information Science Conference Proceedings. Available: www.cais-acsi.ca/proceedings/2007/mackey_2007 .pdf/. Accessed Retrieved February 25, 2008.

Mackey, Thomas P., and Jinwon Ho. 2005. "Implementing a Convergent Model for Information Literacy: Combining Research and Web Literacy." *Journal of Information Science* 31: 541–555.

Mackey, Thomas P., and Trudi Jacobson. 2004. "Integrating Information Literacy in Lower- and Upper-level Courses: Developing Scalable Models for Higher Education." *The Journal of General Education* 53, no. 3–4: 201–224.

Mackey, Thomas P., Trudi E. Jacobson, and Deborah Bernnard. 2007. "Promoting Teamwork and Critical Reflection: Collaborative Information Literacy and Technology Instruction." In Trudi E. Jacobson and Thomas P. Mackey (Eds.), *Information Literacy Collaborations That Work* (pp. 221–242). New York: Neal-Schuman.

O'Reilly, Tim. 2005. "What Is Web 2.0: Design Patterns and Business Models for the Next Generation of Software." Available: www.oreillynet.com/pub/a/oreilly/tim/news/2005/09/30/what-is-web-20.html/. Accessed February 19, 2008.

"Our History." The Honors College. University at Albany, SUNY. Available: www.albany.edu/honors college/who_we_are_history.shtml/. Retrieved February 14, 2008.

PBwiki. "About PBwiki." Available: http://pbwiki.com/content/team/. Accessed March 9, 2008.

Reda, Vinny. 2007. "Honors College Students Take Course to Community Service and Scholarship" (May 15). Available: www.albany.edu/main/features/2007/0507/birnbaum/birnbaum.shtml/. Accessed March 9, 2008.

Ronald McDonald House Charities of the Capital Region. "Welcome to the Ronald McDonald House." Available: www.rmhcofalbany.org/. Accessed March 8, 2008.

Seigenthaler, John. 2005. "A False Wikipedia 'Biography.'" *USA Today*, November 29.

Shneiderman, Ben. 2002. *Leonardo's Laptop: Human Needs and the New Computing Technologies.* Cambridge, MA: The MIT Press.

"Social Science Courses." 2007–2008. SUNY Albany. Available: www.albany.edu/gened/dp_socsci.shtml/. Accessed March 1, 2008.

Stephens, Michael and Maria Collins. 2007. "Web 2.0, Library 2.0, and the Hyperlinked Library." *Serials Review* 33, no. 4 (December): 253–256.

Tuominen, Kimmo, Reijo Savolainen, and Sanna Talja. 2005. "Information Literacy as a Sociotechnical Practice." *The Library Quarterly* 75, no. 3: 329–345, 376–378.

"Undergraduate Bulletin 2007-2008." Honors College, SUNY Albany. Available: www.albany.edu/undergraduate_bulletin/honors_college.html/. Accessed February 14, 2008.

University of Pennsylvania. "What Is PennTags?" Available: http://tags.library.upenn.edu/help/. Accessed March 1, 2008.

Upper Hudson Peace Action. "Upper Hudson Peach Action." Available: www.peaceact.net/. Accessed March 8, 2008.

Warshauer, Mark. 2003. "Demystifying the Digital Divide." *Scientific American* 289, no. 2: 42–47.

Wesch, Michael. 2008. "ELI Podcast: Human Futures for Technology and Education." Educause Learning Initiative Annual Meeting 2008, January 30, San Antonio, Texas. Available: http://hosted.mediasite.com/hosted4/Catalog/?cid=cd40888eed5940f2bbd8daa8c09b4ecc. Accessed February 29, 2008.

Chapter 2

A Conversation about Collaboration
Using Web-based Video Streaming to Integrate Information Literacy into a Research Assignment for a Large Blended Class

Flavia Renon, Timothy A. Pychyl,
and Christopher P. Motz

INTRODUCTION

Our libraries and classrooms are now deeply enmeshed in an age of "networked intelligence" as foreshadowed by Tapscott (1996) and numerous others (e.g., Bates, 2000; Katz, 1999; Luker, 2000). Information has never been more widely available. Tools for information searching and computer-mediated interaction have never been more commonplace; so commonplace in fact that "Google" is now a verb and "Facebook" a place (not a dynamic database) in our students' lives.

Of course in writing this we hesitate a bit, because we know some of these tools will be dated referents, at least in our students' lives, as this chapter goes to print. Try as we may, we cannot keep up. Even our online courses always seem to fall short of the latest trends in the use of technology. For example, just as we get our lectures on the Web as podcasts and create blogs for class discussion and chat rooms for virtual office hours, students are expecting more of Web 2.0 inter-action tools as a new space for their learning. It seems an impossible chase. More importantly, we hesitate because as educators, irrespective of the current tools or trends, we recognize the need to bridge a gap between using Internet-based tools in the everyday forms of information literacy (IL) that are required to find new music or friends online and the information literacy skills we hope to foster within the scholarly context of our students' intellectual lives.

In this chapter, we present a summary of our approach to bridging this gap. We explain the context of our teaching, which is rich in the use of technology to support student learning, and we take you on our own journey of collaboration as we designed and implemented a research assignment within the discipline of psychology that was intended to develop students' information literacy skills.

We defined information literacy broadly, and our approach may best be understood within the categories presented by Shapiro and Hughes (1996). Our assignment included basic "tool literacy" as we demonstrated (live and through streaming video) how to use various tools to find appropriate information as well as how to submit the assignment with specific tools within the course management system. With this as a propaedeutic task, we then turned our attention to "research literacy," as the assignment required students to identify and locate specific types of content, and to "social-structural literacy," as students were required to make sense of what they found in their research in terms of information and resources within the course textbook. In sum, our students had to find peer-reviewed research articles that related to information from an item in the popular press and then place all of this within the context of our course and the subdiscipline of personality psychology. Of course, this important epistemological task of researching a knowledge claim is not discipline specific, so everything our students did in the context of psychology is relevant to other disciplines and areas of study.

All of this gets us a little ahead of our story, however, which is first and foremost about collaboration. For us, this was our greatest challenge, as we believe that there are systemic obstacles to overcome in creating collaborative relationships for teaching in higher education, particularly in research-intensive universities. So, we begin our chapter with our three individual voices, solo, as is so often the case in teaching. We also combine our individual narratives to present a conversation among an instructional librarian, senior faculty member, and new faculty member. Together, we examine how our focus on student learning brought us together to enhance the information literacy skills of our students.

THE LIBRARIAN'S PERSPECTIVE

Academic libraries in recent years have undergone significant changes that have redefined the role they play on a university campus. As access to a greater portion of collections is now available "virtually" to users, this frees up physical space and creates opportunities for libraries to reexamine services and roles they can play in the broader context of the university. A shift from the static image of an information store to a dynamic learning center such as the "learning commons" is a welcome change. This environment relies on partnerships between various groups on campus, such as staff from student learning support groups, computing services, educational development groups, and library reference services.

Library instruction is evolving in a similar way by engaging students in both physical and virtual learning spaces in the library and throughout campus. In particular, the traditional pedagogical practice of the one-shot library session is slowly being superseded by more engaging approaches to teaching, often mediated by technology. This change in the teaching-learning context creates opportunities for changes in our present teaching practices to the benefit of students. By examining areas that are problematic for instruction, we can harness new technological tools coupled with appropriate teaching techniques to create a meaningful learning environment for students that promotes deep—as opposed to surface—learning.

For example, let's revisit the one-shot library session. If not timed and planned carefully to meet students' information needs, it has been shown to be ineffective (Colborn and Cordell, 1998). Students leave the session feeling they have wasted valuable class time, particularly if the session is generic, presented outside of the course context, and at a time when students are not engaged in research. In this "just in case" as opposed to "just in time" context, the onus is placed on students to make a quantum leap between the librarian's presentation, the course content, and the learning expectations for the course. The one-shot session also has an impact on librarians who feel a sense of disconnect with the course content, with students, and with faculty when their role is restricted to that of a guest speaker in a course. The key is to find ways to integrate both librarian and IL into the curriculum and the class, taking into account the new learning environments that are appearing on our campuses.

In order to achieve this objective, I needed to step back and to reflect on what roles collaboration, partnered with technology and teaching, played in student learning. How can integration of both the librarian and IL into the curriculum and the classroom be achieved so that students engage in deep learning? As with all technology, a number of questions about pedagogical practice need to be addressed. How can technology be used to teach information literacy? What teaching practices best suit the technology and make learning more meaningful to students and seamless with the rest of the course? Collaborative partnerships when not managed properly could potentially be problematic. How do we avoid the pitfalls while capitalizing on the synergy of a team approach? A second-year psychology class taught by Tim Pychyl provided the ideal teaching and learning environment to explore these questions.

THE FACULTY MEMBER'S PERSPECTIVE

My relatively large second-year course, Introduction to the Study of Personality, represents the culmination of ten years of development of Web-based resources to support student learning in a blended format. In addition to the Web resources for student learning outside of the classroom, this course is unique because it is taught as two different sections: a traditional in-class section in which students attend face-to-face lectures (approximately 120 students), and a section offered through Carleton University Television (CUTV, approximately 300 students) in which students view the live section either as a broadcast on local cable television, via DVD recordings on campus in a dedicated viewing room or DVD recordings mailed to the student (these students actually comprise a third smaller section of the course known as "tapes-to-you" [TTY, approximately 10 to 20 students in any term], but in most respects these students have a similar experience to the CUTV section). Finally and most recently, I pioneered the implementation of streaming video technologies to move the lecture recordings out of the relative confinement of cable television and various forms of recorded video (i.e., videotapes and DVD) to the much more accessible medium of the Internet. As you can see with even this cursory description of the course, students have ready access to course materials, particularly the lectures, any time, any place.

As a consequence of being an introductory survey-type course with a large enrollment, this course presents significant challenges in terms of instructional activities, assessment, and building a cohesive learning community within the class and its sections. In order to address these challenges, I developed a number of resources to assist me as the instructor as well as the students in their learning. These were:

1. Web-based learning activities and assignments
2. Online tutorials, including streaming videos of supplementary materials
3. A cohort of students who had successfully completed the course in recent years to work as volunteer mentors to current students
4. A co-instructor to assist me in the management of student learning (this was done in lieu of a teaching release for my administrative work)
5. Partnership with an instructional librarian, which is the focus of this chapter

Although it is beyond the scope of our chapter to provide details of each of the learning resources and assignments in the course, it is important to provide an overview of how students accessed course materials and completed assignments, as this is the technological context for our information literacy assignment and partnership in teaching. Briefly, the WebCT site for the course provided students with traditional information such as the course outline, a weekly instructor blog about the focus for the week, FAQ page, exam information, practice tests, grade book, and a link to an external site that permits anonymous feedback to the instructor (offered through www.getfast.ca). These general tools, while important, are not the key resources for student learning; the key resources included: (1) archived streaming videos of all lectures with accompanying PowerPoint and Word-format lecture slides; (2) detailed explanations and resources for the assignments (e.g., marking scheme for the course essay as well as sample essays from previous years); (3) an interactive questionnaire tool that provides students with weekly, topical personality questionnaires (the data from which we based a group research assignment); and, most important for this chapter, (4) an extensive section of the Web site that explained and provided resources for the information literacy research assignment.

The research assignment that we designed is explained in detail in a later section, so it will suffice to say at this point that the course's blended-learning environment provided key tools for our work together for information literacy. Specifically, we were able to employ the streaming video technology as well as the resource tools within WebCT to teach the students the relevant information literacy tools and manage the assignment. As well, given the students' familiarity with, even dependency on, the "just-in-time" delivery of course content with the streaming video of lectures and online practice tests, students' expectations for our librarian's participation in the course was equally, "What I need, when I need it!" Designing the assignment to provide the learning resources for students in this just-in-time format, was, I think, an important success factor in our work together and students' learning, and, as noted previously, this just-in-time integration of the librarian's work with the students' learning provided a welcome change from the one-shot library session.

OUR SECOND INSTRUCTOR REFLECTS ON THE STUDENT'S PERSPECTIVE

Carleton University is a midsized institution (approximately 20,000 undergraduate students) that faces many of the challenges common to most universities, particularly research-intensive institutions. One of these challenges is very large first- and second-year classes. To address this large enrollment issue, Carleton adopted a cable broadcast channel for televising some of these larger courses, permitting the university to make maximum room of available class space. Thus, some of the students in this particular course are distance learners.

For students, this physical as well as temporal separation may impact their feeling of connectedness to the class as well as to the course content (Gray, 1999; Mann, 2005). Being removed from the physical classroom prevents them from being able to ask questions (directly) in class and minimizes opportunities to talk with the instructor and fellow students. In-class demonstrations and activities are perceived through the lens of the television or computer screen, and participation in group work or study groups becomes problematic.

One of the ways in which many educators are bridging this separation is by creating active course Web sites, which may contain lecture notes, resources, and communication tools. However, not all students are fully versed in online information technology. Having to learn the various tools associated with course Web sites becomes another task that is added to having to figure out the instructions for various assignments, learning to use the various library systems in order to complete those assignments, and learning the course content.

Another barrier to students' class and course connection is the fact that increasingly larger numbers of students are faced with having to juggle hectic work schedules in addition to school schedules. This increased demand on their schedules may result in students not being available to seek help during regular office hours and diverse or erratic schoolwork patterns producing a need for help at times when faculty and educational support services are unavailable. This disconnect between the needs of students and the availability of support runs counter to a world moving toward increasing connections and "just in time" knowledge.

For assignments that require use of library systems, a supportive educator may seek to include a relevant presentation from a librarian during class time. However, in order to be useful, these in-class presentations may be done well in advance of the assignment deadline. This creates yet another disconnect between what is happening within the class and students' assignment-relevant needs. At the time of the presentation, students may not have had a chance to formulate all of their questions, and when they are ready to ask those questions—evenings, weekends, and nights—the librarian and the instructor may be long gone.

BRINGING OUR CONCERNS TOGETHER: THE GENESIS OF OUR RELATIONSHIP

So far, as is reflected in our writing, our story is one of three separate educators in parallel who were struggling to be more effective, to grow in our practice. This growth, as Parker Palmer advocates so clearly, requires a specific kind of resource, namely community. He writes:

> If we want to grow in our practice, we have two primary places to go: the inner ground from which good teaching comes and *to the community of fellow teachers from whom we can learn more about ourselves and our craft.* (Palmer, 1998: 141, emphasis added)

Each of us did turn to our community to further our own growth as teachers. Interestingly, we began outside of our own institutional community, turning instead to the community of practice in higher education in Canada known as the Society for Teaching and Learning in Higher Education (STLHE). In the end, we returned to our own university now connected together with new ideas and a partnership. Let us explain how this happened, as we believe this connection to the larger community and one another is a crucial challenge for all of us.

The Librarian's Perspective

At the end of my first year as instruction librarian, there were gaps in my knowledge about the dynamics of the academic teaching and learning environment that needed to be addressed. Understanding where student engagement in good research practices and information literacy fit into the whole picture as well as how technology could be used to enhance learning motivated me to attend the STLHE conference.

Given that many, if not most, of the faculty participating in this conference are highly motivated, committed to teaching excellence, and often early adopters of technology, this was a genuine opportunity for me to learn from some of the best practitioners. Between conference sessions I wanted to engage in conversation with faculty, educational developers, and other educational stakeholders to get a sense of how they viewed information literacy, the role of librarians, and student learning. Eventually I was hoping that some form of collaborative partnership would emerge, a partnership that would solidify the librarian's presence and more importantly an information literacy presence in the curriculum. Up to that point, the only success I managed to achieve in my own institution was to post my library PowerPoint presentations on WebCT course pages with permission of faculty since librarians did not have WebCT administrator privileges. I wanted to achieve more than simply focusing my instruction on information-seeking skills, which often leads to superficial learning (Asher, 2003); I hoped to find faculty who were open to creating curriculum-integrated library presence on their course Web page. As it so happens, Tim and I crossed paths that day during lunch and quickly realized that we shared a common interest with respect to information literacy.

The Faculty Perspective

A long-standing member of the STLHE and annual attendee of the STLHE conference, I have always valued the opportunity to hear from other instructors to learn what they are doing in their classes and its effects on student learning. As is often the case at conferences, much of this learning happens between sessions, and this particular year was no exception. A biologist from the University of Ottawa, Dr. John Houseman, who I got to know through his innovative use of technology for teaching, met me at an end-of-day gathering, during which time he told me about a new assignment he was using with his students. As introduced earlier, John has his students read an article in the popular press related to his biology course and then research the original source of the information discussed in the article. The gist of the assignment is to research the knowledge claim on which the popular-press article was based and discuss to what extent the article fairly represented the actual research and knowledge claim as presented in the original (peer-reviewed) journal article.

Although not new, this important epistemological task was missing in my own course, as was the necessary research component on which it is based. My immediate question then became, how can I do this? I needed help both to manage the assignment in a large class, and, most importantly, to support my students' learning of the necessary research skills to do this effectively.

As Flavia has already explained, I had a librarian colleague at the conference who was looking for just this sort of opportunity to achieve some of her own goals in support of student learning. The search for each of us had ended, but the work had just begun. Now we had the more challenging task of working together to create an assignment and support the students through the process.

Fortunately, even though we had not been able to collaborate on curriculum design prior to this, we did not have to embark on curricular innovation without valuable input from others. There is a well-established literature that discusses issues related to successful collaboration (e.g., Kraat, 2005; McGuiness, 2006; Julien and Given, 2003). Perhaps the most important insight we gained was that, although collaboration and curriculum integration are at the heart of successful information literacy initiatives, not paying attention to the dynamics between faculty, librarians, and the learners can quickly undermine positive learning outcomes.

PLANNING FOR SUCCESS THROUGH COLLABORATION AND INTEGRATION

During planning discussions, both faculty and librarians should be on the lookout for what we interpret as signs of perceptual dissonance. By this we mean that faculty may view the role of librarians and libraries, information literacy, or appropriate teaching and learning practices in a different context. We need to be aware that faculty operate in a culture defined by autonomy, time constraints, and a relatively narrow content focus, factors that are often not conducive to collaboration with a librarian (Hardesty, 1995). Of course, this dissonance works both ways, so librarians also need to be aware of their own perceptions and assumptions with respect to faculty, their own teaching styles and philosophies, and their knowledge and interpretation of information literacy.

According to Manuel, Molloy, and Beck (2003), faculty may choose not to include IL in their course because they believe that students figure out library and information research on their own (or should do so). They may also assume that the library and information research skills are being taught elsewhere and are not their responsibility, that individual students will ask for help on an as-needed basis, that they could provide their own teaching of library and information research skills to their students, or that the course curriculum is already too full for library instruction. To this list we can add the difficulty in scheduling instruction with the library/librarian, lack of awareness of library instruction, and concerns over librarians' mastery of their subject content (Doskatsch, 2003; Lindstrom and Shonrock, 2006).

In addition to this notion of perceptual dissonance, we also had to acknowledge that people see teaching and learning differently. It is common for individuals to adopt different views of learning and teaching in different contexts. These views could become problematic when they are not properly articulated (Bruce, Edwards, and Lupton, 2006).

When faculty and librarians are engaged in curriculum planning, students should not be left out of this equation. Generation X and Y share distinct characteristics that define how they do research and how they learn. For example, Brown, Murphy, and Nanny (2003) found that these students are often overconfident about research because they equate their technology savvy with knowledge of information literacy. Bennett (2007) summarizes this succinctly, "We face the challenge of internet-savvy students whose ease of use of on-line resources is not matched with critical judgement about the quality of those resources and whose understanding of research has often been shaped by technical expertise rather than critical questions" (148). And, to further emphasize our challenge, Generation X and Y want customized library instruction, expect to find information quickly, and "have no interest in learning how information is structured or organized" (Costello, Lenholt, and Stryker, 2004: 252). Taken together, these generational issues underscore how knowledge of who students are and how they learn serves to better inform us on our choices of teaching and learning technologies.

Though these collaborative challenges lay ahead for us, it was evident that the four essential elements or behaviors for successful collaborative teaching partnerships were in place: (1) shared understood goals; (2) mutual respect, tolerance, and trust; (3) competence for the task at hand by each of the partners; and (4) ongoing communication (Ivey, 2003). Although these four elements of collaboration are rather comprehensive, Lippincott (2002) identified additional required elements that need to be in place, including: a willingness to shape a common mission outside of the unit-specific mission, interest in sharing jargon and definitions of technical terms, willingness to learn aspects of the other partner's expertise, and the ability to appreciate differences and not to criticize or stereotype others' professions. In sum, successful collaboration depends a great deal on individuals working across professional boundaries in an open, honest fashion, with clear intentions to achieve shared goals. We certainly believed that the three of us had this as a strong base from which to work.

In addition to our positive interpersonal relationships, the WebCT environment played a role in facilitating collaboration and teaching in this blended environment. The literature highlights the pedagogical advantages that elicit faculty to use classroom management systems (CMS) in a blended course. This includes the desire to: (1) augment course content (e.g., handouts, study guides, PowerPoint presentations); (2) increase active learning through online activities that engage learners in reading, writing, and reflecting on course material; and (3) provide feedback through synchronous and asynchronous communication tools (e.g., discussion boards, chat), allowing the opportunity for higher level thinking such as analysis, synthesis, and evaluation (Frey, 2005). These features coupled with the just-in-time access greatly benefit students.

Cennamo, Ross, and Rogers (2002) also found that students taking part in a blended class report they have become more engaged not only in online learning but also when participating in face-to-face class sessions. Student class attendance was high in our own class even though the videostream lectures were available. In addition, students in class contributed significantly to each session. With this knowledge in hand about our students and ourselves, we set out to decide the learning outcomes of the research assignment.

THE RESEARCH ASSIGNMENT: "BEYOND ACCIDENTAL PEDAGOGY"

The research assignment we developed was more than a simple case of accidental pedagogy (McGee, Carmean, and Ali, 2005). When the three of us first sat down together to begin planning this learning task, we discussed the learning outcomes that we wanted the learners to achieve as well as the barriers to their successful completion of those objectives. From a faculty perspective, we wanted our learners to develop an appreciation for the forms of academic communication, research, and publication in the field of psychology. We also wanted our learners to connect and compare this information to the information being communicated to a wider audience through various forms of mass media.

From a librarian perspective, our goal was to promote IL within the academic domain of psychology but also a general IL that would benefit students throughout their academic careers. A primary barrier to this is a traditional disconnect between IL goals and course-specific faculty goals. In our initial planning session we began to discuss how we could structure a research assignment that would achieve our learning objectives as well as what we could do to manage learner anxiety and its impact on our time.

The Research Assignment

As we designed the research assignment, we relied on some knowledge of teaching and learning theory to guide our approach, in particular constructivist theory that draws its inspiration from Dewey's active learning theory, Piaget's assimilation-accommodation theory, and Vygotsky's social learning theory (Weigel, 2002). Segmenting learning tasks into steps such as we did in the research assignment enabled our students to manage cognitive load more efficiently (Templeman-Kluit, 2006). It is important to recognize that many of the learning outcomes that we are working toward with this assignment are "process" outcomes. Students' learning is manifested in their ability to complete various steps of the assignment. As a result, some of the steps of the assignment require students to demonstrate that they were able to master a particular IL–related task. For this reason, we agreed on an assignment segmented into an eight-step approach (see Figure 2.1).

For the first step in this process, students were asked to look at popular press sources they would read in their daily lives (e.g., *Time Magazine*, local newspaper, *Psychology Today*, etc.) to find an article written about the topic of personality. The goal in this step is an epistemological one to get students to think critically about the knowledge claims that are being communicated to them and to compare and contrast this with the knowledge claims that are made within the academic discipline. Thus, once students have found an article in the popular media that discusses personality, they then begin the process of connecting this back to the underlying academic literature. Most importantly from the librarian's perspective is that through this process they are challenged to develop their IL competencies.

Dewey believed that education should be an engaged experience linking discipline with real world social experiences of the learner (Giles and Eyler, 1994). Brazilian educator and critical-pedagogical theorist Paulo Freire describes the shortcomings of "narrative education" where the teacher "expounds on topics completely alien to the existential experience of the students" (Freire, 1970: 57). For this reason, Freire believes educators need to first engage their students in the context of the students' experience (Doherty, 2005). The students' experience is used not only in the first step in the assignment (see Figure 2.1), it is used consistently in a number of formative exercises throughout the course. For example, students are asked to complete personality questionnaires before attending the class where the theory associated with the test is discussed. Looking at their own performance on the questionnaire, students had a personal context on which to build their knowledge. Seamless integration of IL is apparent when it follows the same curricular design approach and style as used by faculty in the

Figure 2.1. Introduction to the Study of Personality–Research Assignment

Step 1. Find an article in the popular press that discusses/presents information related to personality psychology. Provide reference information for the popular press article. Include the following information:

a. The name of the newspaper or magazine
b. The date of publication
c. The title of the article
d. The name of the author of the article (the author of the popular press article = the journalist who wrote the article)
e. The name of the psychological researcher who is mentioned in the article. *Note:* it would be very unusual for the psychologist to be writing his or her own article—the article would usually be written by a journalist who is reporting on the research of a psychological researcher.
f. For articles from Web-based media, please include the URL of the article and the date of retrieval (the date you found it on the Web). If the article is from print-based media, then there is no need for the URL or date of retrieval.

Step 2. Summarize the key ideas of the popular press article (two to four sentences).

Step 3. Include details about what is said in the popular press article regarding the psychological RESEARCH in particular (two to four sentences).

Step 4. Which of the six domains of the study of personality (as presented in the text) relates to this popular press article? Justify your decision by describing how this article relates to one of the topics covered in the text and lectures (two to four sentences)

Step 5. Use the subject index from the back of the textbook to determine if the research described in the popular press article (or something similar) is covered in the textbook (you may need to look for synonyms). If so, provide page numbers (and the name of the "subject"). If not, what subject from the text is most closely related? (provide page numbers). And why is it related?

Step 6. Use the name index (this is an index of the names of researchers mentioned in the textbook) from the back of the textbook to determine if the psychology researcher discussed in the popular press article is mentioned in the textbook. If so, provide page numbers. If not, what other researchers might work with this researcher (called collaborative research)? (provide page numbers). What other researchers discussed in the textbook might attend similar conferences? (provide page numbers).

Step 7. Conduct a Web-based search for biographical information about the psychology researcher described in the popular press article. Write a brief summary about the researcher (who, where, what does he or she do/study?). This section should be a maximum of 500 words. Do not cut and paste the researcher's biographical information from the Internet (put this into your own words).

Step 8. Find a recent academic publication (an article in a peer-reviewed journal) by this researcher that relates to the topic from the popular press article. This will involve using a psychology-specific search engine available through the Carleton Library (e.g., PsycINFO). Select ONE publication by this researcher that *is related to* the topic covered in the popular press article.

a. Provide a reference for this academic publication (see format provided in the assignment instruction sheet). This reference should be in APA style (see examples).
b. Submit an electronic version (e.g., a PDF file) of this article (the Carleton Library has access to electronic versions of most of the major psychology journals). *If the article you have found is only in print format,* then submit the Carleton Library call number and location in the library stacks (i.e., what floor of the library). For this section, it is a requirement that you find a publication in an academic journal that you can get through the Carleton Library.

Submit the assignment and electronic article

Note: The steps in the figure are the same as the steps in the research assignment, but in the research assignment these are presented in question and answer format.

course, and the first step in the process clearly began with the students' own personal reading.

Steps two to six of the assignment were designed to encourage students to make meaningful links between the theory learned in the classroom and the information they encounter in their everyday lives. Step seven allowed students to make connections with the wider context of the university, that of faculty engaged in research. Finally, step eight provides a counterpoint to step one by allowing students to develop an understanding of the peer-reviewed source. It was interesting to see in class, through e-mail as well as discussion groups within WebCT, that many students experienced an "aha" moment when they understood that journalists were often the authors of the popular articles, whereas the peer-reviewed article was written by faculty engaged in research.

By the end of the assignment, students successfully managed their way through a number of objectives. These include: using online search tools to locate course-relevant popular media articles, using the author and subject indexes at the back of the textbook, using the library's information systems, using the CMS, and making fundamental distinctions between academic and nonacademic forms of communication.

Managing Student Anxiety in the Learning Process

The research assignment requires the student to develop competencies in Web-based searching as well as use of the library's systems. In our planning sessions, we recognized that students would differ in their experience and proficiency with these various skills. Thus, we were faced with the need to provide detailed support but also the need to permit students to access those aspects of the support that were personally relevant as their needs arose.

Well in advance of the assignment due date, the faculty set aside some class time for Flavia, the instructional librarian, to conduct an in-class presentation that introduced IL competencies relevant to students as outlined by the ACRL standards (Association of College and Research Librarians, 2000). Specifically, this included:

1. Determining the nature and extent information needed
2. Accessing information effectively and efficiently
3. Evaluating information and its sources critically and incorporating information into his or her knowledge base and value system

However, because the creation of this assignment was a team effort, Flavia was able to go far beyond the typical "librarian in the classroom" presentation. As explained, having the librarian involved from the inception of the project allowed for the creation of an assignment that met goals that were larger and more relevant than what our faculty members might have accomplished on their own, and also allowed for Flavia to provide an in-class presentation that was perfectly tailored to meet students' needs for this assignment. And thanks to our established working rapport, Tim and Chris, the co-instructors for the course, were able to provide complementary perspectives on the nature and meaning of the assignment.

We decided on a range of media options to provide support to students to help them throughout their assignment. In addition to the in-class presentation, we also provided a rich support environment through our course Web site including:

1. Detailed instructions
2. The assignment template
3. Tips for problem solving
4. A copy of the librarian's presentation
5. A discussion board for interactive communication
6. Streaming instructional videos

All of these support tools were thus available to students "just in time" to meet their learning needs.

The development of our assignment-specific streaming instructional videos deserves further elaboration. In our first semester with our new research assignment, we were confronted with just how unusual this type of learning task is for students. Their level of anxiety and uncertainty was more than expected, and we found that we were investing a significant amount of time in fielding questions. Many of the questions concerned the same aspects of the project and were questions that asked for support in completing some of the specific IL processes of the assignment. It is neither feasible nor desirable to need to address the same questions repetitively. Thus we made the decision to add another level of support to our existing materials, and this resulted in the filming of a series of short resource videos that would explicitly walk students through each of the steps of the process.

This support tool was made possible through the collaborative efforts of several individuals, each of whom were dedicated to advancing our ability to provide new and technologically enhanced ways of supporting our students.[1] Although we utilized a team of individuals in the creation of some of our tools, it should be noted that current technology makes much of this possible for the average individual to produce these tools on their own. Further, a self-produced homemade video might provide a level of "personalization" that carries more meaning for students than something with higher production costs. Based on our long experience at Carleton University with instructional television, we have come to believe that just-in-time capture and delivery of course content is more appropriate than expensively produced video segments that are renewed only periodically.

These instructional videos featured the three of us (Flavia, Tim, and Chris) having a conversation about the research assignment. Parts of the conversation were similar to our planning process, where we were able to share with students our objectives for their learning. Other parts of the conversation focused on specifics of the assignment, elaborating on strategies for mastering the various learning outcomes. Some of these video segments showed us in front of a computer so that we could demonstrate the processes on the library systems or demonstrate the features of the course Web site. By chaptering the videos to reflect the assignment structure, students had the flexibility and ease to select the video stream segment that corresponded to their knowledge gap as they proceeded to work through the steps in the assignment.

Video streaming in this course was not selected simply for the convenience of providing students with 24/7 access through the Internet to learning resources or as a form of "edutainment" but was a choice based on pedagogical practice. According to Mayer and Sims' (1994) dual coding theory of multimedia, video streaming utilizes two working memory modalities, animation and narration, that when coupled together allow the learner to create meaning (Templeman-Kluit, 2006). Though our students are immersed in this learning environment rich in technology, we cannot assume that learning has taken place unless we conduct some form of assessment.

ASSESSMENT

There are a couple of different ways to approach an evaluation of the success of this sort of learning project. One is to examine whether our students have grown as learners and whether they have successfully developed their IL abilities. In conjunction with this, we can also examine whether students were adequately supported during their negotiation of this learning objective. The other way of assessing the value of this learning project is by the response of other educators in the teaching and learning community—in other words, peer review.

Understanding how our learners have grown through this project begins with noting that the majority of them are not coming into our second-year course with preexisting IL skills. In our first semester with the research assignment we were inundated with e-mail and questions about the assignment. Students clearly needed more support and scaffolding (stepwise levels of support) than we had initially predicted. However, this was addressed early on by adding a few extra layers of scaffolding to our existing system of supports (e.g., the streaming-video resources explained previously).

Consistently across several semesters, class averages on this assignment were 90 percent or higher. Thus, with adequate support, our students were able to master the processes involved in this IL project. The students themselves were able to recognize the value of these newly acquired IL skills. For example, one student, through the FAST[2] assessment tool (www.getfast.ca), noted, "I would like to say that there is a lot of work to do . . . but I see now that these things are helping me to learn and understand this material."

The overall value to our students of engaging in these collaborative projects, including a well-integrated team of professionals and a rich learning community, is best expressed through the voices of two students who provided anonymous feedback. The first student writes, "I feel more eager to participate in the class knowing that a ton of effort has been put into the organization of this course even though I am only in the CUTV section. Seeing all the efforts of 'team personality' makes me want to put in the effort." The second student notes, "The concern of your team for the class is apparent always. Even though I have never attended a class lecture, I find myself saying 'We talked about . . . in class today.' Usually I would say 'the instructor talked about . . . ' It is very important to me to feel part of the class, and I do."

The other way of assessing the value of these collaborative projects is to examine the response of the professionals in the teaching and learning community. We have made several well-received conference presentations, and these have led to an invitation for a follow-up talk at a neighboring university as well as a feature article on a technology and culture blog. However, the best indicator of the community's response to a project is adoption by other members of the community; the spread of this approach to teaching IL has already begun among our colleagues.

REFLECTIONS ON OUR CHALLENGES

Given our general introduction to the chapter with our lament of the impossible "technology chase" to keep up with latest tools and techniques, one might be quick to assume that we think that technology is our greatest challenge. We don't. Despite the work involved, we are keeping up with technological change and we have, as advocated by Bates (2000), among others, managed this change quite well. Of course, we don't do this on our own, and we have wisely partnered with anyone and everyone with the skills to help us, including our on-campus educational technology group as well as private sector businesses who offer services not yet widely available on campus (e.g., streaming video expertise). In addition, we have drawn on a growing body of scholarship of teaching that deals explicitly with teaching more effectively with technology (e.g., Bates and Poole, 2003). These resources provide much needed theory and best-practice approaches to guide our implementation.

What remains our greatest challenge, what we grapple with each term, is our collaboration—our teaching with and through community. Again, Parker Palmer has identified the source of this challenge best. He wrote:

Resources that could help us teach better are available from each other—if we could get access to them. But there, of course, is the rub. Academic culture builds barriers between colleagues even higher and wider than those between us and our students. These barriers come partly from the competition that keeps us fragmented by fear. But they also come from the fact that teaching is perhaps the most privatized of all the public professions (Palmer, 1998: 142).

These two barriers, our individual fear and the private lives we live as teachers once the classroom door is closed, are the most significant challenges we face in collaborative teaching. It is important to address each of these challenges in the context of our own work.

First, the "culture of fear" that Palmer (1998) describes in his book *The Courage to Teach* became real to each of us to some extent as we opened the door to collaboration. Despite our willingness, even our eagerness, to forge a partnership, we each had many fears. For our senior faculty member, the primary fear was the fear of letting go of control (and this certainly is related to the relatively privileged position of our private classroom, which we address below). With a librarian now in our classroom and also working with us to design curriculum through the research assignment, we had to "let go of the reins" and listen to someone else; someone who didn't always share the same opinions and definitely didn't share the same disciplinary background and assumptions.

This issue of control has become particularly salient to many faculty members with the growing use of technology and partnership with skilled others such as Web or database programmers and instructional designers. Where once everything revolved around the instructor and his or her decisions, we now have well-intentioned instructional support staff say things like, "don't worry, we keep the professor in the loop." As a faculty member, the usual response, albeit reactive and a little hostile, is "but I *am* the loop!" In other words, faculty resent any threat to the integrity of their role or their centrality in it. We are not just "content providers" in a process. Our way of knowing is deeply entrenched in our disciplinary training, and this way of knowing is itself part of what we call education. To the extent that collaborative teaching poses a threat to *who* faculty are and their role in the classroom, collaboration is a great challenge.

In addition, given our differing backgrounds and expertise, we also had to face the fear of admitting to a colleague that we didn't know something or that we didn't understand. For example, as faculty we had to admit that we didn't know the best way to conduct this type of research, or even that we didn't know what we could reasonably expect students to learn in relation to information literacy. Fear at a basic interpersonal level influenced each interaction, and we had to deal with this as individuals at every meeting in order to be successful.

Finally, the private lives we lead as faculty and instructional librarians—that is, our lives behind the closed door of the classroom—did not prepare us well for the relatively public act of working collaboratively. So often we work with tacit assumptions and "fly by the seat of our pants," and here we had to negotiate our learning outcomes explicitly. This is and continues to be a challenge for each of us. Even when we face our fears, admit our ignorance, and, in fact, use it as a base for real learning, we still had to struggle with basic collaborative skills like being able to make explicit ideas and processes that have, for years, remained unspoken assumptions in our planning. We are getting better at this, but it takes patience by each of us at different points in the process (and a great deal of tactful intervention at times).

OUR NEXT STEPS TOGETHER

Doing something once, like creating a new assignment for a course, can be a creative, fun process. Doing the hard work of assessing your efforts, learning from the experience, and then redesigning your assignment to be more effective is just plain hard work. This is where we're at in our own process now. The course continues in multiple sections with both Tim and Chris teaching separate sections. Our enrollment is well over 1,500 students per year, and the logistics of managing the assignment is another significant challenge. That said, we remain undaunted in our commitment to having students engage in this type of assignment within the context of a large second-year course.

One of the changes we are considering is another approach to our streaming-video assignment tutorials. In place of, or perhaps in addition to, the "talking head," we may employ software that allows voice-over of the actual online research process so that students can see this unfold in real time. Of course, every tool has its limitations, and we do wonder about how quickly these learning materials will become dated and require updating, but this remains our task eternal in the age of networked intelligence. We are also considering assignment blogs so that students can help one another interactively in the format of an archived resource, adding another social constructivism dimension to the learning experience.

The number of choices for supporting student learning is quite large, so we look to the students to guide this implementation. What is it they say they need? To this end, we are also conducting focus group interviews with small, representative sample groups of students in order to get the students' perspective on the research experience and learning.

At the same time that we are refining the assignment, we are also taking a more refined approach to the assessment of student IL learning. Specifically, we are now conducting formal research using pre- and postmeasures of IL knowledge and skills in order to assess just what our students are learning through this assignment. This is part of our own scholarship of teaching, which will take us full circle back to our community of practice where we can share our results with colleagues in order to facilitate the growth and development of our teaching practice.

SUMMARY AND CONCLUSION

In this chapter, we have explained how we created an IL research assignment within the context of a large, second-year psychology class. Using the rich online environment already created to support student learning of content in this blended course, the librarian and faculty team focused on three types of IL, namely tool, research, and social-structural literacy (Shapiro and Hughes, 1996).

The epistemological task of the research assignment required students to develop IL skills in order to trace back the knowledge claims made in a popular press article to the original source in a peer-reviewed journal article. Students were required to demonstrate knowledge of their reading and situate the content from their articles within the context of the course materials, particularly the course textbook and research cited within. The assignment was structured in a scaffolded series of tasks that were explained in a stepwise fashion by the instruction librarian and available to students through streaming video in a "just-in-time" format.

Although technology involves a constant "ever-greening," replacing hardware and software to keep current and relevant, this did not present the biggest challenge to us in the development of this IL research assignment. In fact, the social aspects of collaboration outside of the boundaries of the department and content knowledge of the discipline presented unexpected challenges to both the faculty and librarian. Within the chapter we have drawn on relevant literature to explain and document how to best facilitate these collaborations successfully, and we focused explicitly on the need to draw on the larger educational community to support our growth as educators.

In sum, our greatest challenges remain the social aspects of human interaction within a system of higher education that has thrived on individual scholarship and success. This is not a trivial matter that technique or a particular technology might address. To the extent that we can embrace the kind of courage of which Parker Palmer speaks so eloquently, we might engage ourselves in the kind of community from which we can collaboratively develop the type of IL learning activities that will matter to students. It is clear that the resources we need to do this are available now.

The resources we need in order to grow as teachers are abundant within the community of colleagues. How can we emerge from our privatization and create a continuing conversation about pedagogy what will allow us to tap that abundance? Good talk about good teaching is what we need—to enhance both our professional practice and the selfhood from which it comes. (Palmer, 1998: 144)

We believe that this book and our colleagues' contributions truly represent "good talk about good teaching." That said, a conversation about collaboration is not one sided, so we invite your comments, questions, suggestions for revisions, whatever, really, on our chapter blog at http://.goodtalkaboutgoodteaching.ca

NOTES

1. When animation and narration are used in close proximity or through spatial and temporal contiguity, the result is meaningful learning (Kalyuga et al., 2003). Video technician Kevin Burton applied this principle when designing the lecture slides and archived video lecture streams. He created a window where students could simultaneously view the lecture video and PowerPoint presentation used during the lecture.
2. The Free Assessment Summary Tool (FAST) is a free, online tool for instructors to solicit anonymous feedback from students about their learning and the instructor's teaching. This tool was developed by Bruce Ravelli, lead researcher, and Zvjezdan Patz, lead programmer, at Mt. Royal College, Alberta, Canada. As Ravelli and Patz note in their introduction to FAST at www.getfast.ca, "Traditionally, teaching assessments are conducted at the end of a course—a practice precluding students from offering constructive feedback while they are still in the course. However, conducting instructor-designed and administered Web-based course assessments opens a proactive dialogue with students about teaching, the course, and the entire learning process." We employ this approach in all of our teaching, and thank Ravelli and Patz for the creation of this important tool for our use.

REFERENCES

Asher, Curt. 2003. "Separate but Equal: Librarians, Academics and Information Literacy." *Australian Academic Research Libraries* 34, no. 1: 52–55.

Association of College and Research Librarians. 2000. "Information Literacy Competency Standards for Higher Education." Available: www.ala.org/ala/acrl/acrlstandards/standards.pdf.

Bates, Anthony William. 2000. *Managing Technological Change: Strategies for College and University Leaders*. San Francisco: Jossey-Bass.

Bates, Anthony William, and Gary Poole. 2003. *Effective Teaching with Technology in Higher Education*. San Francisco: Jossey-Bass.

Bennett, Scott. 2007. "Campus Cultures Fostering Information Literacy." *Portal: Libraries and the Academy* 7, no. 2: 147–167.

Brown, Cecelia, Teri Murphy, and Mark Nanny. 2003. "Turning Techno-savvy into Info-savvy: Authentically Integrating Information Literacy into the College Curriculum." *Journal of Academic Librarianship* 29, no. 6: 386–398.

Bruce, Christine, Sylvia Edwards, and Mandy Lupton. 2006. "Six Frames for Information Literacy Education: A Conceptual Framework for Interpreting the Relationships Between Theory and Practice." *Italics* 5: no. 1: 1–18. Available: www.ics.headacademy .ac.uk/italics/vol5-1/pdf/sixframes_final%20_1_.pdf.

Cennamo, Katherine, John Ross, and Cosby Rogers. 2002. "Evolution of a Web-enhanced Course: Incorporating Strategies for Self-regulation." *Educause Quarterly* 25, no. 1: 28–33.

Colborn, Nancy Wootton, and Rosanne Cordell. 1998. "Moving From Subjective to Objective Assessments of Your Instruction Program." *Reference Services Review* 26, no. 3/4: 125–137.

Costello, Barbara, Robert Lenholt, and Judson Stryker. 2004. "Using Blackboard in Library Instruction: Address the Learning Styles for Generation X and Y." *The Journal of Academic Librarianship* 30, no. 6: 452–460.

Doherty, John. 2005. "Empowering the Intentional Learner: A Critical Theory for Information Literacy Instruction." *Library Philosophy and Practice* 8, no. 1. Available: www.webpages.uidaho.edu/~mbolin/doherty-ketchner.htm.

Doskatsch, Irene. 2003. "Perceptions and Perplexities of the Faculty-librarian Partnership: An Australian Perspective." *Reference Services Review* 31, no. 2: 111–121.

Freire, Paolo. 1970. *Pedagogy of the Oppressed.* New York: Continuum.

Frey, Barbara Ann. 2005. Enhancing Face-to-face Courses with a Course Management System. Available: www.eric.ed.gov/ERICDocs/data/ericdocs2sql/content_storage _01/0000019b/80/1b/c1/29.pdf.

Giles, Dwight, and Janet Eyler. 1994. "The Theoretical Roots of Service-learning in John Dewey: Towards a Theory of Service-learning." *Michigan Journal of Community Service Learning* 1: 77–85.

Gray, David. 1999. "The Internet in Lifelong Learning: Liberation or Alienation?" *International Journal of Lifelong Education* 18, no. 2: 119–126.

Hardesty, Larry. 1995. "Faculty Culture and Bibliographic Instruction: An Exploratory Analysis." *Library Trends* 44, no. 2: 339–367.

Ivey, Ruth. 2003. "Information Literacy: How Do Librarians and Academics Work in Partnership to Deliver Effective Learning Programs?" *Australian Academic & Research Libraries* 34, no. 2: 100–113.

Julien, Heidi, and Lisa Given. 2003. "Faculty-librarian Relationships in the Information Literacy Context: A Content Analysis of Librarians' Expressed Attitudes and Experiences." *Canadian Journal of Information and Library Science* 27, no. 3: 65–87.

Kalyuga, Slava et al. 2003. "The Expertise Reversal Effect." *Educational Psychologist* 38, no. 1: 23–31.

Katz, Richard. 1999. *Dancing with the Devil: Information Technology and the New Competition in Higher Education.* San Francisco: Jossey-Bass.

Kraat, Susan. 2005. *Relationships Between Teaching Faculty and Teaching Librarians.* Binghamton, NY: The Haworth Press.

Lindstrom, Joyce, and Diana Shonrock. 2006. "Faculty-librarian Collaboration to Achieve Integration of Information Literacy." *Reference & User Services Quarterly* 46, no. 1: 18–23.

Lippincott, Joan. 2002. "Developing Collaborative Relationships; Librarians, Students, and Faculty Creating Learning Communities." *College & Research Libraries News* 63, no. 3: 190–192.

Luker, Mark. 2000. *Preparing Your Campus for a Networked Future.* San Francisco: Jossey-Bass.

Mann, Sarah J. 2005. "Alienation in the Learning Environment: A Failure of Community?" *Studies in Higher Education* 30, no. 1: 43<en>55.

Manuel, Kate, Molley Molloy, and Susan Beck. 2003. "What Faculty Want: A Study of Attitudes Influencing Faculty Collaboration in Library Instruction." ACRL Eleventh National Conference, April 10–13, 2003, Charlotte, North Carolina. Available: www.acrl.org/ala/acrl/acrlevents/manuel.pdf.

Mayer, R. E. and Sims, V. K. (1994). "For Whom Is a Picture Worth a Thousand Words? Extensions of a Dual-coding Theory of Multimedia Learning." *Journal of Educational Psychology*, 86, 389–401.

McGee, Patricia, Colleen Carmean, and Jafari Ali. 2005. *Course Management Systems for Learning: Beyond Accidental Pedagogy.* Hershey, PA: Information Science.

McGuiness, Claire. 2006. "What Faculty Think—Exploring the Barriers to Information Literacy Development in Undergraduate Education." *The Journal of Academic Librarianship* 32, no. 6: 573–582.

Palmer, Parker. 1998. *The Courage to Teach: Exploring the Inner Landscape of a Teacher's Life.* San Francisco: Jossey-Bass.

Shapiro, Jeremy, and Shelley Hughes. 1996. "Information Literacy as a Liberal Art." *Educom Review* 31, no. 2. Available: www.educause.edu/pub/er/review/reviewarticles/31231.html.

Tapscott, Don. 1996. *The Digital Economy: Promise and Peril in the Age of Networked Intelligence.* New York: McGraw-Hill.

Tempelman-Kluit, Nadaleen. 2006. "Multimedia Learning Theories and Online Instruction." *College & Research Libraries* 67, no. 4 (July): 364–369.

Weigel, Van. 2002. *Deep Learning for a Digital Age.* San Franscisco: Jossey-Bass.

Chapter 3

The World War II Poster Project
Building a Digital Library through Information Literacy Partnerships

Abby Clobridge and David Del Testa

INTRODUCTION

During the fall semester of 2006, 39 students at Bucknell University enrolled in History 100: Thinking about History (HIST100). This was a new introductory course for the Department of History, the theme of which would change, depending on the instructor teaching it, but whose core goals would remain the same—that is, the development of good historical practices and reflections among its primarily first-year students. A major component of the course was the World War II Poster Project, a unit targeting information literacy skills. In addition to drawing on traditional methodologies to teach students these skills, instructors incorporated a broad range of information and digital image technologies in their approaches to reach students and broaden the scope of skills the unit encompassed. A description of that unit and an analysis of its outcomes serve as the focus of this chapter.

For two months, the students in this course cataloged, digitized, analyzed, and reported on an original World War II–era poster from the library's Special Collections Department. The general goal of HIST100 was to encourage student excitement about the field of historical inquiry from their first day of class. This unit was designed to get students immediately involved in the process of research. Library instruction sessions were built into the framework of the course from the onset. Throughout these sessions, technology was used primarily in two ways: through the use of personal response systems and by having students build

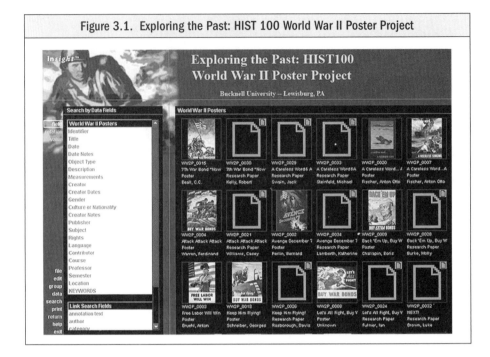

Figure 3.1. Exploring the Past: HIST 100 World War II Poster Project

a digital library related to their posters and research. Figure 3.1 illustrates the digital library students built.

Instructors sought to make these sessions hands-on, intensive, and concrete. This approach was seen as potentially interesting to students because it involved them directly in the process through interactivity, research, and design. Technology was one tool used to accomplish this objective. The specific goals of the World War II Poster Project were as follows:

- Gauge incoming first-year students' information literacy skills by pretesting students using personal response systems.
- Teach students the basics of historical research at a level appropriate for entering first-year undergraduate students.
- Provide students with an in-depth introduction to services available at a university library.
- Give students a hands-on opportunity to work with archival materials and other rare or fragile objects held in library collections and the intellectual tools to think about them.
- Teach students the basics of digital imaging technology, including using digital cameras and working with photo editing software.
- Create a publicly available digital library to share the university's World War II poster collection and students' research papers about the posters.

- Prepare students for their culminating unit assignment: to write a research and analysis paper.

In short, this unit was designed to introduce students to a broad set of tools professional historians use in the production of both traditional print and born-digital scholarship.

THE PROJECT TEAM

The project was initially conceived by David Del Testa, Assistant Professor of History, and was implemented as a collaborative effort between Del Testa and several members of the library and information technology staff who hoped to use a sensitive mix of "analog" historical sources and technology as a vehicle to promote student engagement in the standards and methods of historical practice. The core project team included Del Testa, Abby Clobridge (Digital Initiatives Team Leader and Library Liaison to the History Department), and Doris Dysinger (Curator of Special Collections/University Archives). The complete project team from Information Services and Resources (ISR) also included Debra Cook-Balducci, Instructional Technologist; Mary Beth James, Instructional Technologist; Daniel Mancusi, Digital Projects Technologist; Laura Riskedahl, Metadata Librarian; Jason Snyder, Integrated Online Services Consultant/Librarian; Barbara Stockland, Metadata/Research Services Librarian; and Mary Ann Williard, Assistant Curator for Special Collections. At Bucknell, individual unit members are used to working with one another and with faculty, and careful coordination between the course schedule and these staff members ensured a smooth presentation of lessons to students.

INSTITUTIONAL CONTEXT

Bucknell University is a highly selective, liberal arts institution located in Lewisburg, Pennsylvania. Lewisburg is in the Susquehanna Valley, approximately three hours away from Philadelphia, New York City, Baltimore, Pittsburgh, and Washington, DC. The university is home to approximately 3,400 undergraduate students, 150 graduate students, and 300 full-time faculty members. Students come from 46 states and 41 countries. Small class sizes and an emphasis on teaching at the undergraduate level are hallmarks of a Bucknell education.

Information Literacy and Technology Fluency at Bucknell University

Like several other liberal arts institutions, Bucknell has a merged library-technology organization and ISR. The merger occurred during 1997, leaving one large umbrella organization with nearly 90 full-time equivalent staff positions. Since the merger, most work has been reenvisioned. During spring of 2005, a group of librarians, technologists, and an ISR administrator began working to reexamine and expand information literacy efforts. In the past, library instruction consisted of a series of one-shot, traditional bibliographic instruction sessions. Based on data collected from surveys, faculty members were generally pleased with individual sessions. However, the approach as a whole led to isolated, inconsistent information literacy instruction for students.

Furthermore, regional accreditation authorities had begun to examine information literacy closely at Bucknell University. The Middle States Commission on Higher Education (MSCHE) began examining information literacy programs as part of its regular review process in 2004; Bucknell was part of this first cohort of institutions for which information literacy was evaluated as part of its accreditation review. MSCHE's interpretation of information literacy is outlined in two publications: *Developing Research & Communication Skills: Guidelines for Information Literacy in the Curriculum* (Middle States Commission on Higher Education, 2003), which is devoted exclusively to best practices in information literacy, and *Characteristics of Excellence in Higher Education* (Middle States Commission on Higher Education, 2006), which includes a section on information literacy and technology fluency. In its 2004 accreditation report to the university, the Middle States Commission Evaluation Team suggested that staff from ISR should:

> Lead an effort in conjunction with Academic Affairs and faculty to develop a clear definition of "information literacy"; this effort . . . would be a starting point for informing discussions of a University-wide standard for information literacy, as well as framing assessment efforts.

As a result of the MSCHE's review recommendations for academic departments, ISR, and the university as a whole, information literacy has attracted the attention of campus administrators. While a university-wide program that is truly integrated into the curriculum is still in the early planning phases, individual faculty members and librarians are working together to create in-depth, longer assignments or projects that clearly address the ACRL (Association of College and Research Libraries) and MSCHE information literacy standards.

The Development of HIST100: Thinking about History

At the same time, the faculty of the History Department had begun to revise their curriculum, in part based on recommendations from the MSCHE review and also because the department had been making an effort to expand its offerings at the introductory survey level. This was an effort to attract more students to the history program and ultimately to draw in more history majors. Furthermore, in response to uneven information literacy among students in upper-division courses, faculty within the department had sought ways to solidify all students' basic historical research skills in these introductory courses so students can, regardless of their majors, progress to more advanced historical research.

As a first step toward a general improvement in information literacy, faculty created HIST100. The original goals of the project were these:

- Give students hands-on opportunities to work with archival materials.
- Get students interested in historical research by creating a more engaging, involving assignment than a typical research term paper.
- Instruct incoming first-year students on several aspects of research, drawing on resources available to them at a college or university library.

After an initial brainstorming meeting, additional facets were added to the project related to technology integration, specifically the idea of having students create a digital library. The project was expanded, more clearly defined, and tied to MSCHE (see Appendix 3.1) and ACRL standards for information literacy (see Appendix 3.2). As mentioned previously, it also occurred within the context of a broader internal review by history faculty of history students' information literacy and application. The World War II Poster Project assignment within HIST100 is one example of how a specific faculty member tried to integrate some of the MSCHE and ACRL information literacy standards into a course.

THE PEDAGOGY OF THE POSTER PROJECT

HIST100 served as a pedagogical laboratory for the collaborative and project-based learning methods in an environment crafted specifically for students at the start of their undergraduate education. The subject matter, the history of World War II, coupled with the design of the course itself, helped to elicit great interest from students. As such, it was possible to create a course designed to provide students with the necessary foundations for good historical practices and research skills without the stigma sometimes associated with required classes.

Educational literature has celebrated the positive consequences of "collaborative learning" and "learning teams" for a long time (Atkinson, 2001; Barkley, Cross, and Howell Major, 2005; Bruffee, 1993; McKeachie, 1999; Meyers, 1993; Stein and Hurd, 2000). Instructors at Bucknell have certainly put such techniques into practice in their classrooms successfully for as long as these techniques have been current.

In planning the course, however, it became apparent that a pure "guide on the side" format that generally works well in conjunction with learning teams would not function as well in this particular environment. The materials required for the project as well as an institutional culture that demanded authoritative, instructor-based student evaluation encouraged a hybrid between the instructor serving as a "guide on the side" and a "sage on the stage." This hybrid "master craftsperson" model emerged in which students received instructions from experts to learn new skills but then practiced those skills as teams. The final written report was then evaluated by an expert. Thus students had a responsibility as "journeymen" and "journeywomen" to become "masters" by producing a "masterpiece" and thus enter the guild of historians.

In part because of the fragility of documents being handled, it was necessary for the lead instructor to remain in a position of authority. The instructor needed to preserve the integrity of the materials while also ensuring that one team member would not—or could not—let the other team member down since grades were assigned to teams, not individuals.

While the instructor did retain some authority over the class as a whole, students absorbed more organizational leadership than is possible in a traditional class. Students worked in pairs. Teams, which were formed of the multiple pairs, were encouraged to work together to share information when relevant. For example, several pairs of students worked on posters featuring war bonds; these teams joined together specifically so they could swap information. In this way, they were not treading on the same ground on common issues or competing with one another for precious written materials in the library's collections.

The pedagogy of learning teams under expert guidance worked, but it is likely that a more student-directed model than designed for this project could function if the fragility of the documents were not in question.

Characteristics of Today's College Students

Much research in recent years has focused on the characteristics of the current generation of college students. In their book *Millennials Rising*, Neil Howe and William Strauss researched and analyzed the generation of students born between 1982 and 2002, the generation whose first cohorts graduated from high school in the year 2000, thus giving them the name the Millennial Generation (Howe and Strauss, 2000). Howe and Strauss depict this generation as having seven core traits: a strong sense of being special, sheltered, confident, team-oriented, achievement-oriented, pressured, and conventional. In *Millennials Go to College*, Howe and Strauss follow up their original research by focusing specifically on what these generational characteristics mean for higher education (Howe and Strauss, 2003). This generation is also sometimes referred to as Generation Y, the Net Generation, or the Digital Generation. Susan Gardner and Susanna Eng, in "What Students Want: Generation Y and the Changing Function of the Academic Library," conducted a library user survey in 2003 at an undergraduate institution as a case study to initiate discussion about whether library services are meeting the expectations of Generation Y, specifically in terms of four of their characteristic attributes: "they have great expectations," "they expect customization," "they are technology veterans," and "they utilize new communication modes" (Gardner and Eng, 2005). Thus, instructors may anticipate a high degree of information literacy and good team working skills, but perhaps without the creativity seen in the approaches taken by the age cohorts that preceded them. One resounding theme throughout all of the literature is the need for these students to be actively engaged, especially in classroom activities. The World War II Poster Project was created as a means of promoting student engagement in learning information literacy and technology skills within these perceived desires and capabilities.

Jeffrey Jensen Arnett, in *Emerging Adulthood: The Winding Road from the Late Teens through the Twenties*, argues that there is a stage of life lasting from around the time people graduate high school through their mid-twenties, which he refers to as "emerging adulthood." This stage has five key characteristics: identity exploration, instability, an inward focus, a feeling of being "in between," and an abundance of possibilities in terms of life choices (Arnett, 2004). Diana G. Oblinger and James L. Oblinger also examine this generation of students within the context of their experiences in higher education. Specific focus is placed on library services, the usage of technology for instruction, development of learning commons, and implications for faculty skills development (Oblinger and Oblinger, 2005). Given this, coaxing and coaching students toward identifying with the experiences of others in different contexts would be essential to creating effective analyses of the time-specific historical meanings the posters contained.

THE WORLD WAR II POSTER PROJECT

The World War II Poster Project was the first of two major projects that served as the cornerstones of HIST100. The poster project unit lasted for approximately two months toward the start of the fall semester and included instruction in library research methods, technology, organization of information, and preservation methods. (See Appendix 3.3 for schedule and breakdown of class sessions.) During this time students participated in several sessions held in the library that were led by members of the library and technology staff, attended class lectures and participated in discussions, read assigned books and articles, participated in classroom-based activities including building a digital library, and, finally, wrote a research and analysis paper drawing on their experiences over the course of the unit. In-class sessions and out-of-class assignments were designed with the goal of making students budding historians. Instructors taught students skills and exposed them to experiences within the context of creating authentic historical scholarship, both in a traditional sense and by working with new models of digital scholarship.

Throughout the unit, students worked in self-selected pairs called learning teams. Ultimately, each team presented their poster in two ways: through the digital library and in detailed, analytical written reports in which teams figuratively dissected their posters. Students were asked to present their posters as a series of layers: a "historical layer cake" of base material, presentation, composition, intention, context, analysis, and interpretation. In-class sessions were designed so students could develop or hone the skills necessary to complete this assignment and help students to understand, discuss, analyze, and present their posters. (See Appendix 3.4 for a schematic representing in a visual fashion how students were instructed to think about the project.) The submitted reports were to be limited to no more than 20 pages of double-spaced text, supported by footnotes prepared using the Chicago/Turabian citation style. Figure 3.2 details the format and content of the final paper.

First Impressions

Students began the unit by selecting the posters they would be working with for the rest of the project. Immediately after viewing posters for the first time, learning teams were instructed to make notes in their journals about their first impressions and observations about their posters. They were asked to write down all of the information and descriptive notes they could about it, possibly including a sketch of the poster itself. They were asked to consider what was most striking about that poster, and why they selected their particular poster. They were encouraged to make notes about subject matters, words or messages displayed on the poster, colors used, or anything else about the poster that stood out.

Since the students kept a journal and research log throughout the project, it served as a way for them to track their partner's progress and to prevent duplicating research efforts while individuals were working alone. The journal also required students to reflect on their approaches and choices and opened a neutral venue for discussing research approaches with one another.

Working with Materials

Throughout the project, students were encouraged to work directly with the posters and with other materials from Special Collections/University Archives (SCUA). The

Figure 3.2. Sections of the Paper
Understanding the image itself, the apparent "text" and subject
The image's physical properties and dimensions
The image's author/artist and his or her background
The institutional background for the image
The image's historical context, audience, and (changing) message
Commentary contemporary to the image, its author(s)
Your presentation, interpretation, discussion—including presenting the posters from the perspective of today

in-class schedule included three sessions in the archives for each of the learning teams: the initial visit in which students selected their posters, a second session in which students were introduced to various types of primary source materials, and a third session that focused on handling objects. For the session focusing on primary sources, Doris Dysinger, Curator of Special Collections/University Archives, displayed Bucknell-owned materials along with the posters. Dysinger gave an overview of why scholars use primary sources to better understand history, reinforcing what Del Testa had discussed in the classroom earlier in the semester. The overarching question of the session was, "what can you learn from different types of materials?" Students had hands-on time with materials from the vault, many of which were documents and objects from the university itself. Students were encouraged to try to make connections between their posters and what had been happening on the Bucknell campus at the time when their posters were displayed. Students were also given instructions in handling rare and fragile materials.

During the last scheduled session in the archives, the focus was on preservation and display of materials. For professional archivists, preservation and access of materials requires working with both the objects themselves and with technology to represent the materials in the digital environment. Students again had hands-on time with their posters so they could collect data such as their poster's physical measurements, data that would later be included the digital collection. Dysinger led the class in a discussion about how to create exhibits to display and increase access to materials. In many instances, exhibits can be manifested in two forms: a physical exhibit displayed in glass cases at the library and an electronic exhibit, such as a Web site or digital library that is publicly available on the Internet. This discussion of exhibits was the first step toward creating a digital library and accompanying Web site. Various components of the digital library and Web site were brought together later in the process.

Building a Digital Library

Toward the end of the unit, the class worked together to build a digital library to make images of the posters and the students' research publicly available. Building the collection occurred over the course of several weeks and was carried out largely within class sessions. Each pair of students created a digital surrogate of their poster along with data describing it; the compilation of the digital images and metadata formed the framework for a small digital library the students built to present their posters and make them more widely accessible. The students' research papers have also been included in the final version of the digital library.

Technology Competency: Working with Digital Images

Two instructional technologists worked with the class to teach students the basics of creating digital images of their posters. The instructional technologists had students assist them in setting up lighting and displaying the posters in optimal ways before using digital cameras to take photographs of the posters. Technologists discussed photography issues such as lighting, dealing with oversized objects, and handling fragile, curled materials.

After the posters were photographed, the digital images were distributed to the students. The technologists demonstrated several basic processes in Adobe Photoshop such as rotating images by 90 degrees and cropping images. Digital images were saved in two formats: uncompressed, as a tagged image file format (TIFF) and in a compressed format, as a JPEG (Joint Photographic Experts Group). Students used the smaller JPEG files to work from while they referenced their posters throughout the research process. The larger, uncompressed files were later used for the digital library. Students were encouraged to use their shared spaces on the campus network, which also opened up opportunities for instructors to discuss how to access the campus network and the differences between public and private file spaces.

While many students already knew how to open digital image files and perform basic editing functions, we assumed that not all students would be familiar with these techniques. We felt that these skills were technology competencies that all students should know, so they included these basic digital image manipulation techniques into the learning outcomes for this unit. Student surveys indicated that their assumption was accurate, and that students appreciated the time in class in which they worked with digital images.

Metadata

During one of the final class sessions, after the digital images had been created, Clobridge led a discussion with students concerning issues surrounding the procedures for building a digital collection. Topics for discussion included describing materials according to library and archival standards, Dublin Core and VRA Core 3.0 metadata standards, collection access points, digital preservation, and copyright.

Metadata provided the biggest challenge for students. Each team was given two handouts. The first handout listed Dublin Core fields; the second handout included fields from VRA Core 3.0. The class discussed the idea of a digital surrogate versus the object itself; that is, does a "date" field refer to the date when the poster was originally created or the date when the digital image was created? The class decided which fields to use from the two standards and created some additional fields. The class also discussed metadata issues such as formatting and consistency of data. For example, how should titles be capitalized? In what format should proper names appear: Firstname Lastname or Lastname, Firstname? Appendix 3.5 delineates the metadata schema ultimately used for the digital collection as decided by the class. This exercise made students participate, however lightly, in a larger professional technical process. It was hoped that this exercise encouraged reflection on professional standards and the informed, ongoing debates that encourage the evolution of international standards. Having students rigidly conform to human subject requirements and oral history standards in a subsequent project achieved similar goals.

The digital image collection was built using Luna Imaging Incorporated's Insight software. Clobridge created the database structure and uploaded the students' images into the collection. Students then used Inscribe, the cataloging component of the Luna suite of software, to create metadata for their poster.

Using Technology to Gauge Students' Information Literacy

In addition to analyzing the objects and gathering information from primary sources, students needed to use secondary sources, which inherently required using various library services such as interlibrary loan and the reserves desk. Evaluation of student learning and students' general understanding of library research skills was an important part of the conceptualization of this course from its inception. Clobridge used personal response systems ("clickers") as the medium for collecting baseline information about students' comprehension of basic information literacy skills and library services. Clobridge had two goals for using clickers in library research instruction sessions: to incorporate active learning techniques into library instruction to get students more engaged in library sessions and to gain a more accurate picture of students' understanding of research techniques.

Students were each given a device and were asked to answer a series of questions that had been prepared in advance. The first questions posed were designed to get students familiar with and comfortable using the devices. For the rest of the session, Clobridge led the class in an exercise to assess students' basic research skills. Students' answers were used as a jumping-off point for a class discussion following each question. When most of the students correctly answered a question, a volunteer was asked to explain the answer. When most of the class answered incorrectly, Clobridge led the class in a longer discussion or showed examples pertaining to the question in the library catalog or a bibliographic database to demonstrate the topic. A full list of questions used in class is available in Appendix 3.6.

Anecdotal evidence suggests that students enjoyed participating in class discussions by using clickers. During the course of the semester, several students from a number of classes mentioned to librarians how much they enjoyed the sessions, that it was fun to play a kind of "Who Wants to Be a Millionaire." Clobridge used clickers in several other courses throughout the semester. In two of these other courses that incorporated the clicker technology, students were

Figure 3.3. Students' Responses—How Useful Was This Session?		
This session was:		
	Student Responses	Percentage
A Extremely helpful	(4)	11.4%
B Very helpful	(19)	54.3%
C Helpful	(11)	31.4%
D Not particularly helpful	(1)	2.9%
E Not at all helpful	(0)	0%

asked how useful or helpful they felt the session was. The results are shown in Figure 3.3.

As the question of how useful or helpful students felt that the session had been was asked only in two courses, only a small subset of students was sampled. Even so, having data demonstrate that students were positive about these sessions was useful in encouraging librarians to continue to experiment with clickers in instructional sessions. Writing the questions and answers in advance took some time, particularly for the first few sessions. Advantages of using the clickers included having students more engaged in class sessions, being able to gauge students' understanding of a particular topic, and as a result of gauging students' understanding, being able to adapt the session on the fly. If students have already mastered a skill, the instructor can move on and focus on another topic; if, on the other hand, students are not grasping a skill, the instructor can commit more time to that topic. While using clickers was generally successful in this and other sessions, instructors should expect a learning curve to adjust to using the new technology and writing questions and answers in advance. Furthermore, while getting instant feedback from students can be quite helpful, instructors should be prepared to change the direction of a class session on the fly to accommodate students, either by moving on to another topic or continuing to discuss the issue at hand.

For this article, we drew our conclusions from three sources: the results of this initial survey in which the entire class (39 students) participated; the outcomes indicated in standard university course evaluations (38 responses); and an online questionnaire Clobridge solicited from students during early Summer 2007 (18 responses).

The World of the Historian: Intertwining Analog and Digital

One of the major themes throughout the unit was the idea that a historian's work is firmly embedded in both the analog and digital worlds. Students ultimately presented their findings in both formats: a written paper and electronically, through the creation and distribution of a digital image collection that provided access to images of the posters along with students' analysis. This process allowed students to engage in historians' work: finding new materials and presenting them in a professional manner to an interested audience.

HIST100: A FACULTY-STAFF COLLABORATION

Historically, mechanisms have been in place for faculty-librarian collaboration; a formal faculty liaison program has been in existence since 1990 and a formal user education program has been in place since the early 1980s. Each academic department is assigned a librarian who serves as the liaison to this department. Responsibilities include leading instructional sessions, working with faculty to ensure that collection development needs are met, and serving as the point person to field questions or work on special projects. Likewise, each academic department has one faculty member who serves as that department's representative to the library. In some instances, liaisons have worked extremely closely with departmental representatives or the departments as a whole.

Clobridge and Del Testa began working together as library liaison and departmental representative during the 2004–2005 school year. During the fall semester of 2004, Del Testa asked Clobridge to host each of his classes for one or two sessions. Del Testa worked actively with Clobridge in these sessions to boost student competency in library research skills, and Clobridge made herself available to students for individual appointments on an as-needed basis. Students were brought to the library, and Clobridge led sessions introducing students to various aspects of library research. Some sessions focused mainly on having students work in the reference and book stacks; other sessions were research workshops for students to have hands-on time at computers to search particular databases.

Over the next three semesters, Del Testa and Clobridge continued to experiment with the format of class sessions, in-class exercises for students, and the number of sessions in which a librarian was invited into class. One particular class included three library-led sessions over the span of two months. For that course, Clobridge was able to introduce various topics and work with the students throughout the length of a particular assignment—a scenario that worked well.

Clobridge's main job responsibility is to manage the university's digital library program. In this capacity, she works closely with members of the ISR instructional technology team. Upon his arrival at Bucknell in 2004, Del Testa submitted a proposal to build a digital image collection and Web site related to his scholarship and teaching of French Indochina. The resulting project, *Adieu Saigon, Au Revoir Hanoi: The 1943 Vacation Diary of Claudie Beaucarnot* (www.bucknell.edu/beaucarnot), was the result of a great deal of collaboration between Del Testa, Clobridge, and Michael Weaver, an instructional technologist. Like the poster project, it originated in the connection of archival materials to student researchers and their analysis, albeit in a much more specialized and intensive project.

The success of in-class collaborations and the digital image collection gave Del Testa and Clobridge the confidence to experiment with a more ambitious project. During the summer of 2006, Del Testa, Clobridge, and Doris Dysinger, Curator of Special Collections/University Archives, began brainstorming ways to integrate the World War II posters and other objects from Special Collections into Del Testa's HIST100 course. Del Testa was aware that the posters had been collected and maintained in the library and had ideas for creating a multiweek, intensive project for students to "dissect" the posters.

While Del Testa and Clobridge had worked together on several projects in the past, the World War II Poster Project involved many more components—the sheer number of staff members necessary to support such a project, working with nearly 40 students to build a digital image collection, and the logistics involved in keeping so many students, staff, and faculty all on the same page.

LESSONS LEARNED

In the execution of the poster project, certain challenges arose along the way. The organization of the course, the assembly of materials, and the preparation for lectures presented no particular challenges beyond what instructors might normally face. However, the actual execution of the unit required extraordinary amounts of dedicated staff time, much more than anticipated. Having nearly 40 students working directly with fragile documents led to many more hours of staff work than is typical, although with very satisfying results. We anticipate that ways to streamline the processes involved will be developed in the future as similar projects are repeated for other courses (World War II–era diaries from Bucknell students, antiwar materials on file for the Vietnam War, etc.).

Beyond the dedication and hard work of its instructors, students had the fortune to have access to original World War II–era posters that former university president Arnaud C. Marts (acting 1935–1938, 1938–1945) had collected during his tenure. Having students complete the same exercise using materials related to World War II freely available on the Internet would have been possible and would have required less staff time to execute, but this approach would not have given students the same sense of responsibility gained by handling the original documents. Another issue that many students noted in course reviews was a perceived disconnect between the relationship of the poster project and its successor, an oral history project, to classroom lectures, readings, and evaluations. Special care needs to be taken to coordinate and make explicit the relationship between classroom and laboratory. For humanities courses, the laboratory typically cannot occupy extra class time as a hard sciences laboratory would. In retrospect, emphasizing the involvement of the United States in the war would have provided plenty of material to discuss and perhaps would have made the links between poster and history easier for students to connect.

Of course, students' expectations for a thematic course do not always coincide with those of the instructor. Although Del Testa knew that many of his HIST100 students, heavily weaned on a hagiographic view of World War II, expected a great deal of discussion about the machinery of warfare, battles, and violence, these were not the focus of the course and left many students asking, "Okay, when do we talk about the war?" Indeed, only some fairly graphic World War II anti-Japanese propaganda films shown late in the course seemed to have the effect of making the realities of the war clear for students and led students to connect the propaganda they were researching with brutal realities. Furthermore, making the meaning of the posters come alive for the students, who pretended to have traveled down the road to the history of World War II too many times, took some careful planning and discussion. The responsibility of students to serve as protector for the posters and instructors' insistence on a professional approach in working with the objects helped in this task.

The postcourse survey confirms the overall success of the course, the achievement of its main aims, an improved and "concretized" set of historical skills for students, and a general enthusiasm for history. From both the instructor's perspective and that of the students, it seems the single greatest improvement in the course would be the articulation of the larger course with the specific projects. Del Testa barely had the time to touch on the texts and themes they addressed within the context of the larger history of World War II, and the students became fatigued trying to do well in the projects and course readings.

However, some students also expressed anecdotally that they had started to become bored with the poster project by the end, even if 72.2 percent of students said they strongly agreed or agreed that they preferred this to a traditional research paper. A significant majority (83.7 percent) of student respondents said they agreed or strongly agreed that they learned more than they otherwise would have in a traditional research paper. Consistent with that finding, 82.3 percent of responders said they would agree in assigning this over a traditional paper. A small segment of the class, 1.2 percent, disagreed or strongly disagreed that they preferred the poster assignment to traditional research papers often assigned in courses like these. These data reflect not only some disconnect between student expectations of what a course on World War II should address but also the limitations a predetermined assignment presents. Finally, it is apparent that students did not have a clear understanding of the link between the posters and Special Collections—that is, what made the posters so special that they needed isolation from the general circulating collection in the library.

For the instructors, using technology was successful. First, having students use personal response systems allowed instructors to quickly get the class to a common ground in terms of research methods. By not needing to spend time on topics students were all familiar with, class time was focused on issues students had not mastered. Having students answer questions and get them wrong also served to clearly indicate students' areas of weakness to the students themselves. After students answered questions incorrectly, they were more involved in the discussion afterward. In short: students tend to assume they know how to conduct research and use the library, but after they incorrectly answered questions, they tended to pay more attention to the instructor explaining research processes and library services.

Building the digital library was also a successful endeavor. Students indicated that they appreciated instruction on working with digital images, a skill that hopefully will be integrated into the university's information literacy and technology fluency plan. The creation of the digital library serves as a legacy to the course. Students, their families, and other researchers are now able to access digital representations of the posters housed at Bucknell. This group of students was instrumental in taking items housed in Special Collections/University Archives and making them more broadly accessible to the public.

The course strengthened links between the instructor and various members of the library staff, creating professional bonds and cross-disciplinary connections as colleagues that had not existed before. Such courses take an enormous amount of time, but the positive results are evident. We are sure that, in addition to a broader and deeper understanding of specific aspects of World War II and its textual legacy, students will take away a stronger sense of information literacy, a greater appreciation for library materials and their use and preservation, and a clearer sense of themselves as active historians.

REFERENCES

Arnett, Jeffery Jensen. 2004. *Emerging Adulthood: The Winding Road from the Late Teens Through the Twenties.* New York: Oxford University.
Atkinson, Jean. 2001. *Developing Teams through Project-Based Learning.* Burlington, VT: Gower.
Barkley, Elizabeth F., K. Patricia Cross, and Claire Howell Major (Eds.). 2005. *Collaborative Learning Techniques: A Handbook for College Faculty.* San Francisco: Jossey-Bass.
Bruffee, Kenneth. 1993. *Collaborative Learning: Higher Education, Interdependence, and the Authority of Knowledge.* Baltimore: Johns Hopkins Press.
Gardner, Susan and Susanna Eng. 2005. "What Students Want: Generation Y and the Changing Function of the Academic Library." *portal: Libraries and the Academy* 5, no. 3: 405–420.
Howe, Neil and William Strauss. 2000. *Millennials Rising: The Next Great Generation.* New York: Vintage.

Howe, Neil and William Strauss. 2003. *Millennials Go to College: Strategies for a New Generation on Campus: Recruiting and Admissions, Campus Life, and the Classroom.* Washington, DC: American Association of Collegiate Registrars and Admissions Officers.

McKeachie, Wilbert J. 1999. *McKeachie's Teaching Tips: Strategies, Research, and Theory for College and University Teachers.* Boston: Houghton Mifflin.

Meyers, Chet. 1993. *Promoting Active Learning: Strategies for the College Classroom, The Jossey-Bass Higher and Adult Education Series.* San Francisco: Jossey-Bass Books.

Middle States Commission on Higher Education. 2003. *Developing Research & Communication Skills: Guidelines for Information Literacy in the Curriculum.* Philadelphia: Middle States Commission on Higher Education.

Middle States Commission on Higher Education. 2006. *Characteristics of Excellence in Higher Education.* Philadelphia: Middle States Commission on Higher Education.

Oblinger, Diana G. and James L. Oblinger. 2005. *Educating the Net Generation.* Boulder, CO: Educause.

Stein, Ruth Federman and Sandra Hurd. 2000. *Using Student Teams in the Classroom: A Faculty Guide.* Boston: Anker.

Appendix 3.1. HIST100 Learning Objectives Mapped to MSCHE—Phases in the Process of Teaching Information Literacy

MSCHE Phase	Selected Details of Phase	Selected Details of Phase
Phase 1: Preparing Students for an Information Literacy Experience	At beginning of class, provide a clear presentation of: • What students will learn in the course • How information literacy relates to those learning goals	During Session 2, instructors provide overview of project and intended outcome.
Phase 2: Teaching Students to Find and Evaluate Sources	Address basic principles of finding and evaluating sources. Can be addressed via formal lectures, discussion sections, library visits, writing workshops, computer labs, or classroom management systems.	In-class exercise during Session 2 using personal response systems to discuss the basics of finding and evaluating sources. Selected topics included: • Understanding citations • Finding materials in a university library • Interlibrary loan
Phase 3: Teaching Students to Evaluate and Understand Content	• Framing the research question • Identify and access information sources • Evaluate the information • Use the information effectively to accomplish a specific purpose.	In class during Session 2, students begin to work in pairs to frame their individual research questions and strategies. Throughout project: Students work to identify, access, and evaluate information sources.
Phase 4: Producing New Information	"Students gain critical insights about information literacy through their own production of information, which is likely to be the result of some form of active learning opportunities—those that go beyond lectures and require students to make critical decisions about the information they evaluate and produce, especially as they try to formulate a response" (MSCHE, 2003: 35).	Students write research/analysis paper to place posters within historical context, make connections between poster and broader World War II experience, and draw connections between posters and current events. In class: Students create a digital library with surrogate images of posters and data related to posters.

Appendix 3.2. HIST100 Learning Outcomes as Mapped to the ACRL Information Literacy Standards		
ACRL Standard	Performance Indicators (PI)– The information literate student does the following:	Integration into HIST100 Poster Project
Standard One: The information literate student determines the nature and extent of the information needed.	PI 1.1: Defines and articulates the need for information.	Students worked together in pairs to identify research topics and a thesis statement for their final papers.
	PI 1.2: Identifies a variety of types and formats of potential sources for information. • Identifies purpose and audience of potential resources (e.g., popular versus scholarly, current versus historical) • Differentiates between primary and secondary sources.	Students' basic understanding of information sources was gauged during a pretest exercise using personal response systems ("clickers") during Session One.
Standard Two: The information literate student accesses needed information effectively and efficiently.	PI 2.1: Selects the most appropriate investigative methods or information retrieval systems for accessing the needed information.	Students selected appropriate research sources for the papers. In addition to using the Internet, students were encouraged to use subject-specialized databases related to history and, to a lesser degree, art. Students needed to balance using primary sources available through Special Collections with secondary source research collected elsewhere.
	PI 2.2: Constructs and implements effectively designed search strategies.	During Session Two, students worked in pairs to identify key concepts and terms to use for their research. Students participated in class discussions and discussions with smaller groups of peers about their information needs and plans for research. During Session Two, students participated in a brainstorming session to create keywords, synonyms, and related terms that were used in search strategies. Students discussed their intended search strategies with each other and their instructors. Research logs were maintained by all students. Del Testa placed the emphasis on "process over product," encouraging students to consider how they approached their research.

(Continued)

Appendix 3.2. HIST100 Learning Outcomes as Mapped to the ACRL Information Literacy Standards *(Continued)*

ACRL Standard	Performance Indicators (PI)— The information literate student does the following:	Integration into HIST100 Poster Project
Standard Two *(Continued)*	PI 2.3: Retrieves information online or in person using a variety of methods.	To complete their papers, students needed to use materials from Special Collections along with library-licensed databases. Some materials were available in person at Special Collections, in the reference collection, at the reserves desk, and in the library's main book collection. Most students also needed to order articles or books through an interlibrary loan system.
Standard Three: The information literate student evaluates information and its sources critically and incorporates selected information into his or her knowledge base and value system.	PI 3.1: Summarizes the main ideas to be extracted from the information gathered.	The research/analysis papers required that students were able to extract and synthesize information from various sources, evaluate information and sources, and construct new ideas based on all of the information gathered.
	PI 3.2: Articulates and applies initial criteria for evaluating both the information and its sources.	
	PI 3.3: Synthesizes main ideas to construct new concepts.	
Standard Four: The information literate student, individually or as a member of a group, uses information effectively to accomplish a specific purpose	PI 4.1: Applies new and prior information to the planning and creation of a particular product or performance. • Organizes the content in a manner that supports the purpose and format of the product or performance. • Manipulates digital text, images, and data, as needed, transferring them from their original locations and formats to a new context.	The digital library, created over the course of several class sessions, required students to create a new product. As a class, students decided how to organize the content for their collection. They created digital surrogates of their posters, manipulated digital images, and used specialized information technology applications to create the digital library.

(Continued)

Appendix 3.2. HIST100 Learning Outcomes as Mapped to the ACRL Information Literacy Standards *(Continued)*		
ACRL Standard	Performance Indicators (PI)— The information literate student does the following:	Integration into HIST100 Poster Project
Standard Four *(Continued)*	PI 4.2: Revises the development process for the product or performance. • Maintains a journal or log of activities related to the information seeking, evaluating, and communicating process. • Reflects on past successes, failures, and alternative strategies.	As part of the initial written instructions for the poster project that were distributed to students, Del Testa directed: Remember that process is as important as or more important than product in this assignment, therefore you **must** collectively keep a diary/journal of all actions you take related to this project and submit it to the instructor along with your poster report. Your instructor recognizes effort as much as outcome. The best proof of this effort, especially if you don't come up with much supporting material in the end, is your diary/journal. You are encouraged to make notations in this diary/journal every time you meet to discuss your poster, examine your poster, research your poster, and so on. This will provide valuable "proof" of your efforts to your instructor. Once you and your partner have selected a poster to investigate, you should immediately get out your journal/diary, note the date and place, and then proceed write down all of the information you can about it, perhaps even sketching out roughly what you see. You should write down all of your first impressions and observations and take notes on all of the text you can find on the page. None of these impressions or observations are "wrong" . . . what you're doing is bringing your combined knowledge together to provide a basis for investigating the image further and analyzing it for others. These first impressions and initial information is critical, for it will help guide you. Journals were submitted as part of the final project, along with the formal research paper.

(Continued)

Appendix 3.2. HIST100 Learning Outcomes as Mapped to the ACRL Information Literacy Standards *(Continued)*		
ACRL Standard	Performance Indicators (PI)— The information literate student does the following:	Integration into HIST100 Poster Project
Standard Four *(Continued)*	PI 4.3: Communicates the product or performance effectively to others. • Uses a range of information technology applications in creating the product or performance. • Incorporates principles of design and communication	The digital library, created over the course of several class sessions, required students to create a new product. As a class, students decided how to organize the content for their collection. They created digital surrogates of their posters, manipulated digital images, and used specialized information technology applications to create the digital library. Students were also involved in making recommendations for the look and feel of the online exhibit showcasing their work that would be created at a later date.
Standard Five: The information literate student understands many of the economic, legal, and social issues surrounding the use of information and accesses and uses information ethically and legally.	PI 5.3: Acknowledges the use of information sources in communicating the product or performance.	Students were required to use Turabian or *Chicago Manual of Style* for footnotes and bibliographies. Copyright was discussed in class within the context of the digital library.

Appendix 3.3. Schedule of Class Sessions

Tuesday, September 12: Project Kickoff

ISR Staff: Abby Clobridge, Doris Dysinger. Entire class meets together in Library Lab.

- Professor Del Testa introduces project, assignments, and ISR staff involved in the project. Overview of next four weeks. Etiquette for scheduling appointments.
- Class divides into pairs. Each pair selects a poster. Posters will be displayed in Special Collections/University Archives. Three groups at a time will go into SCUA to select a poster.
- Rest of session: Introduction to Research.
  - While pairs are going into SCUA to select project, the rest of the class will work on a short "quiz" to assess knowledge of the organization of a college library, what is a reference book, etc.
  - Searching the library catalog
  - Library of Congress classification, subject headings
  - Search strategies—keeping a search log

Thursday, September 14: Advanced Historical Research

ISR Staff: Abby Clobridge. Entire class meets together in Library Lab.

- Review from Tuesday's session
- Types of research—primary sources (available in SCUA) versus secondary sources
- Hands-on time in reference collection and stacks
- Databases: America: History and Life; Historical Abstracts; other relevant databases
- Citations

Tuesday, September 19: Doing Research in SCUA and Creating Digital Surrogates

ISR Staff: Doris Dysinger, Deb Balducci, Mary Beth James. Class splits into two groups.

Group A meets in SCUA. Group B meets in Library Lab.

Group A: Doing Research in SCUA (Doris)
- Using primary sources to understand history—what can you learn from different types of materials?
- Research using the WW2 materials from SCUA

Group B: Creating Digital Surrogates (Deb and ITEC)
- Capturing the posters using digital cameras
- File formats for digital images and image resolution
- Using Photoshop for image cleanup and correction: cropping and rotating images

Thursday, September 21: Doing Research in SCUA and Creating Digital Surrogates

ISR Staff: Doris Dysinger.

Repeat of Tuesday, September 19 sessions.

Group B: Doing Research in SCUA
Group A: Creating Digital Surrogates

(Continued)

Appendix 3.3. Schedule of Class Sessions *(Continued)*

Tuesday, September 26: Preserving, Archiving, and Displaying

ISR Staff: Doris Dysinger.

Group A: Preserving, Archiving, and Displaying
- Handling materials
- Measuring posters
- Differences between archiving and preserving
- Materials preservation techniques
- Planning for displays

Group B: Off. Use time to get caught up working with partners on assignments. The Library Lab will be available for use.

Thursday, September 29: Preserving, Archiving, and Displaying

ISR Staff: Doris Dysinger.

Repeat of Tuesday, September 26.

Group B: Preserving, Archiving, and Displaying
Group A: Off.

Tuesday, October 3: Building a Digital Collection

ISR Staff: Abby Clobridge. Entire class meets together in Library Lab.
- Components of a digital image collection
  - Collection access points
  - Standards
  - Digital preservation
  - Access issues
  - Copyright issues
- Describing materials following library and archival standards, cataloging rules

Thursday, October 5: Wrap-Up

ISR Staff: Abby Clobridge. Entire class meets together in Library Lab.
- Catalog data for posters and final steps to build the collection in Insight
- Rest of session: Research, Part 3
  - Group discussion about sources

Appendix 3.4. Historical Layer Cake: Analyzing a Poster

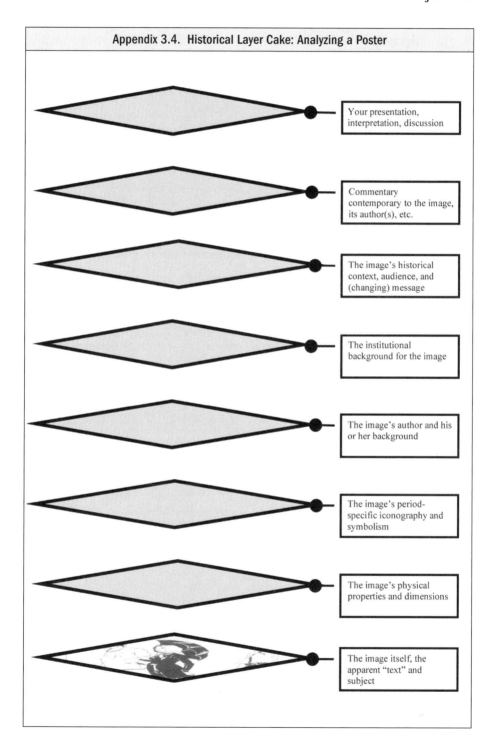

Your presentation, interpretation, discussion

Commentary contemporary to the image, its author(s), etc.

The image's historical context, audience, and (changing) message

The institutional background for the image

The image's author and his or her background

The image's period-specific iconography and symbolism

The image's physical properties and dimensions

The image itself, the apparent "text" and subject

Appendix 3.5. Metadata Schema for the World War II Poster Project

Field:	Identifier
Required:	Yes
Description:	Unique alphanumeric identifier for linking metadata with image data.
Format:	"WW2P_" + *four digit number with leading zeros*
Field:	Title
Required:	Yes
Description:	Indicates the title of the poster; if the poster has a given title, record it exactly as given.
Format:	Capitalize all words, except articles, prepositions, and conjunctions.
Field:	Date
Required:	No
Description:	Print or copyright date of the work.
Format:	Single year given in full four-digits. If a more specific date is given, the format should be *month + dd + yyyy*.
Field:	Date Notes
Required:	No
Description:	Provides additional date-of-event information pertaining to the work that does not appear in another field. Appropriate information for this field is an indication whether the date is approximate or where the given date can be located on the poster.
Format:	Complete sentences or strings of complex nouns. Always punctuate. The final phrase must end in a period.
Field:	Object Type
Required:	Yes
Description:	Indicates the type of object.
Format:	One or two words. Capitalize all words.
Range:	This field utilizes a controlled vocabulary.
Field:	Description
Required:	No
Description:	Unique information that adds descriptive value or historical context that is not already appropriate for other specified fields.
Format:	Use complete sentences or phrases, and end each with a period.
Field:	Measurements
Repeating:	Yes
Required:	No
Description:	Dimensions or other measurements representing the size of the work.
Format:	British and SI units are both appropriate. Centimeters should be abbreviated as *cm*, and inches should be abbreviated as ". Do not use fractions (i.e., "8 1/4") and always use the same number of significant figures or decimal places in the measurements of any single aspect of the object. When noting two dimensions, combine them with " ×," denoting *width × height*.

(Continued)

Appendix 3.5. Metadata Schema for the World War II Poster Project *(Continued)*

Field:	Creator
Required:	No
Description:	Indicates the name of a person or entity responsible for the creation of the work.
Format:	For personal names use *last-name* + "," + *first-name* + *middle-names*. Do not include personal titles. For clarification use ULAN and the LC Name Authority. Use the preferred index name when possible. Capitalize all proper nouns.

Field:	Creator Dates
Required:	No
Description:	Indicates the lifetime of the creator.
Format:	*birthdate* + "-" + *deathdate*. Make sure to include the spaces around the dash. This information is taken from the LC Name Authority or ULAN when possible. This field is strictly for ranges of years.

Field:	Gender
Required:	No
Description:	Indicates the gender of the creator.
Format:	Male or female. In cases of gender-ambiguity from the name, use ULAN to clarify.

Field:	Culture or Nationality
Required:	No
Description:	Indicates the creator's nationality or ethnic background.
Format:	Adjective. Refer to ULAN to determine the creator's nationality, when possible.

Field:	Creator Notes
Required:	No
Description:	Provides additional information about the author that might be pertinent to the record. Relevant data for this field may include a brief biographical note.
Format:	Use complete sentences or strings of complex nouns. Final phrase must end in a period. Sentence case capitalization applies.

Field:	Publisher
Repeating:	Yes
Required:	No
Description:	Name of the publisher, printer, or distributor of the work.
Format:	Capitalization is in sentence case. Capitalize all proper nouns. Separate hierarchical entities by a comma, followed by a space. Personal names are *last name, first name, middle name* or *initial*. For clarification use the LC Name Authority.

Field:	Subject
Repeating:	Yes
Required:	Yes
Description:	Terms that identify, describe, or represent the content of a work. Subjects will be topical, geographical, names of persons or corporate entities, or based on Rare Book, Special Collections, and Art cataloging standards.
Format:	Capitalization is sentence case (capitalize the first word and proper nouns).

(Continued)

Appendix 3.5. Metadata Schema for the World War II Poster Project *(Continued)*	
Field:	Rights
Required:	Yes
Description:	Statement of the appropriate-usage policy for an individual image.
Format:	Complete sentences or strings of complex nouns.
Range:	This field utilizes a controlled vocabulary.
Field:	Language
Required:	Yes
Description:	The language of the text on the poster.
Field:	Contributor
Repeating:	Yes
Required:	Yes
Description:	The name of the person or group who donated the object to Special Collections and University Archives.
Format:	For personal names use *last-name* + "," + *first-name* + *middle-names*. Do not include personal titles.
Field:	Course
Required:	Yes
Description:	Indicates a course that uses a particular image or collection.
Format:	Use the course number as published by Bucknell University.
Field:	Professor
Required:	No
Description:	Indicates the instructor who lectures the course given in the *Course* field.
Format:	*last-name* + "," + *first-name*. Do not include the instructor's title (PhD, MA, etc.).
Field:	Semester
Required:	No
Description:	Indicates the year and semester (Fall, Spring) of the course indicated in the Course field.
Format:	*yyyy* + "–" + *semester*
Field:	Location
Repeating:	Yes
Required:	Yes
Description:	The location housing the object.
Format:	Capitalize proper nouns.
Range:	This field utilizes a controlled vocabulary.

| Appendix 3.6. Pretest Questions Used with Personal Response Systems |

1. What is your class year?

A	95%	First-year student (Class of 2010)
B	0%	Sophomore (Class of 2009)
C	0%	Junior (Class of 2008)
D	5%	Senior (Class of 2007)
E	0%	None of the above

2. What is your primary area of study?

A	0%	Engineering
B	3%	Science or math
C	13%	History
D	5%	Humanities (other than history)
E	41%	Social science
F	38%	Undecided

3. Do you understand the poster/research assignment?

A	18%	Yes
B	59%	Sort of
C	18%	Not really
D	5%	Not at all

4. I think that my library research skills are:

A	8%	Excellent
B	18%	Pretty good—I think I'm prepared for the assignments for this class
C	59%	Okay
D	15%	Not great

5. If you are looking for books outside of Bucknell's library, where would you search?

A	3%	Go to another university's library catalog and directly search their catalog.
B	23%	Search WorldCat
C	13%	Search the Library of Congress Catalog
D	62%	I have no idea

6. The library uses the following form of classification to organize our book collection:

A	36%	The Dewey Decimal Classification System
B	15%	The Carnegie Classification of Higher Education
C	26%	Library of Congress Classification System
D	5%	Hertzsprung-Russell Classifications
E	18%	I have no idea

7. Which of the following is not a primary source?

A	0%	Diary entries
B	23%	Transcription of an oral history
C	49%	Biographies
D	10%	Newspaper articles
E	3%	Letters
F	13%	Census data

(Continued)

Appendix 3.6. Pretest Questions Used with Personal Response Systems *(Continued)*

8. Which of the following is the best way to start if you want to locate good journal articles on a specific topic?

A	3%	Flip through journals
B	51%	Use a research database
C	15%	Use an Internet search engine (e.g., Google)
D	23%	Use the library catalog
E	8%	I don't know

9. If you are trying to obtain a book that the Bucknell library doesn't own, what's the best next step?

A	10%	Order the book from Amazon
B	44%	Order the book from interlibrary loan using EZ-Borrow (PALCI)
C	33%	Order the book from interlibrary loan using ILIAD
D	13%	Ask a librarian to order the book for our collection

10. If you are trying to find an article that we don't have available in paper or electronically, what's the best way to get the article?

A	3%	Buy a copy of the article using an Internet source
B	13%	Order the article from interlibrary loan using EZ-Borrow (PALCI)
C	79%	Order the article from interlibrary loan using ILIAD
D	3%	I have no idea

11. In an online database or a catalog, which search would result in the greatest number of hits?

A	36%	Homosexuals and Holocaust
B	15%	Homosexuals or Holocaust
C	33%	Homosexuals Holocaust
D	15%	All three strategies will produce the same results
E	0%	I don't know

12. To retrieve only items discussing both women and World War II, which search strategy would work best in the library catalog or an article database?

A	77%	Women and World War II
B	15%	Women or World War II
C	5%	Women World War II
D	0%	All three would produce the same results
E	3%	I don't know

13. You have just done a search on "World War II and blitzkrieg" in the library catalog. The search retrieved one book. What step could you take to efficiently find additional books?

A	10%	None, there is only one book on this topic
B	18%	Find the book on the shelf, look for others nearby on the same topic
C	54%	Look at the record for the book, investigate subject, and perform an advanced search using subject headings
D	5%	Search for "world war ii" and scan the list for relevant books
E	10%	I don't know

(Continued)

Appendix 3.6. Pretest Questions Used with Personal Response Systems *(Continued)*

14. For the citation below, what is the article title?
The benevolent empire. R. Kagan. Foreign Policy 11:24–35 Summer '98.

A	59%	The benevolent empire
B	8%	Kagan
C	28%	Foreign Policy
D	3%	No idea

15. For the citation below, what is the journal title?
The benevolent empire. R. Kagan. Foreign Policy 11:24–35 Summer '98.

A	10%	The benevolent empire
B	3%	R. Kagan
C	85%	Foreign Policy
D	0%	I have no idea

16. To what does the following citation refer?
Borozsky, Sue. (1998). "U.S. soldier's health issues in World War II." In Smith, Peter and Malloy, Jennifer, (Eds), International Health and War. University of Pittsburgh Press: Pittsburgh, PA. Pages 34–57.

A	13%	Encyclopedia article
B	31%	Newspaper article
C	38%	Periodical article
D	3%	Book
E	8%	Chapter within a book
F	5%	No idea

17. To what does the following citation refer?
Wilson, Mary P. Psychology of Soldiers' Post-Traumatic Disorder. Boulder: Univ. of Colorado Press, 2001.

A	5%	Encyclopedia article
B	21%	Newspaper article
C	28%	Periodical article
D	41%	Book
E	0%	Chapter within a book
F	3%	No idea

18. How could you track down an article if you have a citation?

A	3%	Search the Internet
B	0%	Find the printed journal at the library
C	10%	Search a full-text article database
D	0%	Order the article through interlibrary loan
E	41%	All of the above
F	44%	Answers B–D

(Continued)

Appendix 3.6. Pretest Questions Used with Personal Response Systems *(Continued)*

19. Which of the following represents a refereed journal?

A	3%	A magazine that is published at regular intervals
B	18%	A journal published by a professional organization
C	8%	A journal with an editorial board
D	10%	A journal that is peer reviewed
E	13%	A journal that publishes only research
F	21%	B, C, or D
G	21%	I have no idea

Part II

Course Management Systems

SECTION INTRODUCTION

Course management systems (CMS) and online learning have a potentially transformative role to play in education, both to enhance and to change the nature of what happens in the classroom. Information literacy courses and programs benefit from this technology and provide meaningful contexts for faculty and librarians to collaborate. When used well, these Web-based systems engage students in the learning process, to deepen the overall course experience, to assess student learning, and to provide a virtual space for librarians to expand their influence. Online learning extends the amount of time students spend on a course, beyond the physical classroom. It also expands the kinds of activities instructors design for an online environment, including tutorials, quizzes, and surveys, as well as writing assignments (in a journal or blog, bulletin board, or online chat session). This technology provides practical tools for grading, assessment, and for uploading course materials such as PowerPoint presentations, Web links, Web-based multimedia, lecture notes, and assignment descriptions. Without an effective institutional strategy for supporting faculty and librarians in learning and using these tools, however, the CMS is underutilized and will not become a meaningful part of the learning experience.

Colleges and universities implement these systems through information technology units, or in collaboration with departments, libraries, or teaching centers. CMS are considered a wise investment because they provide faculty and students with access to Web-based learning tools that are fairly easy to use without requiring users to code complex Web documents or to balance multiple applications. CMS creates both synchronous and asynchronous opportunities for collaboration between faculty and library teams and within student groups. With a

24/7 course delivery mode instructors and students are not limited by traditional or restrictive schedules. For example, librarians can open up chat sessions with students in CMS during times that coincide with their reference desk hours or library office hours. Students can work on collaborative projects at any time, conducting research and posting written responses or scholarly resource links via the Web. Further, the ongoing expansion of mobile devices offers the potential to communicate and collaborate via CMS from any place as well.

The chapters in this section emphasize the need to engage students in course materials, to strengthen their opportunities to learn critical information literacy skills, and to use librarian-faculty collaborations creatively to accomplish these goals. Some of the tools are standardized, but the authors employ inventive strategies for adaptation in specific courses, while some are designed by librarians and could be customized further in new settings.

Laura E. Briggs and James M. Skidmore of the University of Waterloo describe the use of online learning systems in a German cultural and intellectual history course that enrolls 50 to 60 students per section. The information literacy component evolved as an integral part of the course when it was recently redesigned. The course is taught both as a distance course and in person, and the online information literacy components are appropriate to both formats. In redesigning the course, the authors "were governed by the guiding principle of the 'classroom flip.' By moving everything possible from a standard lecture course into the online setting, class time would be freed up for revision, practice, and more active and deeper learning." The information literacy component was completely integrated into a research-feedback-reflection assignment through a learning pathway. Library Help! discussion forums and a strategically timed live chat session were also elements of the online learning system. The use of technology in this course increased the communication between the librarian and students and redefined the role of the librarian as a fully integrated partner in the teaching and learning process. It also created tangible connections for students between the analysis of information sources and a specific disciplinary context.

The WISPR (Workshop on the Information Search Process for Research) program at the University of Calgary, described by K. Alix Hayden, Cindy Graham, Shauna Rutherford, Jean Chow, and Claudette Cloutier, was envisaged as a way to teach students more than is possible in a single instruction session and maximize "faculty collaboration by combining the use of a customizable online tool and face-to-face sessions with students." While the chapter focuses on the implementation of this program in science and nursing courses, it has been used in a number of disciplines. The blended approach taken by WISPR involves designing units in which significant learning takes place outside of the classroom, while in-class time is reduced but not eliminated. The "classroom flip" strategy described in the previous chapter is a key element in WISPR. The authors discuss the disadvantages of their previous one-shot approach to information literacy instruction, and the benefits gained from the blended approach. To facilitate its use in a variety of disciplines, "all content in WISPR may be customized, adapted, and changed." This content includes a KWLF (what I know, what I want to know, what I learned, where I found it) chart, screencasts, guided database tutorials, a self-assessment method, and a logbook. The implementation of this modular format for teaching information literacy is based on the specific needs of students within particular disciplines and provides them with an inventive way to expand concrete skills and critical thinking.

Ann Manning Fiegen, Keith Butler, and Regina Eisenbach at California State University San Marcos describe a preparatory capstone business course within the Senior Experience Program that "prepares student teams to work with local businesses and nonprofit agencies to solve real business problems." This course contains a number of technologically enhanced components, many of which are available through the WebCT course management system. Indeed, it is considered to be a hybrid course, given the integral nature of the CMS to the course structure. A series of multimedia video modules on five topics, including library research, is available through WebCT. These information literacy modules are viewed by students at their own convenience, and the nature of the medium allows them to return to the video whenever they feel it is necessary. The video contains not only lecture, enhanced by a PowerPoint slide show with Web links, but also Adobe Captivate demonstrations. Students were thus able to see what they should be doing and were prompted to try it out for themselves, with the video paused. The authors emphasize, "the intent of the online components was to deliver lecture material electronically where the listener could have greater control over when, where, and how often they viewed the material." While the authors note that streaming video is a one-way communication tool that might lessen student interaction, they supported it through discussions on WebCT, lab hours, and reference consultations. The innovative use of technology through this partnership allowed for the complete redesign of a course that contributed to the distinctiveness of an entire program.

Based on these chapters, we recommend considering the following when designing the use of course management systems:

- Decide if the system or module will be used in a single course or whether it might be generic enough for use in a variety of courses given the possibility of customizing the content.
- Determine how the online component of the course will coordinate with the in-person sessions.

- If a course is being redesigned, begin planning for the use of online components right at the start, with close collaboration between librarian and faculty member.
- If online elements are being added to an existing course, expect that the new elements will have a significant impact on existing material and may start you down the path of a complete redesign.
- Consider the issue of "content flip" addressed by two of the chapters in this section.
- Design online elements carefully so that they extend student learning and provide an opportunity to deepen the treatment of information literacy concepts and skills.
- Include personalized elements, such as online discussion forums and chat opportunities, that allow students direct contact outside the classroom with the faculty member and the librarian.
- Seek opportunities to work with technical advisors.
- Look for opportunities for grant funding to encourage ambitious thinking and to procure the technical and design assistance that you need.
- Consider the CMS a portal to other resources such as Web-based multimedia, online tutorials, databases, and research-oriented Web sites.

The three faculty-librarian teams in this second part of the book developed inventive and thoughtful uses of CMS and online learning that challenge students to think critically about content from the fields of German studies, science and nursing, and business. The techniques explored here, however, extend beyond any specific area and are portable to other disciplinary and interdisciplinary contexts.

Chapter 4

Beyond the Blended Librarian
Creating Full Partnerships with Faculty to Embed Information Literacy in Online Learning Systems

Laura E. Briggs and James M. Skidmore

INFORMATION AND THE UNIVERSITY EDUCATION

One could say that a university education is essentially about information—finding it, understanding it, working with it, manipulating it, discussing it, communicating it, disagreeing with it, disproving it, and replacing it with new information. The sophisticated comprehension of information, or knowledge, is also a fundamental aspect of postsecondary learning. These concepts, however, are often taken for granted, ignored by learners and instructors alike because both parties are so busy trying to grasp and define these terms that they do not consider the essential nature of each. But if the postmodern turn in Western culture during the past 50 years has taught us anything, it is to be more self-reflexive, to appreciate not only the content that is the net result of our efforts (be they artistic, scholarly, or otherwise), but also the processes that generate—or impede—those results. These practices have come under scrutiny in the Internet age as the availability of information explodes with the addition of every new database and every new method. The ability to communicate that information also changes with the addition of every new piece of learning software. In real terms, these changes are perhaps most visible in a university library, which is no longer just a physical collection of books but rather an access point for a variety of information available in a multitude of formats. Negotiating the stores of information held by a research library has become an increasingly complex and challenging task, but helping students gain experience and ability with information retrieval can improve not only their university education but also their capacity for coping with a world of information.

Since information storage and retrieval have become so complex, it seems only natural that the efforts to teach a new generation of information users should also gain in intricacy and sophistication. At universities and colleges, collaboration between librarians and faculty members should be instinctive; both can bring their skills, background, and understanding of student abilities and needs to bear on the development of information fluency on the university campus. The added technological expertise of the modern librarian, coupled with the opportunities for online learning in higher education, have resulted in a conducive climate for exploring new methods of teaching information literacy skills. The project described in this essay is the result of such collaboration. The context of this partnership—the academic program in which it took place, the resources available to the collaborators, and the goals of the project—are largely local in nature, but the analysis of the project yields, one hopes, information of common benefit because it addresses questions central to such collaboration, namely how the librarian and faculty member negotiated specific collaborative and technical issues to teach information literacy online in an effective and creative manner.

LITERATURE REVIEW

To understand the context in which this collaboration took place, it is necessary to look at some of the philosophical issues surrounding teaching and learning at universities, the role of the library in postsecondary education, and the role that technology can play in library instruction. One of the central questions facing universities is their understanding of their role with regard to the education of their students. The title of Barr and Tagg's article from 1995, "From Teaching to Learning—A New Paradigm for Undergraduate Education," summarizes this issue. The authors explain that "the paradigm that has governed our colleges is this: A college is an institution that exists *to provide instruction.* Subtly but profoundly we are shifting to a new paradigm: A college is an institution that exists *to produce learning.* This shift changes everything. It is both needed and wanted" (Barr and Tagg, 1995). This is not a new concept; current research describing the notion that lectures provide little room for creative growth and are little more than information transfer sessions is based on research of long standing (Salter, Richards, and Carey, 2004). Nevertheless the consequences of this shift should not be underestimated, since it requires a modification in the attitude of the instructor toward teaching. In practical terms, it demands that specific attention be paid to course organization and structure in ways that are likely unfamiliar to the average university or college instructor. This can be difficult for a member of the academy since the time to investigate and implement changes is scarce when one considers the pressures to prioritize research over teaching. Moreover, the nature of academic inquiry—first establishing the problem, then investigating that problem—does not lend itself well to the study of postsecondary teaching because it would imply that there is a problem with the scholar's teaching, and this is something that most academics are loathe to admit (Bass, 1999). Another consequence of this paradigm shift, and one that has received less attention in the literature, is that it requires a commitment on the part of students to adjust their expectations about their roles in a course that has adopted this new paradigm. It would seem that for the vast majority of students the pressure to succeed at university forces them to place a priority on the external measures of success, on grades, rather than on the internal measures such as increased knowledge or confidence with the material learned (Shepard, 2005).

Admitting a problem or a lack of knowledge is not just a concern for professors. Fear of the library coupled with students' sense of shame at not knowing something that they think they should know has long been identified as a stumbling block to improving student comfort with libraries (Mellon, 1986). A central issue of librarianship has been to address this problem by exploring different models of library instruction in order to find the system that reaches most students and has the best chance of success. Whereas most university libraries rely on some form of group instruction to orient students to the library and its resources, there has largely been consensus that library instruction works best when connected to actual courses (Dewald, 1999; Bordonaro and Richardson, 2004). "Course-integrated" library instruction has long been identified as a type of library instruction (Bhavnagri and Bielat, 2005), yet the question remains as to just how this integration is best structured. "One-shot" classroom instruction is perhaps the least invasive of these methods. More involved models, ranging from librarian-faculty collaboration on one course to a department-, faculty-, or campus-wide integration of information literacy into the curriculum have been discussed in the literature. The notion that information literacy should be introduced into courses at the "point of need" has received support (Southwell and Brook, 2004) and is seen as much more useful than more traditional approaches such as the development of subject study guides (Reeb and Gibbons, 2004). The broad, curriculum-based integration of information literacy has garnered much attention and interest (Grafstein, 2002; Hine et al., 2002; Owusu-Ansah, 2004; Walton and Archer, 2004; Badke, 2005), though the numerous problems and obstacles that come from organizing a number of people with different priorities and competing agendas has been noted (Hepworth, 2000; Snavely and Cooper, 1997). Some have even advocated the establishment of information literacy as its own discipline that can lead to higher order synthesis of library and critical thinking skills (Johnston and Webber, 2003); information literacy should be about learning, and the notion of literacy should be broadened to encompass a range of fluencies needed in today's technologically influenced society (Marcum, 2002).

The integration of information literacy into the curriculum is dependent on the cooperation of librarians and faculty members. The issue of librarian-faculty collaboration occupies a great deal of attention in library scholarly literature, and most of this literature is written from the librarian perspective. Faculty interest in information literacy and the subsequent collaboration required is considered to be rare or nonexistent. The reasons for this are many. Academics may not like to share their time or their classrooms with others, or have fragile egos that resist suggestions regarding teaching methods (Farber, 2004). For librarians, faculty members can appear to be self-centered individualists who do not want to cooperate with others; in the words of one contributor to an electronic discussion list, faculty act like "delinquent children" (Given and Julien, 2005: 32). At the same time, faculty see librarians as obstacles and view the library itself not as a learning and teaching resource but rather more like a utility, merely a part of university infrastructure (Given and Julien, 2005). As a result, librarians can feel like second-class citizens at the institutions they serve (Gilman, 2006). This problem is compounded by the attitude of many faculty that information literacy is a skill and, as such, does not merit consideration as a university subject (Walton and Archer, 2004).

Apart from establishing the emotional friction that factors into the librarian-professor relationship, scholarship on librarian-professor working relationships has also noted that systemic and workplace expectations provide the greatest source of difference between librarians and academics. Badke, borrowing a term often used to describe Canada-Quebec relations, refers to "two solitudes." He states, "Faculty do not respect the roles of librarians, and librarians view faculty as arrogantly ignorant of the functioning of the library, its personnel and its tools" (Badke, 2005: 65). Although Badke is arguing from the librarian perspective—there is no mention of a commensurate lack of understanding on the part of librarians about the role of the faculty member—he is quick to refer to the work done by Larry Hardesty to explain faculty culture. Hardesty has explained for a librarian audience the pressures on a faculty member's time, the focus on content in teaching, and the professional autonomy that can discourage collaboration with those outside the academy (Hardesty, 1995). Others, adopting the librarian's point of view, have defined these cultural differences in more specific terms by arguing that librarians are focused on meeting the general education and lifelong learning needs of students, whereas faculty members center their attention on a narrower range of short-term, course-specific goals (Baker, 1997; Leckie and Fullerton, 1999). Ivey states the difference in slightly different terms, comparing the "holistic" attitudes of most academics (and a few librarians) toward information literacy ("information literacy should be developed in conjunction with discipline specific learning") with the fragmented view of most librarians (and a few academics) on the same topic ("information literacy as a discipline in itself") (Ivey, 2003); Nimon argues that different ways of viewing information literacy have resulted in a gap separating librarians and academics (Nimon, 2000). Roy Tennant has recognized the difference between librarians and users of information, noting quite succinctly in paraphrasing Herbert White that the librarians' interest in process may lose sight of important short-term needs: "Only librarians like to search; everyone else likes to find" (Tennant, 2001: 38).

Despite the literature's librarian-centric approach to the cultural differences between librarians and faculty members, the general but not universal acknowledgment that information literacy needs to be integrated into courses necessitates bridging the cultural gap. The literature offers much advice about how to do this in positive and trust-building manner (Fain, Bates, and Stevens, 2003; Ivey, 2003). But there has also been recognition of the fact that more must be done to make greater use of the skills and perspectives that both faculty members and librarians bring to the table. Bruce argues that librarians recognize "the role of the information professional in fostering student learning" and that academics are beginning to understand "the importance of the world of information and information literacy to student learning" (Bruce, 2001: 108). Bhavnagri and Bielat contend that it is by collaborating on information literacy projects that librarians and professors can become better acquainted with the other discipline's strengths; the librarian can help develop the professor's technical skills while the professor can scaffold the librarian's "knowledge of research and teaching pedagogy" (Bhavnagri and Bielat, 2005: 122). Others envision collaboration at different and varying levels of complexity and purpose that move beyond the nuts and bolts of information literacy education (Bruce, 2001). But any hopes for collaboration will falter if instructors are not willing to incorporate the library into courses. Library instruction "is meaningless unless teaching faculty require students (especially undergraduates) to do research as part of their course-work. . . . [U]ndergraduates typically make little use of the library because their coursework does not require them to do so. This is a critical issue" (Zabel, 2004: 19).

Opportunities for collaboration have increased during the past ten years with the advent of online instruction. Including the library in courses taught using a course management system (CMS) can imply two things, namely that the instructor and the library or librarian view "point of need" instruction as a path to student learning and that the CMS offers a good mode of transportation along that path. Integration into an online learning environment means different things for different people, however. Some are reluctant to discard live instruction because the opportunity for personal outreach and contact will be lost (Martin and Lee,

2003). Others see the point of bringing library instruction to the CMS, but are not convinced that "online tutorials, Web-based classes and electronic user aids will completely replace traditional library instruction in a classroom setting" (Silver and Nickel, 2003: 9). Others echo this view, seeing library involvement in the CMS as a supplement to other library instruction initiatives or offering new points of contact with students (George and Martin, 2004; Hearn, 2005). Dewald notes that "web-based library tutorials are best used in connection with academic classes rather than in isolation" (Dewald, 1999: 31), but she is vague on whether that tutorial should be geared to specific course content or merely a general overview, much like an in-library tutorial, offered through a different medium. If the latter, then this approach may be criticized on the basis that it does not take advantage of online learning's strengths: its ability to enable task-based instruction as opposed to content delivery, and the opportunity to allow students to develop independent learning skills (Salter, Richards, and Carey, 2004), a point made in the information literacy context by Zhang (Zhang, 2002). Some librarians have noted that the CMS presents the possibility of changing the teaching/learning dynamic by occasioning the so-called "classroom flip" in which content delivery goes into the CMS, thereby freeing up class time for discussion, application, and higher-order learning, and going back to the CMS for further discussion (Ladner et al., 2004: 330). Reyes partially reiterates this point by stressing the necessity of using the CMS to facilitate "point of need" instruction. This will not reach every student a library serves, but it will provide good instruction to those it does reach (Reyes, 2006).

The challenge that the CMS is posing, in effect, is the way it raises the question as to what extent information literacy should be integrated into courses offered via CMS. Should CMS–based library instruction replace the traditional methods and become the new norm? Regardless of one's opinion on that matter, the CMS does offer "the opportunity to collaborate with faculty to an unprecedented degree in the development of new online environments promoting active learning and cognitive immersion" (Ladner et al., 2004: 330). The CMS also offers librarians the opportunity of becoming "active members of a course, answering questions, participating in discussions, directing students in the successful completion of their research" (Cox, 2002: 39). It has been noted that CMSs do not offer good library components (Buehler, 2004), and the desire to see library instruction become part of a broader curriculum has also had an impact on the librarian response to CMS use at universities (Jackson, 2007).

THE UNIVERSITY OF WATERLOO

The University of Waterloo was founded in 1957, and during its relatively short existence has become a significant player in the Canadian and international postsecondary landscape. Well-known for its programs in engineering, math, and computing, the university also mounts strong programs in applied health studies, environmental science, and the more traditional arts and science disciplines, and for several years has been singled out as one of the leading comprehensive universities in Canada by the news magazine *Maclean's*. A cohort of 963 faculty members instructs a student body consisting of 21,726 full-time undergraduate students, 2,500 full-time graduate students, and over 2,500 part-time students at all levels. The university was founded with the express purpose of providing its students with a less traditional education, and thus the university's cooperative education program has grown to become the largest of its kind in the world, with 45 percent of the undergraduate population taking part. As a result, the University of Waterloo has three full-fledged terms: Fall (September to December); Winter (January to April); Spring (May to August). Each term is 12 weeks in duration, with an additional three-week examination period.

The University of Waterloo Library serves the UW community through five locations on the main campus and the School of Architecture campus in Cambridge, Ontario. The library contains over 2 million print volumes and receives over 20,000 serials, two-thirds of which are electronic. The UW Library participates in the Tri-University Group of Libraries, a joint venture of the University of Waterloo and its neighboring universities, Wilfrid Laurier University (Waterloo, Ontario) and the University of Guelph (Guelph, Ontario). The main features of this cooperation are a combined online public access catalogue and shared lending practices.

GERMAN 272: GERMAN THOUGHT AND CULTURE

German 272 (GER272) is a course that explores the intellectual and cultural history of German-speaking central Europe from the mid-nineteenth century until today. Taught in English, the course is required of all students pursuing Honors German studies, and it can also be used to fulfill one of the breadth requirements for the Faculty of Arts, thus attracting a number of students from various majors. Close to half of the students enrolled in the course are in their second year of university studies, with the remainder in their third or fourth years with a sprinkling of first-year students. The course is offered both on-campus and via distance education (DE). Apart from a trial version to test the new online configuration of the course in Fall Term 2005, GER272 is offered twice a year, in Winter Term (January to April) in both on-campus and DE versions, and in Spring Term (May to August) as a DE course. Currently each course section has between 50 and 60 students per offering.

The course has been a staple of the German program at the University of Waterloo for many years. Most language programs have similar survey courses, often called "civilization" courses, which touch on various aspects of the target culture's political, social, literary, and artistic history. In the case of GER272, and its sister course GER271 (German thought and culture prior to 1850), the content of the course had been organized in traditional, "civilization course" fashion for many years. One of the main goals of the redesign of the course in 2004–2005 was to update the approach to content to reflect the changes that had occurred in the foreign language disciplines over the previous two decades. This shift can be loosely described as the turn from study of language and literature to more inclusive and interdisciplinary approach that owed a great deal to the "cultural turn" that had taken hold in many university departments of English and foreign languages and literatures throughout Canada and the United States. In the case of German in particular, this turn can be most quickly described as the shift from *Germanistik* (the traditional field of literary scholarship) to *German studies* (the study of the interrelated fields comprising but not limited to literature, the arts, anthropology, history—political, social, and intellectual—women's studies, and gender studies). In short, one of the major goals for the redesign of GER272 was to ensure that its content recognized the more expansive and nuanced view of German-speaking culture as can be found in Denham, Kacandes, and Petropoulos's thorough introduction to this topic (Denham, Kacandes, and Petropoulos, 1997).

INTEGRATED COLLABORATION

Having taught GER272 for three terms before the major redesign of the course in 2004–2005, Skidmore was not only dissatisfied with some of the content, he was also concerned about the level of student achievement, especially in the major essay that comprised 30 percent of the final grade. The students handed in vague, expository essays that made use of inappropriate resources. Judging by the papers, students were unaware of the specialty resources, such as peer-reviewed journal articles, that were available in the library and instead relied mainly on monographs. Students were asked to use MLA style for their in-text citations and bibliographies, but it was clear that most students did not know how to employ this or any other citation method. Most disturbing to Skidmore was the attitude of students; from his vantage point it appeared that many seemed not to care about these matters. When the opportunity arose to discuss the instructional bottleneck with students, they responded with a variety of answers: this class was not part of their major so they were not going to put as much effort into it, they had no idea where to find information on MLA style, or this was their first university class in two years that had a major writing assignment, thus they did not know how to proceed.

Skidmore had had some previous experience at another institution with information literacy, and before the redesign had begun in GER272 he had already implemented, in conjunction with the liaison librarian for German, some tentative measures to address the more obvious trouble spots. But with the complete overhaul of the course came the opportunity to consider more assertive training in information retrieval. It was at this time, in fall 2003, that Skidmore met Laura Briggs, liaison librarian both for chemistry and UW's Centre for Learning and Teaching Through Technology (LT3 Centre). The mission of the LT3 Centre was to support the development of pedagogically sound uses for technology, and it also supported instructor use of UW's course management system, at first UWone (an in-house system) and currently UW-ACE (short for Angel Course Environment since the software used is designed by Angel Learning, Inc.). Briggs was expected to facilitate the inclusion of library instruction in courses that were being taught on UW-ACE. The timing was ideal; working with Skidmore and Pia Marks from the LT3 Centre (an LT3 liaison with responsibility for assisting instructors in the sound pedagogical use of the learning technology), Briggs was able to become intimately involved in the redesign of the course from the beginning. Thus the information literacy component of GER272 was not an afterthought or squeezed into the course but rather evolved as part and parcel of the discussions regarding the writing component of the course.

As the literature review has shown, Skidmore's interest in and knowledge of information literacy is an anomaly for university instructors. But his clear sense of what he wanted—namely course-embedded information literacy instruction that would be so much a part of the fabric of the course that it would eventually be listed on the syllabus as one of the course objectives—provided a good head start for this instance of librarian-professor collaboration, and so the obstacles of disinterest discussed in the literature were never at issue. Skidmore's previous experience with GER272 also gave him a clear idea of what the learning issues for students in the course were.

This collaboration began under a favorable sign since both Briggs and Skidmore shared complementary goals. Skidmore wanted to overcome a learning bottle-neck by getting students "into" the library, virtual or otherwise, by making students acquainted with more suitable resources, and Briggs wanted to get the library "into" the classroom by providing point of need support to students. Neither felt threatened by the other trying to exercise too much control over the course, and both were open to what each could contribute to the enterprise. Obstacles to the collaboration were actually few and minor. Briggs, as a chemistry librarian, was not very well acquainted with German cultural history, although she had worked on other humanities courses. There was some concern among UW librarians that the Briggs-Skidmore collaboration would lead to the exclusion of liaison librarians from participating in such librarian-faculty ventures, even though the library had seconded Briggs for just such a purpose. Time was an issue in two respects: first, the amount of time needed to design an online course had an impact on Briggs and Skidmore's other commitments; second, for part of the development phase, Skidmore was on sabbatical in Germany, and Briggs just could not remember how the time difference worked and would call Skidmore in the middle of the night with questions (and vice versa!).

LEARNING AND THE ONLINE COURSE ENVIRONMENT

Another factor that contributed to the success of this particular collaboration was that both Briggs and Skidmore shared a similar enthusiasm for the using UW-ACE to mount GER272. Neither of the authors wanted to introduce technology into this course for technology's sake, but both could see that the technology could help us achieve our goals for the course. Primary among these goals was the desire to engage the learner at a deeper level. Skidmore was concerned that the poor student performance on some aspects of the course stemmed from the student attitudes toward the course (a course that had to be taken to satisfy the faculty's breadth requirements) and toward learning in general (minimum effort and maximum gain). For her part, Briggs wanted to move the UW Library beyond orientation week information sessions and provide concrete assistance that would have a real impact on student learning. Both of us felt that the key to this change was to instill in the students the sense that they had to be active participants in their learning.

There were also practical considerations that assured the CMS a large role in the development of GER272. The Department of German and Slavic Studies had decided to increase its presence in distance education (DE) and had received two grants from the university to develop online courses. It occurred to Skidmore that it would be a waste of effort to put in hours developing the DE version of the course and yet not use those materials in the on-campus section. The unveiling of UW-ACE, which occurred at the same time the initial plans to redesign GER272 were being discussed, provided a relatively easy method to design one course site for all sections. Though there were some administrative obstacles to this concept stemming mainly from the more rigid course design policies in place at the university's Distance Education Department, the goodwill of the DE administrators helped to smooth out these bumps. For the course in general, a shared course Web site had the advantage of reducing the amount of preparation time for the instructor while improving interaction between on-campus and DE students.

In redesigning the course, Briggs, Marks, and Skidmore were governed by the guiding principle of the "classroom flip." By moving everything possible from a standard lecture course into the online setting, class time would be freed up for revision, practice, and more active and deeper learning. Both on-campus and DE students would benefit: on-campus students would meet one less hour a week (to compensate for increased independent study), and the class times would become occasions for learning rather than teaching; DE students, who had previously not had any access to lectures, would receive an enhanced course package that came closer to approximating an in-class experience. The design team identified elements of traditional face-to-face instruction that would transfer readily to an online environment without loss of learning value to the students. These elements were not merely transferred online as a "content dump" but were completely redesigned in order to create an engaging and interactive learning experience. The lecture component of the course was recast as "Prof Moments." These short e-lectures presented specific course themes and issues via narrated PowerPoint presentations that had been put online as Flash videos. Handouts of the PowerPoint slides formatted for easy note taking were made available in PDF format. Group work was replicated by organizing students into three-person study teams that went on "virtual field trips" to external Web sites that raised important issues related to the course content. Q&A discussion forums provided all students with a space to meet and to share and gain information about course content and housekeeping matters. In short, any element of GER272 that lent itself to replication in the course management system was moved online. This included putting most of the course readings (mainly articles from journals, newspapers, and books) on e-reserve; articles for which e-reserve rights could not be obtained were sold as a courseware package. Assignments were completed online, including the research-feedback-reflection (RFR) exercise, a term essay project that was broken into three stages in which initial research findings were presented, feedback from the instructor on the suitability of the information was provided, and a final stage in which students wrote a short essay that made use of the research undertaken and which was uploaded to the course site for grading. Only the final exam was done on paper since it would have been difficult to invigilate an online exam at a distance.

The course's information literacy component was woven into the RFR exercise, particularly the first component, the research stage. For this component, students had to state a research question and write abstracts of two to three journal articles that would illuminate that question. Students would then receive feedback from the instructor on the suitability of the question and information sources, on the quality of the abstracts, and on the accuracy of the bibliographic information (students were instructed to use MLA style). To prepare students for this task, Briggs and Skidmore discussed (and sometimes argued) at length about what information should be provided to students. Both agreed that the students should be introduced to the research databases and indexes that would be particularly helpful to them, namely the MLA International Bibliography, the Arts and Humanities Citation Index (part of the Web of Science), and Humanities Full Text.

Briggs, who had course editing rights, then wrote HTML documents for the course site that explained the use of these databases in further detail. This included:

- Providing students with an overview of search commands and strategies
- Giving students tips on how to identify appropriate sources
- Using search examples to illustrate key concepts about searching and suitability
- Providing step-by-step instructions for using some of the resources
- Creating two quizzes with detailed automatic feedback and grading to help students evaluate their understanding of the databases and MLA style

All of these documents were illustrated by numerous screen shots. The pages themselves were formatted using the course style sheet. This sheet places content in two columns; the wider left-hand column provides the information, whereas the narrower right-hand column contains the learning pathway, i.e., a list of tasks and activities connected to that particular unit (see Figure 4.1).

For the RFR unit, links to the information literacy pages were incorporated into the learning pathway, and thus students saw the information literacy exercises

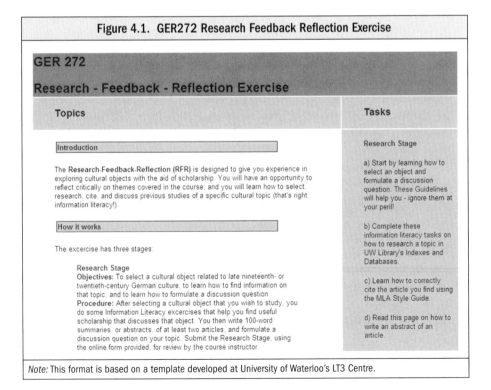

Figure 4.1. GER272 Research Feedback Reflection Exercise

GER 272

Research - Feedback - Reflection Exercise

Topics	Tasks
Introduction The **Research-Feedback-Reflection (RFR)** is designed to give you experience in exploring cultural objects with the aid of scholarship. You will have an opportunity to reflect critically on themes covered in the course, and you will learn how to select, research, cite, and discuss previous studies of a specific cultural topic (that's right: information literacy!).	Research Stage a) Start by learning how to select an object and formulate a discussion question. These Guidelines will help you - ignore them at your peril!
How it works The excercise has three stages: **Research Stage** **Objectives:** To select a cultural object related to late nineteenth- or twentieth-century German culture, to learn how to find information on that topic, and to learn how to formulate a discussion question. **Procedure:** After selecting a cultural object that you wish to study, you do some Information Literacy excercises that help you find useful scholarship that discusses that object. You then write 100-word summaries, or abstracts, of at least two articles, and formulate a discussion question on your topic. Submit the Research Stage, using the online form provided, for review by the course instructor.	b) Complete these information literacy tasks on how to research a topic in UW Library's Indexes and Databases. c) Learn how to correctly cite the article you find using the MLA Style Guide. d) Read this page on how to write an abstract of an article.

Note: This format is based on a template developed at University of Waterloo's LT3 Centre.

as a completely integrated portion of the RFR assignment. Briggs also helped create the information on how to write abstracts (see Figure 4.2). In fact, it quickly became evident to both of us that we shared a similar outlook on how to structure the course, and many parts of the course, though not related to information literacy in any obvious way, were more or less coauthored by both of us. In order to add variety to the Prof Moments, for example, Briggs joined Skidmore in the narration of some of them, and students have remarked that they like the witty and jocular banter in the Prof Moments on Vienna's Ringstrasse or Peter Schneider's book *The Wall Jumper.*

Briggs also contributed a great deal of feedback and personalized assistance in the course. She did not mark the first stage of the RFR; Skidmore, as the course instructor, felt responsible for that aspect, and since his knowledge of MLA style is legendary in his department, was qualified to do so. Briggs, however, set up a separate Library Help! electronic discussion forum to provide students with a space to raise research questions (for example, queries about suitability of

---

Figure 4.2. GER 272 Sample Abstract

GER 272: **Sample Abstract**

Article:

Welch, David. "Hitler's History Films." *History Today* 52.12 (2002): 20-25.

Abstract:

This article discusses how propaganda was used in history films as a means of "reteaching" history with a Nazi slant. The article argues that the most pervasive attribute of these films was the use of historical figures as an analogy to Hitler. Such analogies emphasized the consolidation of power into the hands of the Fuehrer, promoting the willing sacrifice of individual rights for the good of the whole. The article maintains that these films had a profound influence on indoctrinating the population in general, youth included. As evidence, the article relates these assertions to several historical films, the focal ones being: *Der grosse Koening; Bismarck, Die Entlassung; Friedrich Schiller; Heimkehr; Ohm Kruge.* That these history films composed the Hitler Jugend's list of top five films further attests to their particular hold on young minds. Through these films, the article also shows specific examples of how the Nazis ever so delicately brought up common points of dissent to the regime, only to tactfully discredit them. This further enhanced the effectiveness of film as a form of propaganda.

Comment [JMS1]: This sentence summarizes the article's topic.

Comment [JMS2]: This sentence contains the main argument put forth in the article.

Comment [JMS3]: The rest of the abstract contains examples that are used to bolster the article's argument.

Why is this a good abstract?

* It is clearly and concisely written.
* Only pertinent information is included.
* It is structured very simply: first the topic of the article is introduced, then the main argument/thesis, then examples used to defend the argument are mentioned.
* After reading this abstract, you have a concrete idea about the article and its scope.

Note: It is not enough to provide an example; instructors must point out the elements that make the example worth following.

sources, how to overcome a research impasse, and assistance on research topics, etc.). The advantage of the forum is that a question can be answered once, yet everyone reading the forum can take advantage of that answer. A week before the first stage of the RFR was due, Briggs and Skidmore held a real-time live Library Help! electronic chat session where students could come with their research questions. These were held on a weekday in the early evening, and Briggs and Skidmore sat together so that they could communicate orally about the questions. Since the questions were both about research process and content, it was beneficial to have both Briggs and Skidmore involved in the live session.

ASSESSING RESULTS AND ATTITUDES

At the time the course was redesigned, Briggs, Marks, and Skidmore received a grant from the University of Waterloo Learning Initiatives Fund to support a study of the course's new configuration. The ongoing research study, titled Transferable Skills Acquisition and Retention in Blended and Wholly Online Course Environments, analyzes the mediation of transferable skills, namely information literacy and cultural literacy skills. We are looking at whether online activities provide effective instruction of targeted transferable skills and trying to determine if the type of course environment (wholly online versus blended) affects that acquisition. The study has covered four terms. Approximately one-third of the 272 students have participated by giving us permission to use their assignment results and comments in our analysis. We have gathered qualitative and quantitative data by the following means: beginning- and end-of-term questionnaires, beginning- and end-of-term cultural analysis exercises, reflection questions on the final stage of the RFR, discussion forum comments, comments from focus group sessions, results from the final exam, the database and MLA quizzes, and the RFRs.

Though much of assessment of the success of the information relies on the students' own reflections about their experiences in the course, some more objective indicators suggest that embedding the information literacy tasks into the course resulted in gains for the students. As the students became better users of the library's information resources, the quality of the information they used for their term assignments (the RFRs) improved, and this in turn enabled them to interact with ideas and issues of German cultural history on a more sophisticated level. The vast majority of students made use of more recent academic literature to frame more specific discussions of issues related to the course content. Even their use of MLA style improved. Generally speaking, Skidmore believes that the quality of the information used in the term assignments has improved since 2004.

The results from the tasks dedicated solely to information literacy reveal a more complex picture. A database quiz and an MLA quiz during the term, plus three multiple choice questions on the final exam based on those quizzes, provide a snapshot of student learning. There was minimal difference in the grades for on-campus or DE students. Students did best on the MLA quiz, averaging 88 percent over the four terms of the study. The questions were geared toward the lower end of Bloom's taxonomy for categorizing learning behaviors; they tested the students' ability to recognize correct or incorrect citations. In the first stage of the RFR, however, students proved unable to match the high score on this quiz with their own MLA citations, which reaffirms the notion that while citation styles may appear easily understandable in the abstract, they can be difficult to master in practical application.

Generally speaking the students did quite well on the databases quiz, averaging 73 percent across all sections. In this quiz, when responding to a question on truncation symbols, the overwhelming majority of students got the correct answer, but when answering a similar question on the final exam, less than a third of the students over four terms were able to answer correctly. We infer from this that the students either did not review the information literacy component for the final exam (even though they were informed that all material covered in the course would be on the final, it could well be that students did not think that the information literacy component constituted course content), or were better able to grasp the concept when it was contextualized—that is, when they were in the middle of the task and not thinking about it theoretically at the end of term (see Figure 4.3).

The database quiz also posed a question about a search strategy that tested the students' understanding of how to combine different terms to narrow the

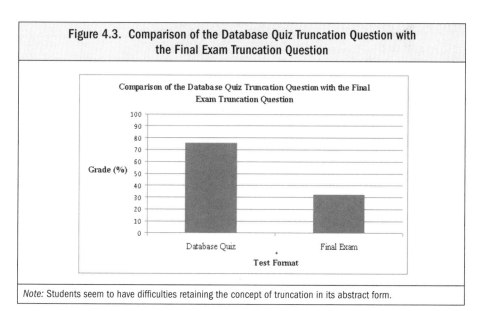

Figure 4.3. Comparison of the Database Quiz Truncation Question with the Final Exam Truncation Question

Comparison of the Database Quiz Truncation Question with the Final Exam Truncation Question

Grade (%)

Database Quiz   Final Exam

Test Format

Note: Students seem to have difficulties retaining the concept of truncation in its abstract form.

search parameters. This proved to be a difficult question, with just over half of the students over the various semesters answering correctly. The database exercise explained which databases were useful and why and gave students hands-on experience with them, but the database quiz did not ask questions about this relevance. A question on the final exam did, however, and students scored poorly with almost half thinking the Web of Science was not a useful resource for this course even though it contains the Arts & Humanities Citation Index. The students were most likely confused by the name of the resource or were unable to recall its usefulness out of context, a problem that would disappear if they were to make more use of it. Two questions on the database quiz and one on the final exam tested student understanding of the use of descriptors or subject headings. The database quiz results were better than the final exam, but even so the exam showed that at the end of term a majority of students understood the concept (see Figure 4.4).

Another source of information about the efficacy of the information literacy component in the course are the records generated by UW-ACE on the number of times students accessed the Library Help! discussion forum. One cannot draw the conclusion that numerous accessions equals learning because one does not know why the student accessed the forum; in some instances, such as when the forum was used for a live electronic chat session, students were required to refresh their screens often, and each time they did this it was recorded as an

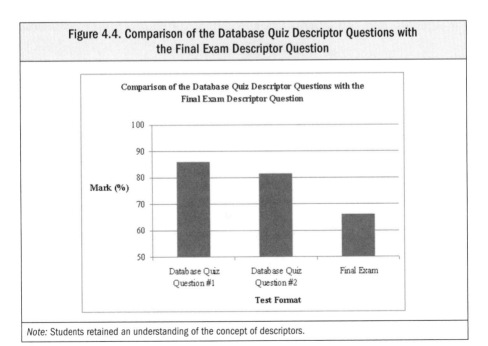

Figure 4.4. Comparison of the Database Quiz Descriptor Questions with the Final Exam Descriptor Question

Note: Students retained an understanding of the concept of descriptors.

accession. But analysis of discussion forum activity does provide insight into the abilities and confidence levels of the students. Briggs would "prime the pump" (Markwell, 2005: 261) by starting off the forum with a couple of common questions. Students did not answer one another's questions but would wait instead for Briggs or Skidmore to respond (unlike the general Q&A forum in the course where students would jump in to answer questions of both housekeeping and content nature). Nevertheless, students were clearly lurking in the forum, that is, reading posts but not posting themselves, an activity that still provides students who are less confident in their knowledge or ability to participate with opportunities for learning (Markwell, 2005: 263; McKendree, 1998: 117; Salmon, 2000: 80). Half of all students taking GER272 access the Library Help! discussion forum, many on numerous occasions, and again one notices minimal differences in on-campus and DE student behavior in this regard. The live Library Help! chat sessions were introduced in response to student suggestions for real-time assistance. These sessions did not attract many posters (two to seven per session), but the number of students lurking during the live session was always equal to or greater than the number of who asked questions, and the logs of the live session were accessed many times up to the deadline for the first stage of the RFR. Thus even though it appeared that the live session was poorly attended, in actual fact the ability to preserve the session in the CMS increased its reach a great deal.

Questionnaires were filled out by students at both the beginning and end of term and were designed to measure any changes in the students' perception of both their information and cultural literacy skills. Results for 82 students who filled out both questionnaires over the course of four terms indicate that students thought their information gathering skills had improved during the course. For example, at the start of term 13 percent of students rated their skills of locating and evaluating information sources as poor or very poor, but by the end of term this decreased to 1 percent. Moreover, 40 percent of students rated their skills of locating and evaluating information sources as good or very good at the start of the term, and this increased to 56 percent by the end of classes. Thus it would appear that students perceive an improvement in their confidence with respect to using the library. At the same time, however, some of the questionnaire results raise questions as to whether student understanding of the library's resources actually improved. For example, a relatively stable percentage of students knew that TRELLIS was the name of the UW Library's OPAC system, but a surprisingly large number of respondents at both the beginning and end of term confused it with other library services or resources. At the start of term 32 percent of the students identified TRELLIS as a library subscribed database, and thankfully this decreased to 13 percent, surely in part due to the emphasis on databases in the course. At the same time, however, the number of students who thought that TRELLIS was the interlibrary loan service increased from 28 percent to 42 percent, an indication that students remain confused about library resources.

Though the previous statistic may seem disheartening, other information provides a more complete picture of student learning. Comments gathered at focus group sessions, on questionnaires, and on the final stage of the RFR itself yield a great deal of information about the students' attitudes toward the inclusion of explicit information literacy learning in the course. Many students welcomed the information literacy component; for too long they had felt overwhelmed by the vast array of resources at the library:

> I feel more confident in searching for resources and I am not as bitter towards research assignments. . . . This course has helped me to apply the information literacy to other classes. I do not fall back on Google as much now, unless looking for quick and easy answers. I use the library's resources to find reliable sources. I also do not mind doing MLA citations as much anymore.

> In the five years I've been at UW, I never fully understood how to search journal articles. I knew there were databases, but never understand what kind of search words to use or how to get the article after reading the summaries. This course and RFR practice has helped me in other classes where journal sources are necessary. I only wish I learned this much earlier in my university career and not the semester before I graduate.

One student seems to have been particularly heartened by the exercises:

> I never thought [I could learn how to find library materials]—I thought I lacked that ability, and everyone else it seemed could. Giving examples and information is the best way that I learn, then having an exercise where I need to do it, and get the answers so I can figure out where I went wrong.

Others, however, felt that they had gained little in the exercises, and felt simply overwhelmed by the immensity of the task: "The ocean was large, but it was hard to catch many fish." Still others felt they had already acquired the skills being taught:

> There were only a few minor things that I learned in the info-lit exercises, as I've had six years of experience with MLA and four years experience with evaluation of sources and finding online journal articles. In my program, it is a necessity to know these things and to be able to evaluate a source and to be critical of it. I would hope that this is taught in other programs aside from Classics.

Ironically enough, this student was unable to cite her sources in proper MLA fashion.

One aspect of the information literacy instruction that garnered general appreciation was the strategy of meeting the previous concern with scaffolded, step-by-step instruction. This reiterates the notion that information literacy instruction, when scaffolded in order to present models of practice (for example, providing tips or teaching with canned searches), can reach learners effectively (Kearns and Hybl, 2005). Students also felt that this would improve the likelihood of their transferring the skills learned to other courses and contexts:

> By printing off "Information #1 Finding Journal Articles for your RFR" and following all the step by step instructions included within I feel better prepared to find electronic sources. . . . These notes will be my guide to finding sources of information for future courses. Thank you.

> Particularly the GER272 Info Lit example for Search Tips for Journal Indexes—a good reference for refreshment on Boolean operators, truncation, wildcards and parenthesis. I keep this article under R for Research in my file folder for quick reference, applicable to other university libraries also. . . .

Additionally, some students commented positively on the required nature of the information literacy exercises, for example the MLA and database quizzes. In order to instill the notion of practicing these skills in quizzes in order to improve the end result (the term essay), the syllabus did not assign any weight to the information literacy tasks but merely indicated that all parts of the RFR could count toward the final RFR grade. Students, grade conscious as they are, took this seriously, and the majority of students completed all tasks, welcoming especially the quizzes for pointing out where gaps in their knowledge lay. The mere mentioning of a relationship between the exercise and the students' grades proved to be a positive incentive.

Student attitudes toward technology, information, and information literacy were especially illuminating. A few students were vociferous in their distaste for online learning. Often, this relates to the student's perception of his or her inadequate computing skills. Though it is a commonplace at North American universities to hear that today's students "plugged in" and disdainful of anything but the latest technology, a small minority of the students in these courses reflected unease with the emphasis on technology in the course. At the other end of the scale were those students who could not hide their frustration that not all the material they found in their research was accessible online:

> The only downside was the lack of availability of the articles listed. Often the searches resulted in numerous articles, but were either not available online or not available at the University library. Also many articles were in languages other than English, which for a student without fluency or understanding of other languages this is a barrier.

Finally, the role and presence of the librarian was commented on by students. Many appreciated the presence of the librarian—"It was very helpful to have

Laura so available in this course"—a presence that was felt thanks to Briggs' willingness to participate in all aspects of GER272. A small number of students, however, missed "flesh and blood librarian help" and decried the lack of in-class library instruction sessions, largely since these better suited their learning style than reading Web pages or trying to follow an online discussion. Appreciation for the live Library Help! session was directly related to its ability to mimic the instant response of actual in-person help—"I really enjoyed the 'live' library help discussion, because I was able to get help with my topic right away and help with search ideas," something that others found lacking in the course: "I feel I need a lot more practice finding things online. The process was rather frustrating. I would prefer to have the assistance of a real librarian." This last comment, made during the first iteration of the course, gave Briggs and Skidmore the idea of developing the Library Help! discussion forum.

SOME CONCLUSIONS

Our analysis of information literacy skills development in GER272 is an ongoing project; the longitudinal aspect of the skills acquisition in the course has yet to be investigated, and the wealth of material already obtained requires further quantitative and qualitative analysis. The initial findings, however, have provided us with some useful information and provocative reminders.

It has become abundantly clear during this project that the literature is correct: students are intimidated by the library, and this intimidation has been compounded by the advent of the electronic information age. It is therefore all the more necessary to teach information gathering skills, even if it is a frustrating exercise for them. It is not a bad thing for students to learn that research is difficult and time-consuming as long as they also have the opportunity to learn the joy of finding quality information. They will learn to appreciate good information only if they learn about that information from within a disciplinary context. What students also need is help getting started, a leg up to the first rung on the scaffold as it were, in order to begin developing the confidence that will enable them to tackle more ambitious information-seeking projects. The gradual, scaffolded approach taken in GER272 is therefore a step in the right direction, as is the effort to expand the acquisition of information literacy skills through broader, curriculum-based initiatives that would reach students earlier in their university careers.

There is the concern that embedding information literacy in online learning systems will lessen contact between librarian and student and that this will result in a less personal form of library assistance. Paradoxically enough, the use of the CMS to teach this course actually increased librarian-student contact. The librarian has access to students that would be unthinkable in the traditional librarian-student relationship. Thus, if information literacy is embedded in the online course in a thoughtful fashion at the point of need, and if this portion of the course is supported by genuine librarian assistance, the chances of making meaningful contact with students at teachable moments in their education increase substantially.

The role of the librarian in this course will remind one of the blended librarian, the academic librarian "who combines the traditional skill set of librarianship with the information technologist's hardware/software skills, and the instructional or educational designer's ability to apply technology appropriately in the teaching-learning process" (Bell and Shank, 2004). We think that this experience has taken us beyond the blended librarian, who in the final analysis comes across as technical support, to the integrated librarian, a librarian who collaborates on all aspects of the course as a member of the instructional team, thereby becoming an integral contributor to the course as a whole. Though it would be unrealistic to expect such integration in all courses—just the question of the time needed to collaborate endangers the viability of such an enterprise—the librarian-professor collaboration in this course yielded great results as the expertise of both was shared with each other and with the students.

REFERENCES

Badke, William B. 2005. "Can't Get No Respect: Helping Faculty to Understand the Educational Power of Information Literacy." *The Reference Librarian* 43, no. 89/90 (Fall): 63–80.

Baker, Robert K. 1997. "Faculty Perceptions Towards Student Library Use in a Large Urban Community College." *The Journal of Academic Librarianship* 23, no. 3 (May): 177–182.

Barr, Robert B., and John Tagg. 1995. "From Teaching to Learning—A New Paradigm for Undergraduate Education." *Change* 27, no. 6 (November/December): 12–25. Available: http://critical.tamucc.edu/~blalock/teadings/tch2learn.htm. Accessed September 23, 2004.

Bass, Randy. 1999. "The Scholarship of Teaching: What's the Problem?" *Inventio* 1, no. 1 (February): 1–10.

Bell, Stephen J., and John Shank. 2004. "The Blended Librarian: A Blueprint for Redefining the Teaching and Learning Role of Academic Librarians." *College & Research Libraries News* 65, no. 7 (July/August). Available: www.ala.org/ala/acrl/acrlpubs/crlnews/backissues2004/july04/blendedlibrarian.cfm. Accessed November 30, 2006.

Bhavnagri, Navas P., and Veronica Bielat. 2005. "Faculty-Librarian Collaboration to Teach Research Skills: Electronic Symbiosis." *The Reference Librarian* 43, no. 89/90 (Fall): 121–138.

Bordonaro, Karen, and Gillian Richardson. 2004. "Scaffolding and Reflection in Course-Integrated Library Instruction." *The Journal of Academic Librarianship* 30, no. 5 (September): 391–401.

Bruce, Christine. 2001. "Faculty-Librarian Partnerships in Australian Higher Education: Critical Dimensions." *Reference Services Review* 29, no. 2: 106–115.

Buehler, Marianne A. 2004. "Where is the Library in Course Management Software?" *Journal of Library Administration* 41, no. 1/2: 75–84.

Cox, Christopher. 2002. "Becoming Part of the Course: Using Blackboard to Extend One-shot Library Instruction." *College & Research Libraries News* 63, no. 1 (January): 11–13, 39.

Denham, Scott, Irene Kacandes, and Jonathon Petropoulos, eds. 1997. *A User's Guide to German Cultural Studies.* Ann Arbor, MI: The University of Michigan Press.

Dewald, Nancy. 1999. "Transporting Good Library Instruction Practices into the Web Environment: An Analysis of Online Tutorials." *The Journal of Academic Librarianship* 25, no. 1 (January): 26–31.

Fain, M., P. Bates, and R. Stevens. 2003. "Promoting Collaboration with Faculty." In Julia K. Nims et al. (Eds.), *Integrating Information Literacy into the College Experience* (pp. 205–211). Ann Arbor, MI: Pierian Press.

Farber, E. 2004. "Working with Faculty: Some Reflections." *College & Undergraduate Libraries* 11, no. 2: 129–135.

George, Julie, and Karl Martin. 2004. "Forging the Library Courseware Link." *College & Research Libraries News* 65, no. 10 (November): 594–597, 613.

Gilman, Todd. 2006. "Show Your Librarian Some Love." *The Chronicle of Higher Education* 3 (October). Available: http://chronicle.com/jobs/news/2006/10/2006100301c/careers.html. Accessed May 28, 2007.

Given, Lisa M., and Heidi Julien. 2005. "Finding Common Ground: An Analysis of Librarians' Expressed Attitudes Towards Faculty." *The Reference Librarian* 43, no. 89/90 (Fall): 25–38.

Grafstein, Ann. 2002. "A Discipline-based Approach to Information Literacy." *The Journal of Academic Librarianship* 28, no. 4 (July): 197–204.

Hardesty, Larry. 1995. "Faculty Culture and Bibliographic Instruction: An Exploratory Analysis." *Library Trends* 44, no. 2 (Fall): 339–367.

Hearn, Michael R. 2005. "Embedding a Librarian in the Classroom: An Intensive Information Literacy Model." *Reference Services Review* 33, no. 2 (February): 219–227.

Hepworth, Mark. 2000. "The Challenge of Incorporating Information Literacy into the Undergraduate Curriculum." In S. Corrall and H. Hathaway (Eds.), *Seven Pillars of Wisdom: Good Practice in Information Skills* (pp. 22–31). London: Standing Conference of National and University Libraries.

Hine, Alison, et al. 2002. "Embedding Information Literacy in a University Subject Through Collaborative Partnerships." *Psychology Learning and Teaching* 2, no. 2 (December): 102–107.

Ivey, Ruth. 2003. "Information Literacy: How Do Librarians and Academics Work in Partnership to Deliver Effective Learning Programs?" *Australian Academic & Research Libraries* 34, no. 2 (June). Available: http://alia.org.au/publishing/aarl/34.2/full.text/ivey.html. Accessed May 22, 2007.

Jackson, Pamela Alexandra. 2007. "Integrating Information Literacy into Blackboard: Building Campus Partnerships for Successful Student Learning." 2007. *Journal of Academic Librarianship*, 33, no. 4 (July): 454–461.

Johnston, Bill, and Sheila Webber. 2003. "Information Literacy in Higher Education: A Review and Case Study." *Studies in Higher Education* 28, no. 3 (August): 335–352.

Kearns, Katherine, and Tracy Thrasher Hybl. 2005. "A Collaboration Between Faculty and Librarians to Develop and Assess a Science Literacy Laboratory Module." *Science & Technology Libraries* 25, no. 4 (May): 39–55.

Ladner, Betty, et al. 2004. "Rethinking Online Instruction: From Content Transmission to Cognitive Immersion." *Reference & User Services Quarterly* 43, no. 4 (Summer): 329–336.

Leckie, Gloria, and Anne Fullerton. 1999. "The Roles of Academic Librarians in Fostering a Pedagogy for Information Literacy." ACRL's 9th National Conference: Racing Toward Tomorrow, April 8–11, Detroit, Michigan. Available: www.ala.org/ala/acrl/ acrlevents leckie99.pdf. Accessed May 27, 2007.

Marcum, James W. 2002. "Rethinking Information Literacy." *Library Quarterly* 72, no. 1 (January): 1–26.

Markwell, John. 2005. "Using the Discussion Board in the Undergraduate Biochemistry Classroom: Some Lessons Learned." *Biochemistry and Molecular Biology Education* 33, no. 4 (July): 260–264.

Martin, Kelli Bellew, and Jennifer Lee. 2003. "Using a WebCT to Develop a Research Skills Module." *Issues in Science & Technology Librarianship* 37 (Spring). Available: www.istl .org/03-spring/article5.html. Accessed April 10, 2007.

McKendree, Jean, et al. 1998. "Why Observing a Dialogue May Benefit Learning." *Journal of Computer Assisted Learning* 14, no. 2 (June): 110–119.

Mellon, Constance A. 1986. "Library Anxiety: A Grounded Theory and Its Development." *College and Research Libraries*, 47, no. 2 (March): 160–165.

Nimon, Maureen. 2000. "Striking the Right Balance: Information Literacy and Partnerships between Librarian, Lecturer and Student." In Di Booker (Ed.), *Concept, Challenge, Conundrum: From Library Skills to Information Literacy. Proceedings of the Fourth National Information Literacy Conference* (pp. 157–164). Adelaide: University of South Australia.

Owusu-Ansah, Edward K. 2004. "Information Literacy and Higher Education: Placing the Academic Library in the Center of a Comprehensive Solution." *The Journal of Academic Librarianship* 30, no. 1 (January): 3–16.

Reeb, Brenda, and Susan Gibbons. 2004. "Students, Librarians, and Subject Guides: Improving a Poor Rate of Return." *portal: Libraries and the Academy* 4, no. 1 (January): 123–130.

Reyes, Verónica. 2006. "The Future Role of the Academic Librarians in Higher Education." *portal: Libraries and the Academy* 6, no. 3 (July): 301–309.

Salmon, Gilly. 2000. *E-Moderating: The Key to Teaching and Learning Online.* London: Kogan Page.

Salter, Dianne, Leslie Richards, and Tom Carey. 2004. "The T5 Design Model." *Educational Media International* 41, no. 3: 207–218.

Shepard, Alicia C. 2005. "A's for Everyone!" *Washington Post*, June 5, p. W19.

Silver, Susan L., and Lisa T. Nickel. 2003. "Taking Library Instruction Online: Using the Campus Portal to Deliver a Web-based Tutorial for Psychology Students." *Internet Reference Services Quarterly* 8, no. 4 (Winter): 1–9.

Snavely, Loanne, and Natasha Cooper. 1997. "Competing Agendas in Higher Education." *Reference & User Services Quarterly* 37, no. 1 (Fall): 53–62.

Southwell, Karen, and Judith Brook. 2004. "Embedded Assignment Guides: Point of Need Instruction on the Web." *Georgia Library Quarterly* 41, no. 1 (Spring): 5–8.

Tennant, Roy. 2001. "Avoiding Unintended Consequences." *Library Journal* 126, no. 1 (January): 38.

Walton, Marion, and Arlene Archer. 2004. "The Web and Information Literacy: Scaffolding the Use of Web Sources in a Project-Based Curriculum." *British Journal of Educational Technology* 35, no. 2 (March): 173–186.

Zabel, Diane. 2004. "A Reaction to 'Information Literacy and Higher Education.'" *The Journal of Academic Librarianship* 30, no. 1 (January): 17–21.

Zhang, Wenxian. 2002. "Developing Web-enhanced Learning for Information Fluency." *Reference & User Services Quarterly* 41, no. 4 (Summer): 356–363.

Chapter 5

WISPR

A Constructivist Approach to Information Literacy Education in Blended Learning Environments

K. Alix Hayden, Cindy Graham, Shauna Rutherford, Jean Chow, and Claudette Cloutier

INTRODUCTION

Librarians at the University of Calgary designed the Workshop on the Informa-tion Search Process for Research (WISPR) to change our role fundamentally as information literacy instructors. We realized that students were not developing adequate transferable strategies and skills for conducting academic research through "one-shot" sessions that focused primarily on the mechanics of database searching. WISPR maximizes faculty collaboration by combining the use of a customizable online tool and face-to-face sessions with students. It also maximizes faculty collaboration, puts more emphasis on meaningful interaction with students, and allows participants to acquire both transferable information-seeking skills and a greater understanding of the intellectual process associated with library research. This blended approach to information literacy instruction was launched in fall 2005 and has since been fully integrated into a number of courses in different disciplines. This chapter will focus on two such courses: Science 251: Approaching Science as Scientists and Nursing 207: Nursing Inquiry.

BACKGROUND

The development of WISPR was made possible through a grant that assisted faculty in integrating both inquiry-based and blended learning pedagogies into their teaching. Although the University of Calgary Library does not offer a stand-alone information literacy course, librarians proposed a syllabus that could be incorporated into any course where inquiry-based and blended learning were employed; this syllabus became WISPR. The grant enabled us to hire programmers in our campus Teaching and Learning Centre to create the online modules. It also teamed librarians with an instructional designer who worked with us throughout the entire development process. He acted as a project manager, as a liaison with the programming staff, and provided ongoing support and guidance regarding the workshop's design from a pedagogical perspective. The result is a fully customizable workshop, incorporating both online and face-to-face components. The workshop allows librarians and faculty to collaboratively promote a discipline-specific perspective of the research process that helps students develop transferable strategies for progressing through course assignments and future research projects.

Defining Information Literacy in a Blended Learning Environment

Blended learning, also called hybrid learning, refers to situations where significant learning activities are put online, reducing but not eliminating the amount of time students spend in face-to-face environments. The goal of this approach is to "join the best features of in-class teaching with the best features of online learning to promote active independent learning" (Garnham and Kaleta, 2002: 1). Garrison and Kanuka (2004) point out that blended learning is not merely the addition of Internet-based technology to an existing classroom-based course; rather, it implies a "fundamental reconceptualization and reorganization of the teaching and learning dynamic" (97). In effect, simply adding technology as an extra layer to an existing course does not qualify as blended earning. The technology must be employed in such a way that meaningful educational experiences result, and this necessarily changes the nature of face-to-face meetings as well as the online experience.

A strategy for optimizing the blended learning approach is the "classroom flip" (Ladner et al., 2004: 330), so named because it reverses the traditional division of learning activities done inside and outside the classroom. Ladner et al. (2004) cite Jordan-Baker, who summarizes the "classroom flip" in four steps:

1. Move lecture material out of the classroom through online delivery.
2. Move homework into the classroom where faculty can serve as a guide.
3. Use additional opened-up class time for higher level discussion, application, and practice.
4. Extend conversation out of class through threaded discussion. (330)

In designing WISPR, we thought that a blended approach would allow a more meaningful method for information literacy instruction. Our traditional model involved hands-on one-shots in our library's wired classroom. In a 50-minute session, we usually focused on the mechanics of database searching through the demonstration of databases relevant to the particular class being taught. Librarians on the WISPR design team were unhappy with this approach for a number of reasons: (1) it reduced librarians' role to that of "trainers" rather than educators; (2) it was "just-in-case" instruction rather than "just-in-time" intervention, and students' subsequent visits to the reference desk or appointments with librarians proved that learning had not necessarily taken place; and (3) students did not gain an appreciation of the intellectual process of doing research but merely focused on the narrow step of collecting and retrieving information. We thought we could more effectively teach the concepts, strategies, and skills the students need by using a blended learning approach. By putting much of the conceptual content and the mechanical aspects of searching into an online format, librarians' roles in the course could evolve as guides, assisting with questions, challenges, or roadblocks that students encounter with their particular research questions and addressing their needs throughout the entire search process, not merely with database searching.

The other component supported by the Inquiry Through Blended Learning course development grant was, of course, inquiry-based learning (IBL). IBL has become a major trend in higher education in North America in recent years. Based on a constructivist theory of education, inquiry-based learning puts student curiosity at the core of the learning experience. IBL is not only student centered but student driven, with students choosing which aspects of the curriculum to direct their energy and investigative skills.

In order to be successful in an inquiry-based learning environment, students must be able to formulate good, researchable questions, search widely for materials that inform them about those questions, interpret the information they find, and use it to gain deeper understanding, create new knowledge, or provide innovative solutions to the problem at hand. To librarians, it is obvious that students need a high level of information literacy skills and strategies to perform these tasks effectively, but we recognize that very few students enter university with these competencies.

Inquiry-Based Learning and WISPR's Constructivist Framework

WISPR supports inquiry-based learning within the disciplines and is founded on a constructivist model of learning. According to Good and Brophy (1994), the four underlying assumptions of constructivist learning follow:

1. Learners construct their own meaning.
2. New learning builds on prior knowledge.
3. Learning is enhanced by social interaction.
4. Meaningful learning develops through authentic tasks.

These assumptions reflected our own conceptions of how information literacy should be approached; therefore, we aimed to base WISPR on a constructivist perspective. To ensure that the proposed workshop was founded on sound principles of information seeking of diversified populations (e.g., undergraduates, professionals, etc.), we reviewed the relevant education and library literature.

The literature is peppered with models of information seeking that provide interesting components to consider (Dervin, 1983; Ellis, 1989; Bates, 1989; Eisneberg and Berkowitz, 1990; Wilson and Walsh, 1996); however, the models did not fit with the theoretical, constructivist framework we sought. Carol Collier Kuhlthau's (2004) work spoke to us as a way of conceptualizing our proposed workshop. Kuhlthau's information search process (ISP) model is based on a series of longitudinal studies obtained through qualitative research methodology, specifically case studies of high school students. She, and others (Kuhlthau et al., 1990; Loerke, 1994; Swain, 1996), have validated the model with college students and professionals. Of particular significance is Byron and Young's (2000) study which confirms Kuhlthau's ISP in a virtual learning environment. Their study indicated that "students in a virtual learning environment, regardless of levels of computer skill, exhibit the stages indicated by the ISP Model" (264). Further, the results also suggested that the ISP model is representative of both individual work and group work.

Kuhlthau's (2004) ISP model includes six stages: (1) task initiation, (2) topic selection, (3) prefocus exploration, (4) focus formulation, (5) information collection, and (6) search closure. Further, within each stage, there are three realms: affective (feelings), cognitive (thoughts), and physical (actions and strategies). The model highlights the complex cognitive processes, such as brainstorming, contemplating, predicting, consulting, reading, choosing, identifying, defining, and confirming, that are involved in information-seeking behaviors. The model also emphasizes the feelings experienced by the information seeker, such as anxiety at the beginning of the search, often leading to an increase in confidence near the end of the search process. It is the inclusion of these realms that for Kuhlthau (1991) was "necessary for a model to address a wider, holistic view of information use" (362) and that for us was most meaningful.

Kuhlthau's ISP model is also significant as it encapsulates the iterative nature of information seeking and identifies how students explore the various avenues open to them on their information-seeking journey. Her findings suggest that searchers experience all six stages as they complete a search for information. Although her model is presented in a linear fashion, usually as a table, these stages of information seeking are not always linear; users may go through some of the stages several times, return to an earlier phase as new or conflicting information is encountered, or not complete some stages. Commenting on Kuhlthau's model, Jacobson and Ignacio (1997) explain that the ISP "is complex and requires multiple exposures, pauses for reflection, and opportunities for reiteration with alternative strategies and views" (774). Returning to the four assumptions of constructivism as described by Good and Brophy (1994), we determined that Kuhlthau's model of the information search process was the most relevant.

Goals for WISPR

When we set out to create WISPR we had a number of goals for the project. Our overall learning objective was for students to gain an understanding that research is a complex process, involving far more than gathering and regurgitating information found over the Web. In line with the inquiry model, placing student questions at the core of the process helps them to see themselves as active participants in the research endeavor. As Simmons (2005) writes, "facilitating students' understanding that they can be participants in scholarly conversations encourages them to think of research not as a task of collecting information but instead as a task of constructing meaning" (299). Related to this objective is our goal to have students comprehend that the process remains the same regardless of the specific course assignment or research purpose (e.g., research paper, annotated bibliography, thesis, etc.). A well-known melody may be played by different people, on different instruments, in different times and places, it transcends the unique interpretation and is immediately recognizable because it is familiar. Similarly, basing WISPR on Kuhlthau's ISP model provides a recognizable familiar process regardless of circumstance.

We also had specific goals regarding how the workshop would work and be used. First and foremost, we wanted it to be easy to use, both for librarians and instructors who chose to implement it and for the students who would use it. To this end, we insisted that it be Web based and not involve complicated programming from an end-user perspective. The Web platform allows all users to access it anywhere, anytime, as long as an Internet connection is available. We were also insistent that, within the overall ISP framework, maximum customization should be allowable to permit the content to be shaped in a way that suits the particular requirements of a specific course, discipline, or broad subject area. Research has shown that information literacy instruction is most effective when meaningfully integrated into course content (Australia and New Zealand Institute for Information Literacy, 2004) so we wanted to create a product that would address students' immediate needs and research requirements for the course they were taking. The customization also promotes faculty-librarian collaboration on a much higher level than a generic tutorial ever could, as evidenced by the two case studies to follow. Finally, we wanted to incorporate reflective elements into WISPR so that students would thoughtfully review what they had done and be able to apply that learning to future research projects. The logbook, available as a download for personal use or online as a deliverable assignment, meets this purpose.

WISPR DEVELOPMENT

Framework

As WISPR would be taught in online, blended learning, and face-to-face situations, we focused our attention on developing a graphical interface, or framework, which would support these diverse learning environments. We determined that Kuhlthau's typical tabular presentation of the ISP would not be meaningful or interesting to students, nor clearly representational of the ISP. Fortunately, we were able to adapt, with permission, a graphic developed by two colleagues, to use as the framework for WISPR, as presented in Figure 5.1. It clearly illustrates the complexities of the information search process and reinforces the ISP's recursive nature. As Wilson (1999) points out, "Kuhlthau's 'stages' can be seen not as steps in a single information seeking activity, but reiterated steps that may occur in exploratory loops between each link in the problem resolution chain" (266). Our WISPR graphic responds to this perspective; although information seeking is iterative, one must go through each phase prior to moving to the next. During anytime of the process, however, one may loop back to a previous phase.

WISPR is not a direct representation of Kuhlthau's (1993) ISP model. Based on the research of Hayden (2003) and Bateman (1998), coupled with years of

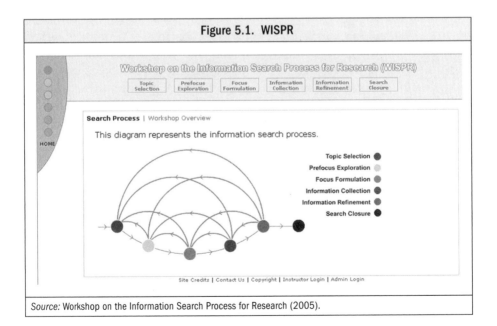

Figure 5.1. WISPR

Workshop on the Information Search Process for Research (WISPR)

Topic Selection | Prefocus Exploration | Focus Formulation | Information Collection | Information Refinement | Search Closure

Search Process | Workshop Overview

This diagram represents the information search process.

Topic Selection
Prefocus Exploration
Focus Formulation
Information Collection
Information Refinement
Search Closure

HOME

Site Credits | Contact Us | Copyright | Instructor Login | Admin Login

Source: Workshop on the Information Search Process for Research (2005).

practical experience, we modified some of the nomenclature. First, we called each ISP stage a *phase*, which reflects a less concrete, more fluid process. We merged Kuhlthau's *task initiation* and *topic selection* into the first phase: *topic selection*. We also divided the information collection stage into two phases: information collection and information refinement so that it is reinforced that students should review the information retrieved and determine where there might be gaps or missing information.

Each phase of the ISP includes standardized components: overview, actions/ strategies, thoughts/feelings, course-specific activities, self-assessment, and logbook, as well as navigation points. Color coding for each phase corresponds to the WISPR graphic. The phase is highlighted in several places: on the top menu, on the left navigation menu, and a small WISPR graphic indicates the phase currently under study. Standardization within each phase assists students in becoming familiar with WISPR's framework and provides a sense of cohesion throughout all phases. Figure 5.2 illustrates the standardized phase layout. To view all phases, connect to WISPR at www.library.ucalgary.ca/WISPR

Ways of Knowing

As mentioned, one of our project goals was to ensure that WISPR's content may be customized to be meaningful to course content and discipline knowledge. Ways of knowing, ways of understanding, and ways of conceptualizing knowledge underpin the ways of producing and acquiring knowledge (Kapitzke, 2001). Through WISPR, we teach students that "research is about constructing meaning through active engagement with the ideas and questions surrounding the information itself" (Simmons, 2005: 308), not just about finding facts or getting

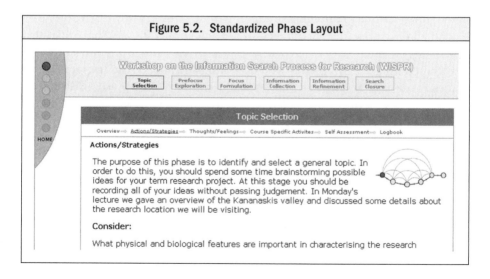

Figure 5.2. Standardized Phase Layout

an A on an assignment. WISPR shows that research is a process of discovery, an uncovering of the unknown, and a journey through the discourse of a discipline.

Simmons (2005) suggests that there are domain-specific processes for reading, writing, and researching that are seen as "normal," "natural," or "correct" by the faculty in the discipline. Often, information literacy instruction is not responsive to the "ways of knowing" in a particular discipline. Simmons (2005) also encourages librarians to focus on the unique discourses of a discipline "by articulating and making visible the epistemological differences in research in the disciplines" (p. 305).

We intended WISPR to model the research process of a discipline through the inclusion of course-specific content within each phase of the ISP. Further, WISPR incorporates specific course concepts, assignments, and information sources. WISPR is not a static online tutorial; rather it is dynamic, fluid, and relevant to the research process of different disciplines. It must be mentioned that currently the WISPR framework nomenclature (i.e., topic selection, prefocus formulation, etc.) cannot be modified to reflect the research process of a specific discipline. Future enhancements will address this and WISPR's six phase headings may be customized to be respectful of discipline nomenclature.

Instructional Technology

During the initial stages of development, we explored multiple means of engaging our learners through the use of technology. Our instructional designer encouraged us to consider ways of addressing different learning styles (e.g., auditory and visual). He suggested two guiding principles for integrating technology into WISPR. First, we review only technologies that promised meaningful authentic learning. He ensured that we did not succumb to slick technologies but rather based our decision to implement a technology on pedagogical purpose. The second guiding principle encouraged us to explore only those technologies that are readily available (either free or inexpensive) and that are user-friendly. We felt that complex technologies would be a significant hurdle for faculty and librarians wanting to integrate WISPR into their curriculum. Further, a study by Derntl and Motschnig-Pitrik (2005) revealed that "blended learning has added value only when facilitated by educators with high interpersonal skills, and *accompanied by reliable, easy-to-use technology*" (111, emphasis added). Figure 5.3 provides a synopsis of the different technologies used to create the various components of WISPR. These technologies will be discussed in detail.

Course management system: In the fall of 2003, the University of Calgary adopted Blackboard as the course management system (CMS) standard. Blackboard is used for both blended learning courses and traditional face-to-face courses. Faculty are accustomed to posting course outlines, assignment details, and PowerPoint lecture presentations. Further, Blackboard facilitates discussion

Figure 5.3. Technologies Integrated into WISPR		
WISPR Component	Technology	Responsibility
Course Management System	Blackboard	Librarians/Faculty
Content	TinyMCE WYSIWYG editor	Librarians/Faculty
KWLF Chart	Macromedia Breeze	Librarians/Faculty
Screencasts	Viewlet Builder Pro & Camtasia Studio	Librarians
Guided Database Tutorials	HTML, Boomer, Javascript adopted from TILT	Librarians
Self-Assessment Scenarios	Quandary 2.2	Librarians/Faculty
Logbook	Jakarta Tapestry	Programmers

boards, assignment submissions, grading, and group work. Jackson (2007) points out that course management systems "make it increasingly possible for faculty and librarians to collaborate on information literacy instruction and outreach to students" (454). She also suggests that a CMS assists librarians in integrating library resources into the systems that students use to access their course content. This marrying of the library with course content facilitates further integration of information literacy into the curriculum. As WISPR is Web-based, it is simple to integrate it directly into the relevant components of the course curriculum through hyperlinking. Librarians can also facilitate discussion boards with students, or groups of students, based on questions raised from using WISPR.

Content: As previously mentioned, in order to be responsive to the ways of knowing in a discipline, as well as to be thoroughly integrated into course curriculum, all content in WISPR may be customized, adapted, and changed. A simple embedded WYSIWYG editor for changing content is available through an administrative interface. The faculty member and librarian are registered for access to this interface. This encourages faculty-librarian collaboration as both professionals may integrate specific course-related strategies and activities, develop meaningful and content-relevant examples, post assignment due dates, and embed links to specific resources. A WYSIWYG editor ensures that changing content is simple and that a knowledge of HTML is not required.

KWLF chart: The KWLF (what I know, what I want to know, what I learned, where I found it) chart is based on the KWL chart, developed by Ogle (1986), and is used extensively in the K–12 environment as a means of improving students' reading comprehension. We wanted to implement a mechanism where students are encouraged to think actively about what they know, what they want to know (or wonder), and what they learned. Given the tendency of students to use Google for academic research, despite instruction on appropriate databases, we added the "Found" component. This additional element provides a way for students to be accountable for the information that they have retrieved. It also encourages good note taking and citation habits.

We felt that providing instruction about the KWLF chart in a table or textual format would be tedious, very long, and most probably skipped by the majority of students. Therefore, our instructional designer suggested we investigate Macromedia's Breeze. This software package, licensed by the university, incorporates narration, animation, and quizzes with Microsoft's PowerPoint (PPT) slides. The file is converted to Flash and, therefore, can easily be delivered via the Web and integrated into WISPR's framework. No plug-ins or additional software are required to view the Breeze file, and the file plays automatically. The ability to pause and rewind enhances student learning. For online or blended learning courses, Breeze offers the opportunity for the students to "meet" the librarians, to hear their voices, and provides the *human touch* that might be missing in the online learning environment.

Keeping true to our principle of user-friendly technology, each PPT's slide narration is a single recording. One does not need to redo the entire PPT narration if words are misspoken during recording. Further, the file can be shared between faculty member and librarians, and both voices may be recorded onto different PPT slides, which provides a more collaborative learning experience for the students.

Screencasts: As mentioned previously, the "classroom flip" is a blended learning strategy where traditional in-class learning activities are completed online. In face-to-face, one-shot information literacy instruction sessions, librarians often demonstrate databases. We wanted to move this "training" aspect to WISPR so that face-to-face sessions with students would focus more on the intellectual aspects of the ISP (i.e., the first three phases of WISPR). We used the concept of the classroom flip for developing screencasts that demonstrate relevant databases, provide orientation to specific tasks (e.g., authentication to access databases remotely), and for using specific resources (e.g., Find It: SFX for accessing full-text articles).

Screencasts are short recordings of a computer screen that show all mouse movements, typing, screen captures, links, etc. Narration is usually incorporated in the screencast. Some interactivity is possible—students may answer a question or click a portion of the screen in response to a question before being able to advance. We used both Viewlet and Camtasia, and while both are user-friendly, they are more complex than other technology in WISPR, requiring the assistance of a local expert. Unlike Breeze, all narration is captured in one session; therefore any errors require the entire narration to be redone. We found that for more complex databases or search demonstrations, writing and reading a script was very advantageous, rather than improvising.

Guided database tutorials: We wanted to provide guided live database training in the online environment. We also needed to create interactive rather than passive demos and provide the opportunity for students to practice hands-on searching within a guided inquiry environment. In essence, we wanted to emulate the successful components of face-to-face database instruction in the online environment. Through adaptation of the Javascript coding for interactivity provided by TILT (Texas Information Literacy Tutorial, n.d.) and the use of a screen split by frames we created hands-on guided instruction database tutorials. On the left side of the split screen, written instructions guide students through practice searches in a live database, which appears on the right side of the screen. Students may choose to search anything as the database is live, but they are encouraged to follow along with the guided instruction, which explores important search features and embeds questions that students must answer (simple radio button questions). The instructions teach proper searching techniques such as Boolean operators, truncation, and subject headings.

We were delighted to discover the tool Boomer, which added audio to the database tutorials. An audio file, recorded as a WAV file, is converted to Flash by Boomer. The embedded Flash audio file plays as soon as the left split-screen loads. The audio helps to lessen the amount of text contained on the split screen by pointing out important concepts or search features. It also addresses the needs of auditory learners and, additionally, brings a personal connection to the online environment.

Unfortunately, our user-friendly principle did not hold for this instructional technology. Creating the guided database tutorials required more expertise with Javascript coding than can be expected of most librarians. We were fortunate that one of the WISPR team librarians acted as programmer and created the database tutorials, using content, examples, and audio scripts developed by subject librarians. We anticipate developing training workshops for this instructional technology.

Self-assessment scenarios: Student formulation of a personal perspective and engaging with information to construct a new understanding is central to Kuhlthau's ISP. We felt it was important for students to feel confident in their understanding and abilities for each phase prior to proceeding to the next phase. We reviewed a variety of assessment methods, finally settling on the idea of a decision-point tool, or "action maze." Quandary software provided us with a simple way to set up self-assessment scenarios at the end of each phase. The purpose of using an action maze rather than a checklist is to provide students with guidance in areas that they did not fully understand, complete, or found confusing. The action maze also reinforces concepts, strategies, and actions that were taught during the phase. Essentially, the action maze simulates the reference conversation between librarian and student in an online, asynchronous environment. Through guidance and direction, the student eventually completes the action maze and is prompted to continue to the next phase. Figure 5.4 provides an example of a portion of the self-assessment action maze for topic selection.

Figure 5.4. Example of Self-assessment Action Maze			
I have thoroughly read through my assignment and am aware of all the criteria required.			
GO	Yes, I understand my assignment and know what I need to do to in order to satisfy the assignment's criteria.	GO	I've only skimmed the assignment and many details are still hazy.
A positive self-assessment results in the next question.		*A negative self-assessment provides guidance on specific actions and strategies that the student should consider.*	
I'm starting to be on the "lookout" for an interesting topic.		Carefully read your assignment. By ensuring that you know all of the criteria for the assignment often results in less wasted time and ultimately less frustration. Read your assignment to find out what types of materials are allowed (e.g., if no Internet sites, don't waste time searching the Internet), currency, topic may need to be approved, primary sources may need to be cited, citation style, etc. If you are unclear on any of the guidelines, speak to your professor or TA.	
GO	Yes, I'm feeling a bit relieved that I've discovered a topic for my paper.	GO	Continue to the next self-assessment question.
GO	I don't even have the foggiest idea of what topic is of possible interest or is related to the course content.	I'm starting to be on the "lookout" for an interesting topic.	

Logbook: We developed an online tool, referred to as a logbook, where students could track their progression through the ISP, much like a research diary or a scientific logbook. The logbook may be used as a course assignment and students must be registered in the course in order to access the logbook. The logbook can be used by individual students as well as groups and may be submitted electronically to the professor or librarian at the end of each phase or at the end of the whole search process. Two levels of questions are included: (1) action-oriented, in which students are asked to recount their actions, strategies, steps, and procedures for each phase, and (2) reflection-oriented, in which students are encouraged to relate their thoughts and feelings during a phase and consider what went well and what is confusing. The logbook is a complex tool, requiring expert programming from our Teaching and Learning Centre.

CASE STUDIES

The WISPR tutorial has been incorporated into several classes in the faculties of Communication and Culture, Kinesiology, Nursing, Science, and Social Work. The following case studies focus on the experiences of two faculty-librarian teams integrating WISPR into first-year classes in science and nursing. Each case study recounts how WISPR was meaningfully customized based on both course content and discipline knowledge. These two divergent case studies emphasize the flexible and adaptive nature of WISPR and the ability to tailor it to a wide array of courses based on discipline-specific ways of knowing.

Case Study 1: Science

Discipline and Course Context

The Natural Sciences Program is a multidisciplinary degree program started at the U of C in 2002; unlike traditional science degree programs that focus on a single area of science, students concentrate their studies in two scientific disciplines. The depth and breadth of this program as well as a unified "capstone experience" provides students the ability to solve problems and ask questions from more than one scientific perspective and gives them the tools to work effectively within a multidisciplinary team. In 2005, a first-year course, Approaching Science as Scientists (Science 251), was added to the Natural Sciences Program roster.

The primary goals of Approaching Science as Scientists are to (1) encourage critical thinking and creativity, (2) promote science literacy and effective communication abilities, and (3) develop abstract reasoning, interpretive, and assessment skills. The course content is framed using inquiry- and problem-based pedagogies as students investigate how good scientific questions are asked, answered, and verified. They dissect and examine the research methodologies used to reach important scientific conclusions and are introduced to basic methods of data analysis so they are able to assess how conclusions are made. Throughout this course, students develop their own ideas about research and science as they discover the fundamental spirit of scientific thought.

A major component of the student experience in Approaching Science as Scientists is the completion of a semester-long, inquiry-based research project. In 2005, students designed and completed a research project aimed at understanding the relationship between water chemistry and biological diversity in Mt. Lorette Ponds located in Kananaskis Country, Alberta. In the first part of the semester, students learned about scientific methodologies and designed their research question and experimental plan. Students carried out their research during a weekend field trip to the University of Calgary Barrier Lake Field Station and then spent the latter part of the semester analyzing data and forming conclusions in preparation for a conference-style poster session.

Based on student feedback from their reflective "scientific notebooks," it was clear that the research project had successfully given students an understanding of the nature of scientific inquiry and that they felt sense of pride and empowerment by the completion of the final project.

This project has shown me that a lot of work goes into planning an experiment, being flexible to change things last minute, and the work that needs to be done after the fieldwork is finished. By experiencing all this, I got the sense of what real scientists do, from planning and fieldwork to analyzing and showing their work to others. (a natural sciences student)

This whole project has in my opinion, opened my mind to asking better questions in all aspects of my education. I also think it has taught me to do better labs in my other sciences courses. I will undoubtedly use my newfound outlook on science throughout my education. (another natural sciences student)

While the first iteration of the course was successful, it was challenging as we had neglected one key part of any scientific research study—information seeking.

So far I have found the library to be more intimidating than useful and journal articles usually more complex and confusing than useful, but hopefully that changes. (another natural sciences student)

Because of the lack of ongoing information literacy support, students struggled in the planning and execution of the research, and in the explanation of the results.

I also feel stuck for sources of inspiration. The books I found from the library and the journal articles I've looked at on the Internet are WAY above and beyond my understanding. (another natural sciences student)

In 2006, the student research project changed from an aquatic to a terrestrial topic and students generated research questions that could be completed along an altitudinal gradient in the Kananaskis Valley. In an effort to address the lack of guidance in the information collection stage, the instructor approached the librarian supporting the Natural Sciences Program to discuss how this oversight might be corrected.

Faculty-Librarian Collaboration

The librarian and faculty member began their discussion by reevaluating the goals of the course and realized that skills-based library instruction was insufficient for students completing an open-ended scientific research project. Students were not able to apply the information search skills they had learned during one-shot library sessions and were not able to apply search strategies learned in one discipline to research in another. Students also had difficulty identifying authoritative sources, regardless of format. There appeared to be a disconnect between the principles and skills outlined in the library instruction and the students' ability to put them into practice; meaningful library research is not just about finding an article, it is about understanding the context and the discipline within which it is created.

One of the challenges that first-year students face is learning to find, read, and synthesize information needed to complete their assignments. Moreover, students struggle because of the lack of context for the information search process, as many do not understand why it is important or necessary to identify more than one source. The instructor and the librarian agreed to customize and incorporate WISPR into the course to address the challenges and issues identified by students from the previous year. Our WISPR customization focused on meaningfully tying information-seeking strategies to the process of scientific research while also providing support for students reading scientific papers for the first time.

WISPR Integration

Students were introduced to WISPR at the beginning of the course in a three-hour information literacy session. The librarian and the instructor demonstrated how to access WISPR, explained how the course research project corresponded to the phases of the workshop, and highlighted how each module would be of use during the course. The rest of the information literacy session focused on how scientific research is created and how, depending on the stage of the research, the data is shared with others. The activities and resources included in WISPR reinforced concepts embedded throughout the course content, research project, and the information literacy session, and aligned the six iterative phases of the information search process with the process of scientific investigation (Figure 5.5).

The formalized model of the processes of science put forward by Uno (1999) recognizes that while scientific investigations, like the information search process, do not necessarily follow a rigid sequence of events, they do have a progressive methodology in which one step builds on and leads to the next. By explicitly aligning the stages of the scientific process with the phases of WISPR, students more clearly understood the nature of the inquiry that they were involved in. Each WISPR phase provided course-specific resources and identified the key library and information resources required for successful completion of the phase.

The goal of the first phase, *topic selection*, is similar in both the information search process and the scientific research process (Figure 5.5). That goal is to identify an area of interest and, in terms of a research project, consider how scientists ask research questions. In this section of WISPR we were able to add information about the project area, the Kananaskis Valley, and add leading questions to get the students on track. The KWLF chart was customized to focus students on the study area and to encourage them to think about what they already knew about the research topic.

In the second WISPR phase, *prefocus exploration*, students were asked to investigate the current state of scientific knowledge about their area of interest. In this phase, students were encouraged to use any and all means to gather preliminary

Figure 5.5. WISPR and the Scientific Research Process		
WISPR Ways of Knowing	Science Ways of Knowing	Student Outcomes for Science 251
Topic Selection	Observing and comparing	How do we ask scientific questions? What do I find interesting?
Prefocus Formulation	Asking questions and identifying problems	What do we already know about the research area? Where are the gaps in the literature? What information do I need to design an answerable scientific question?
Focus Formulation	Forming hypothesis and predicting outcomes	What is the research question? What is my hypothesis? What are the expected outcomes?
Information Collection	Designing and conducting experiments Collecting and organizing data	Conducting experiments Gathering data and information
Information Refinement	Analyzing data and relating ideas Proposing explanations and making inferences	How can I explain what my results mean?
Search Closure	Communicating explanations and applying knowledge	Scientific poster presentation
Source: Adapted from Uno (1999).		

information, including textbooks, library resources, faculty experts, and even Internet searching. Most students were surprised at the amount of information scientists had to read and categorize before even considering the overarching research problem. By having a clear sense of the information that scientists already know, students were well equipped to focus their research toward a novel scientific question in the focus formulation phase of WISPR.

During the *focus formulation* phase, students started to narrow their interest and focus; they began developing a scientific research question. Students collected their independent research and presented a case for their research question to their group during the lab period. Through a series of, at times, heated debates and discussion, students refined and chose a research problem that interested all group members. Students worked closely with instructors and graduate teaching assistants to ensure that their question was not only interesting but also answerable. Students then completed an experimental design worksheet where they gave specific details about their research design, including the number and location of samples, how the samples were to be collected, and how the data would be analyzed. Students carefully crafted their hypotheses and discussed what experimental outcomes would allow them to know if their hypotheses were supported by their data.

The *information collection* phase was where most of the course-specific customization of WISPR occurred. The faculty-librarian team identified specific library and information resources that students would need to explore. For each resource identified, students could read a few lines about its suitability for the project and were linked to the guided hands-on search tutorials and screencasts discussed previously. Information in the WISPR module reinforced what had been covered in an associated face-to-face information literacy session. These resources allowed students to consider their research methodology more carefully, and students were better able to determine the most appropriate methods to use in their study. This phase was the most time-consuming for the students as they not only needed to find library resources to design an effective field study, they also needed to carry out their study and collect substantial data for later analysis.

The *information refinement* phase required students to reflect on the information they collected, and for our students it gave them a chance to consider how to draw conclusions and explanations from their data. In class, students were taught the statistical tools required to make robust conclusions about their data; in WISPR, students were coached on how to find additional library resources to explain how their conclusions fit with the larger body of scientific knowledge. In the final phase, *search closure*, students were given information about how to prepare scientific posters and how professional scientists use them to inform the broader scientific community.

Case Study 2: Nursing

Discipline and Course Context

The University of Calgary offers two undergraduate nursing degree streams. The regular track Nursing Program is a four-year degree program that began in 1970, while the accelerated track Nursing Program began in 2001 in response to a shortage of nurses in the health region. The Nursing Program provides the knowledge and beginning skills for graduates to work within a multidisciplinary health care team and a rapidly changing health care system.

Reflective practice is integral to nursing. Therefore, the program emphasizes learning through reflection, and students are expected to seek resources that reflect the four ways of knowing in nursing (Carper, 1978). Knowledge development in each of the ways of knowing, coupled with philosophy, theory, and research are integrated in the development of responsive nursing practice. The ways of knowing provide pathways through which the fullness of the nursing situation can be known (Boykin and Schoenhofer, 1991). Nursing's ways of knowing include empirical knowledge, aesthetics, personal knowing, and ethics, and in recent years sociopolitical knowing has been added. Empirical knowledge development focuses on knowledge developed using the scientific method (Chinn and Kramer, 1999). Ethical knowledge development encompasses the principles and codes that guide practice and behavior. Personal knowledge development involves reflective processes such as journals, meditation, or autobiographical stories in which the self in relation to others is revealed. Aesthetic knowledge or the art of nursing is the transformation of experiences into realms that could take on the form of stories, poetry, and so on.

The undergraduate nursing inquiry course (Nursing 207) was added to the program in 2001 and was proposed to help students develop foundational inquiry skills that would help them be successful in the nursing program. In the course, students extend their knowledge framework for nursing practice and their theoretical base for understanding various human responses to health and illness experiences. Initially, the course was taught using a didactic approach with guest speakers addressing students about their health/illness experience and a group project illustrating a patient's experience. In 2005, funding from an Inquiry Teaching and Blended Learning grant provided the impetus to consider using technology, online learning, and small group discussions to further enhance learning and to increase student collaboration. The ways of knowing in nursing provide the framework for the course.

Throughout the course, students use realistic case scenarios that challenge them to locate adequate resources with the end view of providing excellent care for patients and their families. Small group and online discussions stimulate critical thinking and provide an arena in which meaningfulness of the content for the student can be achieved. Inquiry skills lead to sound understanding of clinical nursing situations and sound approaches to nursing practice. In addition, students are encouraged to develop multiprofessional linkages in information data sources and practice settings.

Nursing 207 is a blended learning course. Students are placed into cohort groups of eight to ten students for the entire semester. These groups relate to their clinical placements for the parallel clinical course, Nursing 209, which offers students their first exposure to clinical nursing. The curriculum in Nursing 207 is closely aligned with Nursing 209 to ensure that students are provided with the theoretical aspects of patients' experiences of health/illness while exploring hands-on reflective practice. Students extend their knowledge for understanding the patient's experience by completing an annotated bibliography, a learning portfolio, and a class presentation.

Faculty-Librarian Collaboration

The course instructor met with the nursing librarian to determine the best way to foster reflective practice within an inquiry perspective. We were mindful that all of the students had received an introductory one-shot information literacy session that focused on searching the primary database for nursing (CINAHL) during their first semester. We proposed that students involved in the course would learn the value of active learning, self-direction, and group processes. We discussed that understanding clinical nursing situations requires strong nursing inquiry skills and the ability to use technology to access knowledge resources. Inquiry skills in nursing inquiry meant knowing *what* information is needed to understand the case study and knowing *how* to look for it, and making decisions about the resources leads to sound understanding of clinical nursing situations and sound approaches to nursing practice. We wanted students to understand that knowing how to find information is not merely an academic endeavor to get a good mark on a paper, but is also an essential component of competent and safe nursing practice.

We felt strongly that students needed to be introduced to clinical information resources but that these resources needed to be contextualized within nursing's ways of knowing and reflective practice and responsive to course content. WISPR offered us the opportunity to meaningfully integrate these resources within the blended-learning format. Together we developed two library-related assignments: For the first assignment, the students were asked to complete the first three phases of the logbook (i.e., topic selection, prefocus formulation, and focus formulation). The assignment's purpose was to focus students' attention on *coming to the topic*, where information seeking is seen as an intellectual process. This was a group assignment and marked as pass/fail. The second assignment required each student to write a reflection on his or her information-seeking process. The purpose of this assignment, worth 10 percent of the final grade, was to integrate reflection into information seeking, highlighting for students that critical reflection is a central part of inquiry and nursing practice.

WISPR Integration

During the first half of the course, students focused on the play *Wit!* (Edson, 1999), a Pulitzer Prize–winning play that delves into the life of Dr. Vivian Bearing, an English professor diagnosed with terminal ovarian cancer. The play acts as a springboard for discussing the facets of a clinical patient situation and the context for care. In small groups, led by a student facilitator with a graduate student or the professor acting as guides on the sideline, the students brainstormed ideas about the play and chose topics to research. Students reflected on the play both in their face-to-face groups and in online discussion groups via CIS (a locally developed course management system similar to Blackboard), learning about Vivian as both a patient with a complex clinical crisis and as a person who was experiencing the slow awareness of a terminal illness. Further, students often merged their clinical rotation experiences with the theory introduced in Nursing

207 in their online discussions. In order to guide students' inquiry, WISPR provided the framework for students to question what is needed to provide quality nursing care for the fictional patient Vivian. Prior to the beginning of the course, WISPR was customized to reflect the content of Nursing 207, most specifically in the area of information collection. Screencasts of relevant databases were developed along with identification of relevant Internet sites. The previous case scenario provides in-depth description of the level of customization possible with WISPR. Therefore, we will not repeat this information for nursing but rather will focus on how WISPR was taught.

We worked from the premise of the "classroom flip." The students were directed to go through WISPR, from their CIS course, prior to meeting with the nursing librarian. Because WISPR is Web-based and linked to the course curriculum, students could connect to the system at their convenience to go through WISPR. We wanted the students to come to the information literacy class prepared, with an understanding of the information search process and a general knowledge of the actions and strategies for each phase. Specifically, we wanted to avoid an in-class training session or "show and tell" where the librarian simply taught students how to use and navigate specific resources. Students were encouraged to go through all of WISPR, but to focus specifically on the information collection phase, completing the guided database tutorials, prior to the face-to-face session. During this session, we wanted to engage the students actively in discussion, focusing their attention on how to ask clinical questions and how to implement evidence-based practice.

During a class lecture, an overview of WISPR was taught, during which the nursing librarian focused on the first three phases (topic selection, prefocus exploration, focus formulation), providing scaffolds and connections to clinical situations. Discussion ensued on how important it is to ask deep and thoughtful questions. Students were asked if they knew how to ask clinical questions and if they knew where to start with their questions. It was also acknowledged that as novice nursing students they would be required to delve into background information prior to being able to understand a patient's disease or condition.

As with WISPR, the nursing clinical ways of knowing are iterative in nature. As the nurse, or nursing student, learns more about a patient's health, beliefs, and desires and integrates this with evidence-based information, he or she might need to return to the patient to reevaluate and reconsider treatment and care. Figure 5.6 further explicates the ways of questioning in nursing practice.

Throughout the face-to-face component, students were challenged to ask questions in a clinical way, and were introduced to the PICO method (patient, intervention, comparison, outcome) (Brown, 1999). Students were provided with handouts related to PICO as well as links in WISPR to other evidence-based practice tools.

Figure 5.6. WISPR and Nursing Clinical Ways of Knowing		
WISPR Ways of Knowing	Nursing Clinical Ways of Knowing	Clinical Outcomes
Topic Selection	The Patient	Start with the patient—recognize a clinical problem or question that arises out of the care of the patient.
Prefocus Formulation	The Question	Question the clinical problem—highlight areas of concern; obtain background information.
Focus Formulation	Focus the Question	Reframe the question using PICO (patient, intervention, comparison, outcome) to focus and clarify the clinical problem.
Information Collection	The Resource	Select the appropriate resource(s) and conduct a search.
Information Refinement	The Evaluation	Appraise the evidence for its validity (closeness to the truth) and applicability (usefulness in clinical practice).
Search Closure	The Patient	Return to the patient—integrate that evidence with clinical expertise, patient preferences, and apply it to practice.

After the class session, students broke up into their cohort groups. Each group consisted of eight to ten students. Health science librarians from the University Library then facilitated the small groups. Students focused their attention on *Wit!* and were required to ask clinical questions about the main character, using the PICO format. Each group of students had access to at least one laptop, connected to the Internet. Prior to jumping in and searching for information on alternative therapies relevant to Vivian's condition (the specific assignment for the day), students were encouraged to discuss Vivian as a patient, with the librarian acting as mediator and guide. The librarians reinforced the idea that nurses must thoroughly understand the patient (topic) before searching for information. It was further emphasized that students would need to conduct literature searches on background information (e.g., ovarian cancer) before linking to evidence-based practice resources. Librarians facilitated the discussion, generated questions, challenged preconceived ideas, and encouraged students throughout the group work process. We wanted students to realize that effective clinical practice is driven by questions and then finding the evidence on which to base practice. During the discussions, students worked collaboratively on completing the first three phases of the logbook. Students submitted the logbook at the end of the day.

Although it was expected that students had already reviewed the clinical resources in WISPR prior to the group discussion, this was unfortunately not always the case. If students were unsure as to how to effectively search within a resource, they were encouraged to review the screencasts in WISPR rather than ask the librarian. We wanted students to be in charge of their own learning and to develop self-sufficiency in determining how to access and search evidence-based resources. Often other members of the group provided assistance, showing the more novice student the best and quickest way to retrieve the required information.

Because of WISPR's ability to be adapted meaningfully to course content and, more specifically, discipline knowledge, students were exposed to the ways of asking questions as a nurse. The small group discussion session facilitated a "zone of intervention" (Kuhlthau, 2004) where the librarian was immediately available to provide opportunities to talk about ideas as they emerged, provide advice and assistance to the group, and to intervene as required. The second library assignment, due two weeks after the group sessions, required students to reflect on their actions, questioning, and their own ISP. Overwhelmingly, the majority of students wrote that they were unfamiliar with the importance of thinking about a topic, reflecting on possible avenues of research or clinical care, and considering conflicting opinions or practices, prior to jumping into information collection. They also felt validated that their feelings of uncertainty, anxiety, and confusion were normal. Through WISPR online and the face-to-face group discussions, the students become more confident in their abilities.

Reflections on Integrating WISPR

Science: Our experience incorporating the WIPSR tutorial into a first-year science class has been very positive. We are convinced that incorporating WISPR into Approaching Science as Scientists enhanced the student's ability to find and use information, and we have given more consideration about how best to integrate it within the course. Because the student research project spans the entire semester, it was difficult to give students enough guidance in WISPR without including more content than students would likely read. Some of the benefits of WISPR can be gained by simply introducing students to how the information search process and the scientific method are aligned at the beginning of the course. By creating context and meaning for information literacy, students should, at the very least, understand the importance of good library research. In order to reduce the amount of information given to students at the beginning of the course, WISPR could be customized specifically for each assignment. This would allow librarians and instructors to highlight specific skills needed for each assignment and would contextualize specific information search processes depending on the assignment outcome. Other changes we have discussed include: dividing face-to-face library instruction into strategic modules and distributing it during appropriate intervals throughout the semester, revisiting WISPR with the students more frequently, and imbedding meaningful course-specific activities into each phase of WISPR or being able to remove sections when they are not needed.

Nursing: As in Science 251, we feel that WISPR offered new ways to explore information literacy strategies within the context of a discipline. From students' reflection assignments it was clearly evident that most students had viewed the research process as purely information collection (i.e., searching, and most often searching the Web). They were unaware of the importance of thinking about their topic, considering different points of views, and really questioning what they want to know. Further, the students stated that, prior to Nursing 207, they had viewed "library research" as a merely academic endeavor, not one that would play a role in their future professional lives. By customizing WISPR to be reflective of the clinical ways of knowing in nursing and providing small group discussion groups mediated by health sciences librarians, students came to understand the information search process and to appreciate that information plays a critical role in professional practice.

We did, as can be expected, encounter some hurdles with WISPR. We found that forcing students to go through the first three phases of WISPR while in their small group discussions and to fill in the corresponding sections of the logbook was not authentic learning. Students felt confined by the time and were anxious to complete the logbook quickly rather than to really think about and reflect on their process and actions. In the future, we will look at ways to explore the first three phases as a group but allow time for completing the logbook in a more natural, less forced, sequence.

We also found that some students in the Bachelor of Nursing accelerated track program (the students enrolled in this program already have an undergraduate degree) were somewhat insulted by WISPR. These students felt that they had already successfully completed a four-year degree and had developed coping strategies for information seeking. They did not like the small group discussions with the librarian, commenting that they felt like they were being "babysat." In essence, we were not mindful of students' past experience and knowledge. For future sessions, we will try to draw these experiences out during either the in-class session or during the small group sessions. We will then build on what they know and link it to ways of knowing and doing research in nursing.

General: Although the success of a faculty-librarian collaboration has been reported previously (Souchek and Meier, 1997), it typically requires a great deal of faculty and librarian time—something that becomes prohibitive when dealing with typically large first-year classes. Where traditional library instruction gives students all of the information they will need to complete their assignments at the beginning of term, the incorporation of the WISPR online tutorial allows students to view the information search process in step with the immediate goals of their assignment as well as the overarching principles guiding the course.

While face-to-face library instruction is beneficial, the success of WISPR in these classes is based on the need for students to have ongoing library support. Because WISPR is available at any time of the day, students are able to return to specific phases of the research process for more assistance, to spend extra time on components with which they are having difficulty, and to explore databases at their own pace with guided instructions and audio—something that would be difficult if students had to approach a librarian each time they were having difficulty. One of the most significant aspects of WISPR is the degree and ease with which it can be customized. Most libraries now have some degree of online support for students; however, they may not deal with information literacy problems in a discipline-specific context. When students hit a snag in their assignment or project, it is possible to direct them back to specific phases of the WISPR module, and because each phase of WISPR included course specific objectives, it is easy to embed instructor and librarian guidance into the online material.

WISPR AND FUTURE DIRECTION

WISPR has opened doors for faculty-librarian collaboration that were previously closed, or even nonexistent. Through customization of content, WISPR is responsive to both course content and discipline knowledge. WISPR goes beyond the one-shot library instruction session, and can be woven throughout the course, and across the discipline curriculum. For example, the Department of History and the history librarian are currently working together, funded by a small internal grant, to customize WISPR to be used in *every* first-year history course. WISPR provides the framework for understanding historical research. This framework will integrate information literacy skills and strategies with course content. It is hoped that this approach will be more relevant and purposeful for students.

In April 2007, we received an additional $27,000 (CAN) through an internal teaching grant to further develop and enhance WISPR. We conducted small focus groups that included librarians and faculty who have integrated WISPR into courses to further delve into areas for revision, reconstruction, and refinement, as well as enhancement. Again, an instructional designer will consult with us throughout the redesign process. It is hoped that a pilot of the new, enhanced WISPR will be available in fall 2007, with the final version ready in time for winter 2008 classes.

The main areas of enhancement and refinement include:

1. Development of an administrative interface so that WISPR may be administrated wholly within the library rather than through the university's Teaching and Learning Centre. Currently we are unable to independently create WISPR courses or register students, which somewhat limits the integration of WISPR into librarians' information literacy instruction.

2. Further customization of components, including nomenclature and the logbook. In order to be respectful and responsive to discipline knowledge, the nomenclature for the phases needs to be customizable. For example, referring back to the nursing case study, *topic selection* might be termed *The Patient* (see Figure 5.2). Currently WISPR's logbook is not customizable as the programming is very complex and beyond the skills of most librarians. With the enhancement, the logbook will be easily adapted and modified for specific course assignments. Multiple logbooks, both for individuals and groups, will also be possible. Further, librarian and faculty members will be able to provide feedback via the logbook. In essence, the logbook will be more dynamic and functional.

3. Integration of additional productivity software such as blogs, e-mail notifications, and discussion groups.

4. "Packaging" of WISPR for other institutions. We hope that WISPR will be available to other institutions, via a Creative Commons license, so that they may meaningfully customize WISPR to be responsive to their institutional environment and course disciplines.

5. Research into WISPR and the student experience. Although we have anecdotal feedback from students through reflection assignments and informal conversations that WISPR has indeed provided them with the strategies required for academic research, we do not have empirical evidence to date. We anticipate developing a mixed methodology research study investigating (1) the student experience of using WISPR, (2) whether WISPR is representative of undergraduate students' information seeking process through the utilization the research instruments developed by Kuhlthau (2004), and (3) whether blended learning and the classroom flip enhance students' learning and retention of information literacy strategies as well as their confidence in their abilities.

We hope that WISPR will become a widely used information literacy model at the University of Calgary and beyond. Through meaningful and authentic integration of WISPR into courses, students will become familiar with the information search process. They will learn that information seeking is an intellectual process, that the six phases of the ISP are iterative, and that feeling anxious and overwhelmed is a normal part of the research process.

REFERENCES

Australia and New Zealand Institute for Information Literacy (ANZIIL). 2004. "Australia and New Zealand Information Literacy Framework: Principles, Standards and Practice (2nd)." Adelaide: Australia and New Zealand Institute for Information Literacy. Available: www.anziil.org/resources/Info%20lit%202nd%20edition.pdf.

Bateman, Judith A. 1998. *Modeling Changes in End User Relevance Criteria: An Information Seeking Study.* Unpublished Doctoral Dissertation, University of North Texas, Denton, Texas.

Bates, Marcia J. 1989. "The Design of Browsing and Berrypicking Techniques for the Online Search Interface." *Online Review* 13, no. 5: 407–424.

Boykin, Anne, and Savina O. Schoenhofer. 1991. "Story as Link Between Nursing Practice, Ontology, Epistemology." *Image: Journal of Nursing Scholarship* 23, no. 4: 245–248.

Brown, Sarah Jo. 1999. *Knowledge for Health Care Practice a Guide to Using Research Evidence.* Philadelphia: W. B. Saunders.

Byron, Suzanne M., and Jon I. Young. 2000. "Information Seeking in a Virtual Learning Environment." *Research Strategies* 17, no. 4: 257–267.

Carper, Barbara A. 1978. "Practice Oriented Theory. Fundamental Patterns of Knowing in Nursing." *Advances in Nursing Science* 1 (October): 13–23.

Chinn, Peggy L., and Maeona K. Kramer. 1999. *Theory and Nursing: Integrating Knowledge Development.* St. Louis: Mosby.

Derntl, Michael, and Renate Motschnig-Pitrik. 2005. "The Role of Structure, Patterns and People in Blended Learning." *Internet and Higher Education* 8, no. 2: 111–130.

Dervin, Brenda. 1983. "Information as a User Construct: The Relevance of Perceived Information Needs to Synthesis and Interpretation." In Spencer A. Ward and Linda J. Reed (Eds.), *Knowledge Structure and Use: Implications for Synthesis and Interpretation* (pp. 153–183). Philadelphia: Temple University Press.

Edson, Margaret. 1999. *Wit: A Play.* New York: Faber and Faber.

Eisenberg, Michael B., and Robert E. Berkowitz. 1990. *Information Problem-solving: The Big Six Skills Approach to Library and Information Skills Instructions.* Norwood, NJ: Ablex.

Ellis, David. 1989. "A Behavioural Approach to Information Retrieval System Design. *Journal of Documentation* 45, no. 3: 171–212.

Garnham, Carol, and Robert Kaleta. 2002. "Introduction to Hybrid Courses." *Teaching With Technology Today* 8, no. 6. Available: www.uwsa.edu/ttt/articles/garnham.htm.

Garrison, D. Randy, and Heather Kanuka. 2004. "Blended Learning: Uncovering its Transformative Potential in Higher Education." *Internet and Higher Education* 7, no. 2: 95–105.

Good, Thomas L., and Jere E. Brophy. 1994. *Looking in Classrooms.* New York: HarperCollins College.

Hayden, K. Alix. 2003. *Lived Experience of Students Searching for Information.* Unpublished Doctoral Dissertation, University of Calgary, Calgary, Alberta, Canada.

Jackson, Pamela A. 2007. "Integrating Information Literacy into Blackboard: Building Campus Partnerships for Successful Student Learning." *Journal of Academic Librarianship* 33, no. 4: 454–461.

Jacobson, Frances F., and Emily N. Ignacio. 1997. "Teaching Reflection: Information Seeking and Evaluation in a Digital Library Environment." *Library Trends* 45, no. 4: 771–802.

Kapitzke, Cushla. 2001. "Information Literacy: The Changing Library." *Journal of Adolescent & Adult Literacy* 44, no. 5: 450–456.

Kuhlthau, Carol C. 1991. "Inside the Search Process: Information Seeking from the User's Perspective." *Journal of the American Society for Information Science* 42, no. 5: 361–371.

Kuhlthau, Carol C. 1993. "A Principle of Uncertainty for Information Seeking." *Journal of Documentation* 49, no. 4: 339–355.

Kuhlthau, Carol C. 2004. *Seeking Meaning: A Process Approach to Library and Information Services*, 2nd ed. Westport: Libraries Unlimited.

Kuhlthau, Carol C., Betty J. Turock, Mary W. George, and Robert J. Belvin. 1990. "Validating a Model of the Search Process: A Comparison of Academic, Public and School Library Users." *Library and Information Science Research* 12 (January-March): 5–31.

Ladner, Betty, Donald R. Beagle, James R. Steele, and Linda Steele. 2004. "Rethinking Online Instruction: From Content Transmission to Cognitive Immersion." *Reference & User Services Quarterly* 43, no. 4: 329–337.

Loerke, Karen. 1994. "Teaching the Library Research Process in Junior High." *School Libraries in Canada* 14, no. 2: 23–36.

Ogle, Donna M. 1986. "K-W-L: A Teaching Model that Develops Active Reading of Expository Text." *Reading Teacher* 39, no. 6: 564–570.

Simmons, Michelle H. 2005. "Librarians as Disciplinary Discourse Mediators: Using Genre Theory to Move Toward Critical Information Literacy." *portal: Libraries and the Academy* 5, no. 3: 297–311.

Souchek, Russell, and Marjorie Meier. 1997. "Teaching Information Literacy and Process Skills." *College Teaching* 45, no. 4: 128–131.

Swain, Deborah E. 1996. "Information Search Process Model: How Freshmen Begin Research." Paper read at ASIS 1996 Annual Conference Proceedings, October 19–24, Baltimore, Maryland. Available: http://asis.org/annual-96/ElectronicProceedings/swain.html.

"Texas Information Literacy Tutorial (TILT)." n.d. Austin: University of Texas System Digital Library. Available: http://tilt.lib.utsystem.edu/.

Uno, Gordon E. 1999. *Handbook on Teaching Undergraduate Science Courses: A Survival Training Manual*. Orlando: Saunders College Publishing.

Wilson, Tom D. 1999. "Models in Information Behaviour Search." *Journal of Documentation* 55, no. 3: 249–270.

Wilson, Tom D, and Christina Walsh. 1996. "Information Behaviour: An Interdisciplinary Perspective." Sheffield, UK: University of Sheffield, Department of Information Science. Available: http://informationr.net/tdw/publ/infbehav/cont.html.

Workshop on the Information Search Process for Research (WISPR). 2005. Calgary, AB: The University of Calgary Library. Available: http://library.ucalgary.ca/wispr/.

Chapter 6

Library Research Video Mix
The Use of Collaborative Multimedia via WebCT in a Senior Experience Course for Business

Ann Manning Fiegen, Keith Butler, and Regina Eisenbach

INTRODUCTION

Competencies for information technology and for information literacy are among the curricular learning outcomes for the business major at California State University–San Marcos. Students must demonstrate that they can successfully apply these competencies as part of their capstone business course sequence called the Senior Experience Program. The Senior Experience Program prepares student teams to work with local businesses and nonprofit agencies to solve real business problems. Faculty in the College of Business Administration redesigned the preparatory course in the program using collaborative teaching modules incorporating course management software and multimedia elements. The use of technology was a significant factor in reducing the program from a two-semester, eight-unit course sequence into a one-semester, five-unit course sequence while integrating information literacy and technology learning outcomes into the capstone course.

The Senior Experience Program now utilizes extensive multimedia for course content, course activities, and course deliverables while also allowing students to retain a high degree of personal interaction with business and library faculty throughout the semester. The Business 492 and 493 course sequence is now offered as a one-unit preparatory course followed by a four-unit project course. This chapter will describe a distributed course model where students in an experiential learning environment are guided and assessed on their ability to produce real business solutions using appropriate research methods. First-phase changes are described that took place prior to initiating the new course sequence. Second-phase changes are explored based on lessons learned from delivering the new sequence for four semesters, and ideas for continual assessment in relation to best practices will also be discussed.

The redesign would still need to maintain high quality guidance for student teams throughout the semester, in a shorter time period and with fewer units than the previous course sequence. The course design challenge for the one-semester course sequence would be to introduce expectations in a much shorter period since the preparatory one-unit course would be delivered over just three weeks at the beginning of the semester instead of the previous 15 week semester-long course. A second challenge was how to retain a highly individualistic experience for a large number of students (approximately 200 each semester). Teams were guided by community business contacts and faculty advisors during the four unit project course. In this distributed setting, the project course has only one hour of scheduled weekly meetings between the students and faculty advisors. The students are then responsible for setting up additional meetings with one another, with company contacts, the business librarian, or others needed to complete the project.

Redesigning the library instruction components created yet another challenge. The projects vary widely across many areas of business research, such as database or Web design, product release plans, nonprofit fund-raising programs, feasibility studies, and economic impact studies. It is difficult to tailor library instruction to such diverse topics when each has its own specialized information architecture requiring different paths of inquiry and distribution channels. The student teams are expected to conduct secondary research as needed throughout the project, but the only opportunity to reach all students at one time is during the three-week, one-unit course. Clearly the three-hour library workshop previously offered would have to be revised. Within these constraints, new uses of technology would be applied to expand course delivery and student deliverables for the research components of the course.

Overall, there are several strategies that guided the first-level design phase and that will direct the effectiveness assessment during the second phase, including the use of:

- Collaborative teams to implement the instruction
- Information literacy competencies and business analysis models to integrate the library research instruction
- Appropriate technology and instructional design principles to enhance instruction.

RELATED LITERATURE

Collaborations between business faculty and business librarians are common, and case studies describing these collaborations are well documented. Less common are case studies of how these collaborations used technology to enhance business instruction. Interactive Web tutorials have been developed to teach business at a number of institutions (Flanagan, 1999). Roy and Elfner (2002) examined student satisfaction of technologies for business instruction. Collaborative efforts between business faculty and librarians with computing and instructional development staff offer more technologically sophisticated methods to improve delivery options (Zhou, 2004). Shank and Bell (2006) see a growing need for a "blended librarian" model where librarians become more adept at instructional design and instructional technology and contribute their information research expertise to instructional design teams comprised of administrators, discipline faculty, librarians, instructional designers, and technologists.

The library instruction design goal was to build on what students already know about business analysis models and add library research strategies into that knowledge base. Reichel and Ramey (1987) advocated designing a contextual relationship between course content and bibliographic instruction. They found that students retain information more readily if new material builds on previously learned concepts. Critical to preparing business students to be independent library researchers is the industry analysis assignment for the BUS302 Business Environments. For this assignment students are required to use either the Griffin (2002) organizational environment model or Porter's (1985) five competitive forces model to research the business environment for their assigned topic. These two models are used to tie course material to library research techniques. Furthermore, since students have already used the models to analyze case studies from *Business Week* articles, the case study technique is used as a bridge to conducting their own independent research for their assigned topic. The Griffin environmental organizational model illustrates this concept. The assignment requires that students research each dimension of Griffin's (2002) task environment (competitors, customers, suppliers, regulators, and strategic allies) and external environment (international, economic, technological, sociocultural, political, legal). A library instruction Web page leads students from each dimension, the familiar, to the unfamiliar print and electronic library resources (California State University–San Marcos Library, 2007). Each dimension has two sets of linked buttons, one labeled "learn more," which directs students to a restaurant case example. Figure 6.1 illustrates how the "learn more" button leads a student through questions to ask and resources to use to research the customer dimension for a family restaurant. The "learn more" button links to suggestions for lifestyle publications, a sample search that leads to trade publications on consumer eating preferences, and to a local

---

Figure 6.1. Learn More—Case Example for Researching Griffin's Customer Dimension

Who is likely to eat at Don's Doggie Diner?

1. Research consumer lifestyle choices:
   • Library catalog subjects: Market segmentation, age groups
   • Lifestyle Market Analyst HF5415.33.U6 L54 REFERENCE
   • Demographic characteristics tied to lifestyle choices by metropolitan area.

2. Read industry news in trade publications:
   • ABI Inform Global/topic guide/restaurant/see other suggested topics
   • Restaurants and consumer behavior

3. Research location for restaurant, where do your most likely customers live and drive?

4. Use SanDAG (San Diego Association of Governments). The county census information and roadway driving volumes can assist in locating an optimal location for the diner.

---

demographics Web site. In another example a user wanting to research the Griffin dimension for strategic allies clicks the "learn more" button and is directed to suggested keyword synonyms for partner, joint, or alliance that may yield news about business alliances. The second option in each dimension links the user to a list of recommended sources. This technique integrates inquiry, searching, and selecting business information directly into the business models and case studies familiar to students. Using these business models as platforms for library research is reinforced in the Senior Experience company and industry report three semesters later.

Chickering and Ehrmann (1996), in "Implementing the Seven Principles: Technology as Lever," described how technology can be used to enhance the seven principles (Chickering and Gamson, 1987). Henninger and McNeil Hurlbert (2006) describe how they used the seven principles as a guide to integrate information literacy and cultural diversity components into a management course. In this case, we apply the recommendations in the Chickering and Ehrmann (1996) essay as a way to assess to what degree technology has served to enhance student learning through the application of the seven principles in the Senior Experience Program. As media options become more available and easier for faculty to develop, they are being increasingly used to enhance student learning.

AN ENVIRONMENT CONDUCIVE FOR TECHNOLOGY AND COMMUNITY

California State University–San Marcos is a Carnegie Master's College and University with the additional voluntary designation for Curricular Engagement and Outreach and Partnerships. Founded in 1989, it is a rapidly growing campus of 9,000 students. The College of Business Administration represents approximately 14 percent of the student body with a faculty of 33. The structure of courses and services offered reflect a largely commuter campus.

Since its inception in 1989, technology has played a central role in the educational mission of the campus. Instructional technology support is centrally administered by the university's Information and Instructional Technology Services Department. This organizational structure as well as a supportive campus culture facilitates close working relationships between knowledgeable development staff and faculty to incorporate technologies into courses. The team assembled to implement the multimedia elements of the course consisted of the College of Business Administration Associate Dean, the Senior Experience Program Director, college faculty, the Career Center Director, the business librarian, instructional technology course designers, and audiovisual technicians.

AACSB, INFORMATION LITERACY, AND THE COLLEGE

The Association to Advance Collegiate Schools of Business (AACSB) requires reflective thinking skills and the use of information technology among its student learning outcomes. Furthermore, the AACSB standards recommend other knowledge and abilities as identified by the individual school. The main requirement for accreditation is that the areas covered in the curriculum are consistent with the school's mission. Given that the College of Business Administration's mission specifically mentions "rigorous and relevant" programs, the faculty believe that information literacy as a learning outcome is very consistent with the AACSB standards. Information competency, lifelong learning, and computer competencies are California State University system-wide requirements, and students are introduced to them in required lower division general education courses. Information competence as a component of critical thinking is formally adopted among the student learning outcomes by the College of Business Administration faculty. College faculty used the Information Literacy Competency Standards for Higher Education (Association of College and Research Libraries, 2000) as a guideline to map core course objectives to the information literacy standards (Fiegen, Cherry, and Watson, 2002). When taken together, these areas point to the need for information literacy as a learning outcome. Thus, to be consistent with AACSB expectations as well as specified learning objectives for the program, it is clear that information literacy is an important learning outcome.

DISCUSSION OF CASE STUDY AND FACULTY-LIBRARIAN COLLABORATION

What Was: Projects and Paper Trail

The Senior Experience Program was designed to take what the students had learned during their undergraduate business education and apply that learning to real-world situations. Student teams are matched with company sponsors that could be public corporations, small businesses, social agencies, foundations, or educational institutions. The sponsors submit real projects describing the business problem, their objectives, and the skills and resources needed to successfully complete the project. The program was initially a three-unit preparatory course, Senior Experience Business 492 (BUS492), meeting for one semester with a five-unit project course, BUS493, following in the next semester. BUS492 was conducted in a seminar format of two large sections of approximately 100 students each and included a review of critical thinking, problem identification, problem solving, and decision-making methods. In a consulting and project-management context, students also learned project design, development, and implementation. Course assessments amounted to several quizzes, a literature review assignment, and a short written assignment. The major deliverables were a draft project proposal, final project proposal, and a final proposal presentation. Not until the second semester in BUS493 did students carry out the proposal, present their final results in a written report, and give an oral presentation to complete the one year Senior Experience Program. The project selection and matching projects to student teams was a paper-based process taking the first three weeks of the BUS492 semester, and as student enrollment grew it become an increasingly complex paper chase.

Once the teams had all been assigned to their projects, their first assignment was a literature review with proposed methodology. The assignment required students to describe their research problem, search and identify secondary research materials, and select and discuss the literature's relevance to project solving methodology and a potential solution (Meulemans and Fiegen, 2006). In week three of the semester, just after students had received their projects, the business librarian conducted a three hour workshop. The first hour was lecture, group discussion, and demonstration followed by hands-on searching in computer labs for the remaining two hours. The format for the session followed traditional methods for library instruction. We provided students with a reminder of the assignment and discussed how secondary research is used in the context of business decision making. This introduction was followed by advanced searching techniques for business electronic sources and references to recommended print and electronic material. Students worked in their groups to develop initial questions and began researching their particular business project. The librarian was available for group consultations and guidance in the use of business Web sites and library databases. Students were given two weeks to turn in the assignment to the librarian for grading and feedback. Student assignments were returned the sixth week of the semester, after which they completed additional research and wrote final proposals to conclude the first semester of the Senior Experience.

Factors Leading to Changes in the Curriculum

Feedback from students, employers, and faculty indicated that the two-semester project timeline was too long. The employers wanted a shorter time period from project submission to project completion, and students wanted preparatory course material delivered more succinctly. The main impetus for change, however, was faculty input based on a major program review. It was determined that too many units were devoted to capstone courses (e.g., a four-unit strategy class along with the eight unit Senior Experience). Faculty believed that additional elective units in the major would provide a better learning experience for the students.

The first, and potentially most important, of these first-phase changes involved the recognition that under the previous format the project scope tended to be modified significantly between the time the projects were originally submitted and when the students actually began work with the sponsoring organization. Typically, this lag time was on the order of eight months. Additionally, the students were responsible for negotiating the scope of the work once they began the projects, a process that could easily take two to three weeks of the semester. Thus in the new format additional effort was put into developing a proper scope for projects prior to teams being matched to the projects. This is accomplished by the Senior Experience director visiting each of the organizations submitting project requests and working with the company sponsor on expectations for the projects so that they offer sufficient learning opportunities for students.

In the redesigned curriculum, therefore, only one unit would be devoted to project preparation for the BUS492 course. The first step was to review what was covered in the three-unit version of BUS492 and decide what was absolutely necessary to keep and what could be removed from the original course without jeopardizing student preparation for their projects. It became clear very quickly that there would not be enough time in 12 class hours to cover the essential topics in a face-to-face manner, thus the idea of using technology became a viable solution. The guiding principle was that if the material to be covered was straightforward, it could be moved into an online format and class time would be freed for those elements where discussion was needed to clarify content. For example, team formation and the project selection are both online pieces, but with different amounts of in-class time devoted to each. The assumption was that team formation could happen primarily online using a discussion board in the WebCT course management software before students even came to class, and thus no class time is devoted to it. However, class time is devoted to explaining to students how to make the best case for their project preference and how the database works in project selection. Where explanation, questions, and clarification are needed and can be conveyed adequately in a large group setting, class time would continue to be devoted to it.

In order to focus only on the essentials in the preparatory BUS492 course, the full literature review was eliminated. In retrospect, that assignment required students to research and report on their projects too early and in too much depth. The new goal would be more on task and require students to quickly become familiar with their respective companies and industry prior to their first company or agency contacts. Students were already familiar with industry analysis research from prior course work and only a review of research strategies should be needed for that assignment. Through this rethinking of the assignment, review material would be a good candidate for electronic delivery.

All students receive ample opportunities to demonstrate aptitude with various personal computing technologies, and such knowledge is also assumed by the senior year with computer and media help widely available. Students must pass a computer competency course their freshman year. Each course in the college includes some type of computing and is included in the instruction for the course, supplemented by an active student help desk with computer labs and classrooms openly available throughout the university. The majority of courses taught in the college use the course management software WebCT. Business students become adept at using the Microsoft office complement, statistical software, and presentation software such as PowerPoint as well as video editing and streaming media. These are important expectations that allow for multimedia distribution of course content to a large class yet retain high expectations for student collaboration, discussion, and deliverables using a range of online tools.

The Technology Fix: Preparing for Projects

Under the new format, most projects are submitted into the project database three months prior to students working directly with the sponsoring organization. Now the director of the program contacts each company or agency prior to the semester to clarify the project description and scope. This has resulted in less workload variability among projects and moved project scoping away from a student responsibility and prior to the semester. Students now focus on the process of choosing and applying appropriate methodologies and researching their projects. The increased specificity of the assignment allows students to focus on those elements for which they will be assessed. The revised project scope allows students to demonstrate that they can work effectively in teams, apply appropriate methods to researching and solving business problems, and do so within the essentially ten weeks allotted to the project.

Today, BUS492 is offered as a hybrid model with many technologically enhanced components. Once a student registers for the course they gain access to WebCT. Students can view information about company sponsors, the scope of the actual projects, required business skills, and faculty supervisor background and office hours for all of the available projects from a database accessible through

WebCT. Figure 6.2 illustrates excerpts for the Vista Community Clinic project description. Students are asked to enter information about their education and work experience into the database, and they can view similar information about other students in the course to aid in team formation. Students are encouraged to use a discussion topic within WebCT to find other potential team members, ask any questions about the course, and to answer one another's questions (moderated by the course instructors). Students are required to submit a reflective statement in a discussion topic within WebCT each week of the preparation course (BUS492) as a process journal (for formative assessment purposes). The reflective discussion topics are intended to coincide with material covered for that week, such as:

1. Starting the Senior Experience project
2. Working on the company and industry report
3. Reflecting on future work for the individual, team, and organization
4. Exploring how it fits into the larger community.

Previously, several guest faculty speakers introduced the preparatory modules in class. These modules are available as multimedia video and linked through

---

Figure 6.2. CoBA Project Information (Senior Experience)

Vista Community Clinic, Health Promotion Center

Sponsor Description

Vista Community Clinic (VCC) was founded in 1972 as a nonprofit, community-based health care organization with a mission—to provide quality health care and health education to the community focusing on those facing economic, social, and cultural barriers. Since that time VCC has expanded into five state-of-the-art clinic sites and over 25 health promotion programs in the cities of Vista and Oceanside, California. VCC provides a comprehensive array of primary health care and prevention services for community residents across all life cycles and serves nearly 46,000 patients in over 185,000 clinic visits annually.

Number of Employees   50

Key Objectives

This project is looking at how to leverage existing services provided by VCC to a new "pay-for-service" demographic. The intent is to take profits from programs delivered to this new demographic to further enhance the current work done by VCC. This project would first focus on a feasibility study for three areas: (1) providing child passenger safety seat inspections and installations, (2) offering court-mandated classes to violators, and (3) providing smoking cessation services. The second phase of the project would be to develop, as much as is possible during the allotted time, a business plan for any of the areas determined as economically viable.

Business Skills Requested

Members should have experience and/or knowledge in conducting marketing research, implementing feasibility assessments, and creating business plans. Additional skills such as computer expertise, statistics, experience in public health and/or working with nonprofits, and knowledge of North San Diego County businesses and resources would also be helpful.

WebCT. They include business writing, survey research, project management, business etiquette, and library research, Students now view these modules as homework assignments to be completed at their own pace, and they have the material available as a resource throughout the semester.
Students deliver their project outputs in several ways:

1. A written report is prepared by the student teams, both in paper and electronic form. If the sponsoring organization agrees, the soft copy can be placed into an electronic portfolio for the student to access and for the student to grant access to potential employers.
2. Team presentations of findings are videotaped using Sonicfoundry's MediaSite software (to capture the presentation as well as any technology used in the presentation).
3. Teams participate in a trade show demonstrating the results of their projects. Virtually all teams have laptops on their tables to show their final presentations. Some displays include the company product or results of project results. Examples have ranged from a small version of a flight simulator to a 54" video display of an organization's project outcome being implemented.
4. Students are encouraged to use a discussion topic within WebCT to provide advice to students who will be taking the course in future semesters.

Four avenues of assessment are undertaken each semester for the Senior Experience Program, each with the intent of evaluating and improving program delivery and outcomes. The first type of assessment is student course evaluations administered by the university in a standardized format. These forms, administered during delivery of the previous course format, were one of the primary incentives for changing from a two-semester to one-semester format. In addition, students have commented that they value the professional manner in which the course is delivered, and they appreciate completing the course requirements during the compressed time frame. These course characteristics model how the business world operates and demonstrates how they should interact with their sponsoring organizations throughout the semester.

Student assessment and sponsoring organizations' assessments are administered by the director of the Senior Experience Program. These assessments are collected at pre-, mid-, and postintervals. Preassessment asks students and sponsors to self-report expectations of the upcoming semester. In addition, students are asked to report existing levels of relevant skills (see Appendix 6.1). Self-reports about progress in these areas are requested at the midpoint of the semester, with the additional question of, "Is the project proceeding on target for completion at the end of the semester?" If students or organizations do not think the project is on target for completion, they are asked to explain why. Typically students report that the project is on target, even when the organization has some reservations.

At this point the director contacts the organization, which typically responds that while the students have been working diligently and making progress they have not been consistent in communicating with the sponsoring organization. The students are then counseled regarding communication requirements for outside consultants working with business organizations.

Students and organizations are also contacted at the end of the semester for postassessment. They are asked the same questions as for the preassessment, with wording changes to reflect the completion of the semester. Students often report gains in their skill sets as measured by the instrument. Sponsoring organizations are also asked the same questions at the beginning of the semester, again with wording changes to reflect the completion of the semester, and they are also asked to give the students a letter grade for the completed project as well as rating the individual team members as to reliability, communication skills, professionalism, and overall contribution to the project. The sponsoring organizations are also given a post-postassessment six months after completion of the project. At this point, after they have had a chance to digest and use the results of the student efforts, they are asked to provide their overall rating of the Senior Experience Program and to determine the value they would place on the project. Over 90 percent of respondents rate the overall program as a four or five on a five-point scale, with five being "excellent" and three being "adequate." They also respond to the question, "If I were to have paid an outside consultant/ organization to deliver the same results as the Senior Experience team did, I would have been willing to pay the following amount:" with respondents providing a median value of "$3,001–5,000."

INFORMATION RESEARCH COMPETENCIES AND THE VIDEO MIX

Along with the other learning modules, the library research segment was redesigned into a video presentation. There was an assumption that senior business students should already know about information research from their previous classes. The presentation needed to reflect the narrower scope of the research assignment, but the learning objectives still needed to include broad business information research principles. The video included more than lecture, and was a mix of tutorial demonstration and some active learning elements. Students were assigned to view the video module, quizzed on its content, and expected to apply it to their research projects.

By the time students are business seniors, it is assumed that they have certain information research and computer competencies for the business major. First, students have a general knowledge of library research strategies through the lower division general education information literacy program. Second, the library instruction learning outcomes introduced during the junior year in the

BUS302 Business Environments course became essential assumptions when designing the library video module. For planning purposes it is assumed students have been introduced to some of the idiosyncrasies of locating business information and that they have experience from previous course work applying business analysis models to the information research process. They have researched company and industry information and applied it to Griffin's business environments and to Porter's five forces business analysis models. They know what a trade publication is. They know that local, state, and federal statistics accessible from government Web sites are important additions to business research. They have used the North American Industry Classification codes and the United States Census Bureau's Web site (www.census.gov) for business research. They have learned that some business information is value-added and comes with a cost for access as they struggle to find relevant information through free Web searches. Subscription-only library databases such as LexisNexis Academic's Company Dossier or Inside Prospects serve to illustrate how these business directories can be used to analyze small private companies.

In order to emphasize time on task, the project definition, scope, and company expectations of student responsibilities are completed between the program director and company contacts prior to the start of the BUS492 course. The research assignment for the BUS492 course is now a one week intensive exercise that challenges students to articulate their research project, gather basic data on the company (sales, employees, etc.) and research its industry, all prior to the first contact with the company or agency. The industry review directs students to apply the business analysis models of Griffin, Porter, or strengths, weaknesses, opportunities, and threats (SWOT). Students continue project-specific research in the BUS493 course.

Given the change in scope, the lesson plan for the multimedia library module was revised. Since the video presentation would be the only opportunity to reach the whole class, the learning objectives would need to address both the company and industry background assignment and also strategies for researching the actual project later in the semester. The library instruction agenda no longer needed a segment on problem definition or research question formation but rather would emphasize efficient and relevant searching and selecting. The video challenge was to design a succinct, highly pertinent session and keep viewer attention. The library research video objectives then would be to convey three business information research principles illustrated with examples and cases showing how to apply the principles to a typical Senior Experience topic.

Steps in a Research Process

The video narrative included a short story about increasing lunchtime sales to illustrate how one would apply the research steps outlined in the textbook *Designing and Managing a Research Project* (Polonsky and Waller, 2005).

- *State the problem:* Lunchtime sales are slowing.
- *State the business objective:* Increase lunchtime sales by delivering to local businesses.
- *Design methods to solve the problem:* Identify criteria for profitability.
- *Gather data:* Locate business customers by zip code in a business directory. Search trade news using the terms "lunch and workers," which yields an article from the Centers for Disease Control and Prevention about trends in foods for healthy meetings.

Collection, Production, and Distribution of Business Information

Students are required to use their critical thinking skills by asking "who cares and why" in order to understand how business information is collected, produced, organized, and distributed. They also need to address "who cares about vehicle registration." Since vehicles are registered with state agencies, this information can be searched through state government Web sites. Students also examine "who cares about vehicle model sales." Since car dealers and car manufacturers collect these data, it can be accessed through industry distribution sources such as trade publications and industry reports.

Structure of the Firm and Its Relation to the Distribution of Information

Finally, students are reminded that the structure of the firm will affect what and how information is distributed. Hawbacker and Littlejohn's (1988) company research finding aid is shown as a series of slides that illustrates what information is available for either public, subsidiary, or private companies, and highlights the limitations of accessing private company information. Through the process of applying the finding aid to their research projects, students learn how company ownership structure affects the distribution of information.

The library research video mix was comprised of a Microsoft PowerPoint slide show with Web links and an Adobe Captivate demonstration embedded into the slide show. The scripted slide show was loaded onto a teleprompter and instructional technology staff used Windows Media to film the presenter and Microsoft Producer to synchronize video, audio streams, and presentation material. The video mix was then loaded into WebCT. This process was repeated for all five modules. In this setting it became especially desirable to provide enough variety in the presentation to hold the viewer's attention by imitating, where possible, the interactivity that would have occurred in a computer lab setting. To do this, simple learning activities were embedded. In one, a slide leads the viewer through a step-by-step Factiva search and instructs them to pause the video and try it themselves. In another activity, an Adobe Captivate file holds a demonstration of how to search for industry statistics in the Economic Census using the North American Industry Classification schedule. A discussion topic in WebCT is devoted to library research and serves as a substitute for the question-and-answer dynamic that occurs in a live classroom. Students are encouraged to use it to post and respond to one another's comments, and the discussion is monitored by the business librarian.

ASSESSMENT OF TECHNOLOGICAL INNOVATION AND PEDAGOGICAL APPROACH TO STUDENT LEARNING

After two years of the redesigned program there is now opportunity for reflection. For the purposes of this chapter, the authors have chosen an assessment model that embodies more than the classroom experience because of its similarity to the goals for the Senior Experience Program. Chickering and Ehrmann (1996) recommended appropriate uses of technology in "Implementing the Seven Principles: Technology as Lever." Those recommendations can serve as a benchmark for reflection on whether the Senior Experience preparatory course and the redesigned library research components are meeting best practice guidelines for technology uses in the course.

Good Practice Encourages Contacts between Students and Faculty

Communication is enhanced between faculty and student and between student and student when multiple exchange channels are available. The hybrid course provides multiple channels for communication depending on the level and need for clarification. The instructors use in-class time for elements that require clarification and/or discussion about the project specifics, for areas where students needed immediate feedback, for team formation and management, and for project management and research methods. In contrast, the intent of the online components was to deliver lecture material electronically where the listener could have greater control over when, where, and how often they viewed the material. The online environment also created an expectation for students to "be in class" via the course page throughout the three-week period as the faculty post announcements and updates and expected students to complete discussion board and reflective assignments on a continual basis.

On its own, the library research streaming video is a one-way communication technology that decreases opportunities for interaction. When this Web-based technology is combined with the library components, however, which include discussion topics, open lab hours, and reference consultations, students have access to multiple communication options.

Good Practice Develops Reciprocity and Cooperation among Students

The Senior Experience Program teaches students how to operate effectively as a team in a challenging environment. In BUS492 there are multiple discussion forums within WebCT that require team postings. Students are given general themes to address each week in these process journals such as comments about getting started in Senior Experience, issues regarding completing the main written assignment of a company and industry analysis, or advice to the next Senior Experience class. There are three pedagogical reasons for the discussion boards:

1. Instructors are made aware of current issues facing the students and can provide timely content and/or guidance.
2. Students internalize progress toward assignment completion in multiple dimensions through reflective posts and discussion topics.
3. Students collaboratively create learning by answering one another's concerns.

Student collaboration was evident when they posted comments and tips about getting the most out of a library database for their industry research and helped one another with team formation and time management challenges associated with the course. When students are about to complete Senior Experience, they are invited to post advice to the incoming class in WebCT and to offer suggestions for improvement in the course. Student suggestions are reviewed by the course instructors and presented to the next group of students in class to highlight student-generated success strategies for project completion.

Good Practice Uses Active Learning Techniques

The entire Senior Experience Program is constructivist in that students are required to plan, research, and present their own projects using the resources that they collect and create. The faculty are there as facilitators of the process just as the course management software now serves as a facilitator for the projects.

Since the library video was 30 minutes long, it was important to incorporate variety in the presentation techniques and add short learning activities. Short stories illustrating how others have applied research strategies were sprinkled throughout the audio portion to add variety and encourage retention. The viewer was instructed to: "pause the presentation," "click to review," "compare the next set of slides," etc. In one segment they are instructed to click on links in a PowerPoint slide to explore the library business subject Web guides and to try out suggested subject terms in the library catalog. Factiva and LexisNexis Academic searching techniques were demonstrated through a slide that instructed them to pause the presentation and try the searches themselves. On one screen they are asked to "click the U.S. Census page to open a short Captivate demonstration of how to use the economic census." The viewer also has the opportunity to apply the activity to their own topic.

Students remarked that while the video was long and slow to download they liked the interactive elements. Revisions are scheduled on three-year cycle, and a number of improvements are planned. The library research segment will be shortened into multiple topics of separate video clips, which will aid in shorter download time rather than confine the listener to their computer for long periods, and it will allow learners to grasp key points more easily. Additional interactivity will be possible as technologies advance in video production and editing software, course management software, and end user access.

Good Practice Gives Prompt Feedback

The program redesign incorporates prompt feedback on e-mail and discussion board postings with instructors and the librarian responding within 24 hours during BUS492. The course faculty and librarian are available through WebCT, e-mail, and in person by appointment. This requires the librarian to clear his or her schedule for a one-week period where there is a heavy time demand from up to 45 teams researching the company and industry report. In addition, given the three-week time period for the class, all student assignments are graded and returned at the next class session.

Good Practice Emphasizes Time on Task

The redesign moved much of the course management out of the classroom and into a database to occur prior to commencement of the course. The development of the research question for each project was also moved from the student teams to the program director. The students can then spend their time addressing methodology and the research process. This is consistent with real world business situations in which higher level management form the question and deliverables then delegate to a team. Teams can then spend more time on providing quality recommendations and solutions. In addition, the redesigned library research components were deconstructed into segments that matched the specific information needed during the research process. The first assignment asks the students to do no more than identify the relevant NAIC (North American Industry Classification) industry code and its description. The second assignment requires students to do a thorough report on the company and industry prior to their first company contact. Students will not research the business problem until BUS493. The authors believe this clarifies the expectations and highlights the importance of background research prior to exploring potential project solutions.

Good Practice Communicates High Expectations

Students are given five weeks to complete the first company and industry report in their introductory course, while in this course they are given one week. They are expected to articulate their project and to have prepared a thorough industry and company analysis prior to the first company contact. Significant factors used to assess the students' work are the depth of research about the company and a solid understanding through evidence about the makeup of the industry in which the company is situated. We expected them to have mastered the material in all of the video presentations to complete their assignments. Students are instructed that they have a "contractual agreement" with the librarian to review any supporting material prior to requesting a reference consultation. This is known to all librarians and student assistants working the reference desk, and works remarkably well.

The library research video mix was designed with an expectation that students given a reminder would recall and apply prior knowledge to company and industry research. We also expected them to assimilate and apply the new material conveyed in the video presentation to their research projects later in the semester. For this reason, high expectations required that the video presentation would facilitate the self-confidence the students would need in order to apply library research methods to successfully complete their assignments. However, a video presentation is inherently a passive activity, and as such could not on its own ensure the retention and mastery of new concepts expected for professional quality deliverables. For this reason variety was added to the video module. Besides listening to the talking head librarian and viewing PowerPoint presentations, students saw captioned text of the lecture, could interact with the slide show, and had access to downloadable print handouts. This combination of media elements is essential to how the course content is delivered and understood. Students favorably commented on the ability to review the presentation later.

The system of team meetings with faculty advisors and company contacts ensures regular feedback on the kind and quality of information being gathered. Faculty referrals to the librarian are common during intermediate due dates of the projects. Students are expected to use high quality, up-to-date technology resources to present their materials. All of these expectations are communicated to students both in class and in WebCT. The instructors give students information on past groups (i.e., that they have been successful) to enhance their confidence in being able to meet these high expectations.

Good Practice Respects Diverse Talents and Ways of Learning

Multiple learning styles need to be considered so that students can assimilate the course material in the best way for them. The course design is a dynamic mix of face-to-face, audio, video, readings, print material, small group meetings, and lecture. The WebCT audio portions are text captioned, and supporting material is available for printing. Assignments may be written or oral, and the presentation requirement may use technology. Students are quick to point out what works best for them, and those suggestions are considered in revisions.

CONCLUSION

The business instruction design techniques used in this case are not new; most have been used regularly in one form or another in faculty-librarian collaborations. The innovation was in changing established practice (condensing one semester's worth of information) and using technology while still meeting all course learning objectives. After teaching the course for four semesters, the use of multimedia appears to be a successful method of delivery.

Communication options have increased owing to the redesign of the course but also because of functionalities within WebCT. There is built-in journal reflection, increased timeliness of feedback to students, and there are additional channels for communicating with other students, faculty, and the librarian. Much of what was previously presented face-to-face in a large lecture hall is now online in multimedia modules: library research, survey design, business writing, business etiquette, and project management. Students regularly report that they review the material throughout the course sequence for reference to specific problems in completing their assignments. Students have also commented frequently that they would like access to this material at the beginning of their course work within the College of Business Administration, and a feasible implementation strategy is under investigation.

The use of technology has streamlined the project management phase and team selection, so this part of the course has moved to an online environment, freeing up course time. Project descriptions and expectations are already stated and agreed on prior to student participation, so students are able to focus on the learning outcomes of selection and evaluation, not on project formation or negotiation with the company. The librarian has access to the WebCT course and the project database, knows the company names, the problem statement, and the skills and abilities needed. This provides better information for planning adequate resources and for anticipating and preparing for potential questions.

ENHANCEMENTS TO THE CURRENT MODEL

After teaching the course for two complete sequences the instructors and the librarian discussed how to improve course delivery and attainment of learning objectives. These improvements included:

1. Taping the project presentations and using these materials for assessment purposes, with business executives and faculty providing feedback to the students about their performance. This will also be used for overall program assessment.
2. Refilming the five video modules based on feedback, good practice, and technology enhancements.
3. Developing new video modules for decision processes and Internet-based surveys.
4. Instituting more specific assessment, for example, an end-of-semester survey incorporating questions regarding information literacy components; focusing student narratives during the semester with specific topics; and alumni surveys asking how they have used Senior Experience in their careers.
5. Holding a best practices meeting for faculty supervisors.
6. Posting expectations for sponsors and students online on a publicly accessible Web site.
7. Requiring students to come to the second class with the North American Industry Classifications identified so they are better able to do their company and industry analysis assignment.

In summary, indications are that the course redesign has been successful based on feedback from all constituents. Student course evaluations have described the new format as timely, informative, and relevant to their careers. The faculty appreciate receiving more information about available projects and being matched to their project prior to students beginning the course. Participating organizations are delighted by the timely completion of projects and consistently rate their satisfaction with the Senior Experience Program, as demonstrated by 90 percent of them giving a rating of four or five (satisfied or very satisfied) on a five-point scale. Overall the curricular redesign of the Senior Experience Program has enhanced and solidified its place as a "Program of Distinction" for both the college and the university.

REFERENCES

Association of College and Research Librarians. 2000. "Information Literacy Competency Standards for Higher Education." Available: www.ala.org/ala/acrl/acrlstandards/standards.pdf.

California State University–San Marcos Library. "Library Course Guide: BUS 302 Foundations of Business Environments." Available: http://library.csusm.edu/course_guides/business/BUS_302.asp. Accessed October 15, 2007.

Chickering, Arthur W., and Stephen C. Ehrmann. 1996. "Implementing the Seven Principles: Technology as Lever." *AAHE Bulletin*, 49, no. 2: 3–6. Available: www.tltgroup.programs/seven.html.

Chickering, Arthur W., and Zelda F Gamson. 1987. "Seven Principles for Good Practice in Undergraduate Education." *AAHE Bulletin* 39, no. 7: 3–7.

Fiegen, Ann, Bennett Cherry, and Kathleen Watson. 2002. "Reflections on Collaboration: Learning Outcomes and Information Literacy Assessment in the Business Curriculum." *Reference Service Review* 30, no. 4: 307–318.

Flanagan, Deborah L. 1999. "Learning Anytime, Anywhere: Designing Web Based Business Tutorials." *Journal of Business and Finance Librarianship* 4, no. 4: 19–34.

Griffin, Ricky W. 2002. *Management,* 7th ed. Boston: Houghton Mifflin.

Hawbaker, A. Craig, and Alice C. Littlejohn. 1988. "Improving Library Instruction in Marketing Research: A Model." *Journal of Marketing Education* 1: 52–62.

Henninger, Edward A., and Janet McNeil Hurlbert. 2006. "Using the Seven Principles for Good Practice in Undergraduate Education: A Framework for Teaching Cultural Diversity in a Management Course." *Journal of Business & Finance Librarianship* 12, no. 2: 3–15.

Meulemans, Yvonne and Ann M. Fiegen. 2006. "Using Business Student Consultants to Benchmark and Develop a Library Marketing Plan." *Journal of Business and Finance Librarianship* 11, no. 3: 19–31.

Polonsky, Michael Jay, and David S. Waller. 2005. *Designing and Managing a Research Project: A Business Student's Guide.* Thousand Oaks, CA: Sage.

Porter, Michael. 1985. *Competitive Advantage: Creating and Sustaining Superior Performance.* New York: Free Press.

Reichel, Mary, and Mary Ann Ramey (Eds.). 1987. *Conceptual Frameworks for Bibliographic Instruction: Theory Into Practice.* Littleton, CO: Librarians Unlimited.

Roy, Matthew H., and Eliot Elfner. 2002. "Analyzing Student Satisfaction with Instructional Technology Techniques." *Industrial and Commercial Training* 34, no. 7: 272–277.

Shank, John D., and Steven Bell. 2006. "A_FLIP To Courseware: A Strategic Alliance For Improving Student Learning Outcomes." *Innovate* 2, no. 4. Available: www.innovateonline.info/index.php?vidw=article&id-46.

Zhou, Ping. 2004. "Baruch College Guide to Financial Statements." Available: www.baruch.cuny.edu/tutorials/statements/. Accessed April 8, 2007.

Appendix 6.1. Student Precourse Survey
Cal State San Marcos College of Business Administration Student Precourse Survey Fall 2007

I hope you have a beneficial learning experience in the Senior Experience Program this semester. Thank you for filling out this questionnaire—your answers will be very useful in helping us to improve the Senior Experience Program to better benefit students and the sponsoring organizations.

1. How many committed members total are on your team at present?

	1
	2
	3
	4
	5

2. Please briefly list any expectations or concerns you have about the Senior Experience Program at this point:

3. How often do you expect to meet with your **STUDENT TEAM** during the upcoming semester?

	Less than once a week
	Once a week
	Twice a week
	Three times a week or more

4. How often do you expect your team will meet with the **SPONSOR CONTACT** during the upcoming semester?

	Once or twice in the whole semester
	Once a month (about three times)
	Twice a month (about six times)
	Once a week (about ten times) or more

5. Approximately how much time do you expect to spend on the Senior Experience Project each week?

	up to 4.9 hours per week
	5 to 9.9 hours per week
	10 to 14.9 hours per week
	15 to 19.9 hours per week
	20 hours or more per week

(Continued)

Appendix 6.1. Student Precourse Survey *(Continued)*

6. Please describe what you see as your role for this project—what will you need to do personally to help see this project to completion?

7. Please describe the outcomes you expect from the Senior Experience **PROJECT** itself (specific objectives and/or outcomes from completing the project):

8. Please describe any outcomes you expect from working with your Senior Experience **STUDENT TEAM** (other than the PROJECT outcomes):

9. Please describe any outcomes you expect from working with your Senior Experience **FACULTY SUPERVISOR** (other than the PROJECT outcomes):

10. We would like to find out how you rate yourself on certain skills and abilities. Please rate yourself honestly; your answers will remain anonymous and data will be reported only in aggregate form.

	1 = Weak/Ineffective			5 = Strong/Effective	
	1	2	3	4	5
Leadership skills					
Public speaking/presentation					
Managing conflict with peers					
Communication with others					
Ability to understand others different from me					
Coping with change					
Managing complex projects					
Personal confidence					
Working in a team					
Understanding the "world of business"					
Problem-solving skills					
Creativity					
Library research					
Professionalism					
Business writing					

Part III

Online Assessment

SECTION INTRODUCTION

Assessment is a vital aspect of higher education that is influenced by various forms and uses of technology. Faculty and librarians have access to a range of instruments that provide both quantitative and qualitative information about student progress, experience, and success in information literacy courses and programs. When used effectively to measure student learning outcomes, technology provides essential feedback to instructors to improve the learning environment, especially through multiple iterations of any given class or curriculum. The results of technology-enhanced assessments are valuable as a reflective pedagogical practice as well as a resource for mandated institutional evaluations. Both formative and summative assessment can be carried out as part of technology-enhanced initiatives.

Technology plays a dual role in the assessment process. First, it is an aspect of a course that may itself be assessed to determine if it had a positive impact on student learning. Second, it provides a means for assessing any part of a course that may or may not necessarily involve technology.

Instructors may choose from numerous tools that are used to determine, either formally or informally, whether instruction has been effective in meeting its goals. For example, course management systems (CMS) provide online testing measures and surveys for feedback on both student learning and student opinion about their learning. Online tests are subject specific and use multiple choice questions, matching, and open-ended essay formats. A survey instrument may be similar in design to the tests while focusing on students' response to the course or to measure students' perception of their own learning. Technology continues to be infused in the classroom, which offers another potential assessment instrument. For example, clicker devices offer immediate student feedback to enhance interactivity in the classroom while also providing data that could be analyzed throughout a course, or from one semester to another. Writing is another important measure of student learning and is both facilitated and evaluated through many Web-based technologies such as electronic portfolios, blogs, wikis, Web pages, and bulletin boards.

In this last section of the book, two chapters recount very different approaches to gauging student learning. In "Assessement in Small Bytes: Creating an Online Instrument to Measure Information Literacy Skills," Nora Hillyer, Marvel Maring, and Dorianne Richards of the University of Nebraska–Omaha outline an information literacy assessment initiative that grew out of a long-standing institutional recognition of the need for determining the effectiveness of information literacy instruction. Their information literacy curriculum is taught in many sections of their first-year English course, and originally student evaluations were used to determine whether the instruction was effective. However, surveys do not assess what students learn, only what they feel they have learned. It was determined that a new method of assessment was called for, one that measured students' knowledge both prior and subsequent to the information literacy instruction. Their chapter describes a three-pronged approach: a pretest, a posttest, and a survey that is administered following the posttest.

The authors describe a two-step process for developing this initiative: the first involved close collaboration with faculty consultants from several departments to help define the form the assessment would take, developing and testing the questions, writing a survey to be administered to students and the English faculty, and selecting an online product for administering the pre- and posttest. The second phase involves integrating the assessment into all first-year English composition classes and adapting the instruments for upper-level instruction sections. The chapter provides an overview of both the advantages and disadvantages of using Blackboard to implement the assessment.

While the University of Nebraska–Omaha team used their CMS to administer their assessment, a librarian and professor of English as a second language (ESL) at Suffolk County Community College (NY) describe a very different form of technology for both formative and summative assessment in their chapter, "A Constructivist Approach to Instructional Technology and Assessment in ESL Course Design." Penny Bealle and Kathleen Cash-McConnell infused information literacy and technology instruction into a three-credit advanced speaking and listening course. The authors' goals for the students are that they be able to "demonstrate competence with several intertwined components of academic discourse," including critical thinking strategies, information literacy competency standards, and "the targeted language germane to many academic disciplines."

Assessment is accomplished through rubrics, a pre- and posttest, anecdotal information collected during a student discussion, a written evaluation of an Internet source, and three technology-enhanced assignments that students present to the rest of the class. The taping of the presentations motivates students and ensures that they take their assignments seriously. Students view the recordings of their presentations and can use a rubric to assess both individual and team performances. The professor also uses a rubric when critiquing the recording, and in addition is able to add "captions to particular frame images on the CD-ROM, highlighting a student's mastery or errors in usage of the strings of targeted discourse." This chapter clearly explains the scaffolding inherent in the constructivist approach provided by both the professor and librarian as students learn, the extent to which technology is incorporated into the course and the recorded presentations, and the challenges involved in transferring their approach into other courses on campus.

Based on these chapters, we recommend the following ideas for using technology in the design of assessment strategies:

- Assess for student learning outcomes in a way that extends beyond student perception of their own learning.
- Select the right tool for the right job and make sure that the technology matches your goals for assessment.
- Start planning an assessment strategy early in the process of course design and continue to revisit this approach throughout multiple iterations of the curriculum.
- Consider a variety of assessment instruments and think about the ways technology may be used to facilitate or enhance this process.
- Review all aspects of technology integration in the course as potential measures of student learning.
- Maximize the benefits of collaboration between faculty and librarians or among different disciplines as a way to expand different approaches to assessment.
- Separate the assessment of technology in the course from the use of technology as a means to evaluate other aspects of instruction.

Both of the chapters in this section describe valuable strategies that may be transferable to other disciplines and other institutions. While these approaches are included in this section, each chapter is rich in information collaboration ideas that extend beyond the spotlight on assessment.

Chapter 7

Assessment in Small Bytes
Creating an Online Instrument to Measure Information Literacy Skills

Nora Hillyer, Marvel Maring,
and Dorianne Richards

In 2000, Patricia Senn Breivik described assessment as one of the "hottest" topics in American education, and almost a decade later, assessment literature has exploded (2000: 5). Search ERIC (Education Resources Information Center) today for "assessment" and you will retrieve a staggering 92,329 hits; add "information literacy" to that search and you will retrieve 1,709 articles. It is impossible to attend a library conference without some mention of assessment of information literacy skills. Such assessment demands an awareness of the multi-layered influence of the entire academic environment in which we function. Like the embedded attributes of text and hypertext, the voices of many constituencies make up the various layers, including the students, librarians, department faculty, university administrators, and even state legislatures. Effective assessment of information literacy demands cognizance of the various interests that have a stake in its outcome.

In today's educational environment, effective assessment also demands a new approach. Many of the established methods for measuring the library's value are no longer adequate. Collection analysis, door counts, reference desk statistics, and student satisfaction fail to fully demonstrate what students have learned. Ilene F. Rockman and Gordon W. Smith (2005) describe what they call "a new learner-centered approach," which has "shifted the focus from passive learning to what students can actually do" (587). And Nancy O'Hanlon (2007), in discussing how Ohio State University considered the role of instruction, asked:

How does the focus on learning outcomes affect the mission of the library? Like other communities at the University, the library must move from a content view (books, subject knowledge) to a competency view (what students will be able to do). Within the new environment, we need to measure the ways in which the library is contributing to the learning that the University values. (169)

Information literacy instruction and evaluation of its effectiveness have been in place on the University of Nebraska–Omaha (UNO) campus for years. Previous to 2002, library instruction was present but inconsistent; individual English instructors took responsibility for organizing library visits and presenting library information as it intersected with students' research needs. From its inception in 2002, the new information literacy curriculum taught in the first-year English course (ENGL1160/1164) has succeeded because of a strong collaborative vision between the library and the English Department faculty. The course, taught by a reference librarian, usually consists of two one-hour sessions in computer-equipped classrooms in the library. Although not a formal requirement, departmental participation in the sessions is high, and the numbers of classes taught has grown 20 percent in the past year alone.

To evaluate the effectiveness of this information literacy course, student evaluations of library instruction have been gathered after the second session. However, these responses reflect the students' *perceptions* of library instruction; they fail to capture what the students have actually learned. Anecdotally, everyone agrees that information literacy instruction is important to students' success, but until this year, no formal outcome assessment had been implemented.

The primary aim of the information literacy assessment project at UNO was to determine the information literacy skill level of first-year students prior to library instruction and their skill level after library instruction. We entered the multilayered assessment arena with three seemingly small questions: How effective is our library's information literacy instruction in the first-year composition course? What do students know about the library before the library instruction sessions? What do they know after the library instruction sessions?

We chose this population of students because it is a reliably large pool (nearly 300 students in the spring semester, and double that number in the fall semester) and because the curriculum has been firmly established with proven faculty support. We could rely on curriculum materials already developed and simply add the assessment layer over it. Our goal was not to reinvent library instruction at UNO but to add the online assessment piece to an already sound foundation. With this goal in mind, we developed an assessment instrument delivered via Blackboard, our online course management software, which would capture student performance-based outcomes to improve library instruction and, in turn, benefit students.

FOUNDATIONAL LAYER: LITERATURE REVIEW

Assessment of information literacy by its very nature demands that we understand the educational environment, including the collaboration between the library, campus, department, and students, and the practical aspects of test instrument design and technological requirements of online assessment.

Many libraries have already done what we set out to do, and libraries around the country are keenly aware of the complex and multilayered environment this assessment exists within. O'Hanlon (2007) states the importance of linking "outcomes assessment in academic libraries to the institutional mission of the parent organization" (171). Edward K. Owusu-Ansah (2004) suggests that the library be the focal point for information literacy instruction because information literacy extends beyond any discipline-specific boundary. He asserts that librarians should be the key personnel "to define and achieve campus-wide information literacy" (3).

Many institutions have examined the pressures imposed from higher education administrators regarding information literacy and assessment and the ways in which they managed the external pressures within their library environment (Blixrud, 2003). Dorothy Anne Warner discusses the need for programmatic assessment and ways in which librarians and faculty can identify learning problems to improve teaching (Warner, 2003). Rockman (2002) considers the tradition of librarian and faculty collaborations, and Donald Barclay (1993) underscores other challenges such as the lack of institutional support, the perceived difficulty of the evaluation process, and the time constraints.

Other authors present concerns that exist regarding the perceptions of classroom faculty concerning library instruction and the ACRL Information Literacy Competency Standards for Higher Education. Some classroom faculty do not make time to provide library instruction, or they assume their students have a solid understanding of how to use the library from previous experience (Owusu-Ansah, 2004; Gullikson, 2006; Franklin and Toifel, 1994). Many authors admit the challenge of assessment and recognize that "libraries cannot do it alone" (Iannuzzi, 1999: 304). Rockman addresses the collaborative relationships with "discipline-based classroom faculty" and she includes another stakeholder—the future employer. Rockman (2002) quotes Anthony Comper, President of the Bank of Montreal, when he spoke to the 1999 University of Toronto graduating class: "Whatever else you bring to the 21st century workplace, however great your technical skill and however attractive your attitude and however deep your commitment to excellence, the bottom line is that to be successful, you need to acquire a high level of information literacy" (188). Other authors mentioned their concerns regarding students and the lack of adequate preparation they receive in their high school media programs (Kunkel, Weaver, and Cook, 1996).

Students' actual skill level and perceived skill level is also frequently addressed in the literature (Ferguson, Neely, and Sullivan, 2005; Freeman, 2004; Fowler, Berens, and Duby, 1990; Krentz and Gerlach, 1989).

The literature provides excellent examples of online information literacy test instruments. Project SAILS is one that is widely accepted and discussed by Julia C. Blixrud (2003). Rockman and Smith (2005) examine several other collaborative test instruments, including the Information and Communication Technology Literacy Assessment, Bay Area Community Colleges Information Competency Assessment Project, and International Computer Driver's License (ICDL).

In 1989, Roger F. Krentz and Donald E. Gerlach mention the frustration of having "no reliable instrument which educators can use to assess the library media proficiency of graduating high school seniors" (7). More currently, Jessame E. Ferguson, Teresa Y. Neely, and Kathryn Sullivan (2005) describe a 51-item survey they developed with input from campus leaders and faculty across disciplines (61). Others have measured student performance against existing instruments, primarily testing lower-level students and incoming freshmen (Fowler, Berens, and Duby, 1990; Krentz and Gerlach, 1989). Barclay (1993) asserts the need to create test questions that would most closely mirror the act of library research, and he prefers "free-response" questions to multiple choice because "the act of writing an answer to a free-response question . . . has more in common with the unstructured act of library research and so may be a better test of a student's ability to use a library" (197).

Finally, the use of Blackboard is discussed as a portal for links to library resources and beneficial in reaching students where they are (Karplus, 2006). However, few articles discuss the use of Blackboard to deliver an assessment instrument for library-initiated projects. This is one reason we feel that our project can benefit other librarians who are preparing to launch an assessment project. The literature regarding assessment of information literacy is vast and rarely limited to one aspect of assessment or of information literacy, but it also reinforces the complexity of the various constituencies or stakeholders in the higher education environment.

INSTITUTIONAL LAYER: UNIVERSITY OPPORTUNITIES AND EXPECTATIONS

Though information literacy assessment projects can be done without full university support, they are most successful when, as Owusu-Ansah (2004) says, they are viewed as "a campus-wide necessity" (4). The University of Nebraska–Omaha fully recognizes the value of assessment and supports assessment endeavors. UNO recently initiated myMapp, an electronic portfolio designed to measure student, faculty/staff, programmatic, and university performance. Ultimately, the sum of the data will aid accreditation teams as they review the institution's standing. With the inception of myMapp, the university urged campus-wide assessment projects. To enable UNO programs and departments to fulfill assessment expectations, the Vice-Chancellor's Office provided competitive grant funding to develop assessment projects at UNO. Since librarians Hillyer and Maring had recently completed an online ACRL Information Literacy Assessment course that provided understanding of how to measure student performance, the grant offered the means to use their knowledge of assessment to build a meaningful instrument. With this institutional support, Hillyer and Maring were able to obtain funding to implement a straightforward assessment of first-year English composition students' information literacy skills.

The urgency of myMapp was one factor for considering an information literacy assessment project at this time. The myMapp institutional digital portfolio has allowed us to see assessment as an opportunity to show the campus how the library contributes to the educational mission of the institution. As Rockman (2002) states, "it is important to collect appropriate evidence to show the library's impact on campus by including the development of information literacy skills in course learning objectives in order to guide improvements, make informed decisions about instructional or curricular adjustments, and document change over a period of time" (192).

Budgetary concerns provided another reason to demonstrate the impact of library instruction. University administrators have control of budgets, and to make the case for support of information literacy and assessment efforts, the role of the library as central to the institution's mission must be clearly stated. To assure university funding for information literacy instruction, "librarians must be prepared to substantiate the claim that these skills indeed make a difference institutionally" (Blixrud, 2003: 18).

The assessment project was further driven by the library's desire to link information literacy instruction to university values stated in UNO's Strategic Plan, which places academic excellence and student focus as key objectives. Information literacy instruction supports these objectives in the short term by helping students with the assignment at hand. Instruction sessions provide students with transferable skills for searching databases and indexes, broadening their ability to find quality information. Additionally, using a formative rather than summative assessment tool has an impact on student learning. Prequestionnaire results motivate student participation in instruction sessions, and because students are given real-time feedback, they can compare results of their pre- and posttests to gain knowledge of their progress. In addition, instructional sessions promote lifelong learning skills. Senn Breivik (2000) asserts that "within today's information society, the most important learning outcome for all students is their being able to function as independent lifelong learners. The essential enabler to reaching that goal is information literacy" (1).

DISCIPLINARY LAYERS: BLENDING VOICES

Campus Voices

Institutional support and department support are both critical to a program's success. Without a shared vision, a sense of partnership in the development of the assessment, and the commitment to promote the assessment to colleagues and students, our assessment would have floundered. Patricia Iannuzzi (1999) discusses the "four levels at which we can assess information literacy outcomes: within the library; in the classroom; on campus; and beyond the campus. There is an increased need for collaboration at each level and the logistics of assessment become more complex. The measure of student learning also becomes more meaningful at each level" (para. 6).

To consider campus-wide concerns, we gathered five faculty consultants from the departments of Education, English, and Psychology to provide guidance, feedback, and a final consultation of the assessment results. They assisted us in the development of the test instrument, in the decision making regarding online software vendors, and in navigating the murky waters of the Institutional Review Board (IRB). We, as librarians, could not have done this alone. They also provided a broader vision of assessment as they perceived it across campus. All of the faculty consultants shared a particular professional interest in information literacy and assessment and a disciplinary viewpoint that expanded our understanding of the topic.

Department Voices

Support from the English Department contributed in large measure to the information literacy assessment project's success. UNO English instructors are particularly invested in information literacy outcomes since Composition II, the second semester of the first-year composition sequence, focuses on argument and research. Several course objectives intersect with the information literacy agenda: students are expected to gain proficiency in navigating the college library, locating and evaluating print and online information, introducing and integrating sources, and citing sources appropriately using MLA or APA documentation format. Instructors are preparing students to write for the academic discourse community, and information literacy skills play an essential role in such preparation.

Collaboration between English faculty and librarians reaps continuing benefits. Rockman (2002), who wrote frequently about the role of information literacy and strong collaborative partnerships, underscores the benefits of a collaborative approach:

As information choices have become more complex and diverse, libraries have recognized the need to infuse information literacy activities throughout the curriculum, both horizontally and vertically. The general education reform movement on many campuses has provided academic libraries with opportunities and possibilities to weave information literacy into both lower- and upper-division courses, and redesign services, reshape librarian roles and responsibilities, and revisit with discipline-based faculty members about course descriptions and student assignments to include information literacy principles. (195)

Library and English faculties' collaborative efforts model a learning pattern that benefits themselves and their students.

English Department faculty were also instrumental in promoting the assessment. Librarian-led instruction in the first-year composition course is entirely optional, so the assessment's success depended largely on the enthusiasm and support of English faculty. They have primary authority and influence over their students; thus, their response to information literacy plays a key role in how effective library instruction is. Ferguson, Neely, and Sullivan (2005) included on their 51-item information literacy survey a section devoted to questions regarding the students' relationship to their faculty. Faculty and librarians know that we are in this endeavor together, and we all want to see students gain confidence and competence in the library.

Library Voices

Tackling the issue of assessment of information literacy skills of first-year English composition students has been a challenge for us just as it has been for many. How could we begin to measure students' information literacy skills? The problem for the librarians and the English instructors has been that we have no knowledge of students' information literacy skill level as they enter college, and we have no data to prove or disprove that library instruction has been successful. As librarians, we wanted to gather data to improve our own individual instruction and the library instruction program in general.

We knew as we began this project that we had a solid curriculum from which to launch our assessment project. When the information literacy project began in 2002, several librarians and English faculty created handouts and rubrics to assist students in their understanding of information sources, characteristics of information, access tools, and evaluation techniques as well as tools to assist students in defining a topic and logging their research progress. A more concerted attempt to introduce active learning and collaborative learning into the curriculum was added this year. If students have time to practice the skills through interactive learning exercises, the students' skills will more likely improve (Kunkel, Weaver, and Cook, 1996).

Our professional organization, the Association of College and Research Libraries (ACRL), also provided framework for developing assessment questions. Blixrud (2003) notes in her description of Project SAILS: Standardized Assessment of Information Literacy Skills that each of the assessment instrument's 150 items "addresses one of the model learning outcomes identified by the ACRL Information Literacy Competency Standards for Higher Education" (18). Time would not allow for such an extensive test instrument, but the concept of linking the ACRL standards to particular test questions was essential for us. We reviewed various tests in print and drafted questions of our own, and then the English Department reviewed our pool of questions before selecting the final 15 that time would allow. We were also cognizant of Bloom's taxonomy and tried to develop questions that would require higher order thinking skills. Barclay (1993) suggests that "free response is superior to multiple choice," and we provided as many open-ended questions or questions involving recall versus recognition as possible (197).

Within the library, we also reinforced among the three members of the library instruction team—two faculty and one staff—that we must remain as faithful to the curriculum as possible in order to provide a consistent library instruction experience. We all agreed to return to the previously developed handouts, and we discussed possible active and collaborative learning exercises that we might employ to introduce different concepts. We knew total consistency was not possible, but within the variables of each instructor's style we strove to emphasize the same key concepts. A benefit of an online assessment instrument is the ability to review prequestionnaire scores and make adjustments for the class's second session. To preserve the integrity of assessment results, we did not review student data between pre- and postquestionnaires during this phase of the study, but we recognize the instructional benefit of doing so in the future.

PLANNING, DEVELOPING, AND DELIVERING THE TEST INSTRUMENT

A Two-Phase Plan

After considering the various constituencies in this multilayered project, we returned to our original questions. What do students know prior to formal information literacy instruction? What have students learned after formal library instruction? Is library instruction helping students with their assignments? To attempt to answer these questions, we defined the parameters of our project and then focused on creating a solid test instrument.

We initially conceived our project consisting of two phases. The first phase involved working with faculty consultants to further refine our project's scope, to draft the questionnaire, and to navigate the IRB process. Phase I also encompassed developing the pool of questions that met ACRL standards, testing questions before going live, and developing survey questions to be administered to the students and the English faculty. Additionally, and of critical importance, we had to select a user-friendly online software product that would administer the assessment questionnaire. We investigated several products that were Blackboard compatible, which was a key criterion. The second phase of the project will be to integrate the assessment into all first-year English composition classes. Additionally, we want to adapt the assessments for our upper-level subject-specific library instruction classes.

A Three-Pronged Test Instrument

Our initial assessment instrument has three components: a prequestionnaire, a postquestionnaire, and a survey. The pre- and postquestionnaires are identical: they contain the same questions and, therefore, the same degree of difficulty. An example of the questionnaire is attached in Appendix 7.1. Each questionnaire contains 15 questions; each question is worth one point. Decisions regarding the test instrument were based on the ACRL IL standards and were linked to the core curriculum developed by the library and English Department. In designing the questions, we focused on determining which information literacy skills were of highest priority to the English Department and to the librarians and on effective methods to measure those information literacy skills. According to available literature, open-ended, fill-in-the-blank, and multiple-answer questions prove most useful in measuring performance-based learning, so we designed the test questions around this premise (Barclay, 1993; Carter, 2002).

In our initial instrument, students were allowed 15 minutes and three attempts for the pre- and postquestionnaire. The prequestionnaire was made available one week prior to the first library instruction and required completion before the instruction began. The postquestionnaire and survey were made available the day of the last library instruction session. The librarians requested the postquestionnaire and survey be completed within two weeks of the last library instruction.

The third part of the assessment instrument is the survey that we asked students to complete after taking the postquestionnaire. The student survey, shown in Appendix 7.2, contains 11 questions. Questions 1 through 8 are Likert-scale questions, asking students about their computer expertise, their perception of library instruction, and their opinion of the handouts used in the class. Questions 9 through 11 are fill-in-the-blank questions asking for suggestions for improvement and what was most useful about the library instruction. The survey was separate from the questionnaire and available to students after the last library instruction session.

The pre- and postquestionnaires were constructed to measure the key representative standards of the ACRL Information Literacy Competency Standards:

- Standard 1: The information-literate student determines the nature and extent of information needed.
- Standard 2: The information-literate student accesses needed information effectively and efficiently.
- Standard 3: The information-literate student evaluates information and its sources critically and incorporates selected information into his or her knowledge base and value system.
- Standard 5: The information-literate student understands the economic, legal, and social issues surrounding the use of information and accesses and uses information ethically and legally. (ACRL Task Force on Information Literacy Competency Standards, 2000)

Standard 1 is addressed in questions 5, 6, and 7. These questions establish whether students understand the different types of information found in different sources and how information is organized in databases and the catalog. Accessing information effectively and efficiently, Standard 2 is measured in questions 2 and 3. Question 2 asks about primary sources, and question 3 requires the student to match the source to the best tool. The focus in questions 8, 9, and 10 is on students' ability to evaluate sources and understand the types of information found in a book, Standard 1 and Standard 3. Standard 5 is addressed in question 1, where students are asked to define plagiarism.

MODIFICATIONS: TECHNOLOGY AND PEDAGOGY

Technology

Knowing today's technology-oriented students respond more readily to digitally delivered information, we never considered a hard-copy method for the Criss Library Assessment. We also recognized any online software product we used had to have two essential qualities: the capability of producing interactive, animated questions and built-in reporting from the questionnaire and survey data. Our first choice was Perception, a product of Questionmark. Perception's desirable features included the ability to build multiple choice, multiple answer, hotspot, fill-in-the-blank, drag and drop, and Macromedia Flash questions; compatibility with Blackboard; assessment data saved in a Perception database; and reporting that could be developed from the data in the Perception database. In November 2006, the library's instruction team received permission from Questionmark to test Perception software for a three-month trial. The software was downloaded, and the license files that allowed the permissions for the Perception software and Blackboard to communicate were installed. Three computer systems departments—UNO, Criss Library, and Questionmark—worked together from December 2006 through March 2007 to get the Perception software to work with Blackboard. The problems were finally resolved at the end of March 2007 with two solutions: a new license file was built with the correct attributes and the accounts in the Questionmark application were created with the same login/password as is used with Blackboard. We learned from this experience that even Blackboard-compatible software may require time to install; we also learned the importance of having a backup plan.

Since English classes were scheduled for information literacy instruction as early as mid-February, we urgently needed an alternate plan, and Blackboard was an obvious choice. Because Blackboard is the university's online learning management system, it is readily available to all students, easy to use, and equipped with test and survey options. In January 2007, Hillyer and Maring attended the Blackboard testing and survey training offered by UNO's Information Technology Services. In early February, with the Perception software still not working, we decided to use Blackboard to deliver the assessment instrument.

While not our first choice, Blackboard proved to be cost effective and user friendly. Many libraries may not have the funding to purchase a separate assessment software product for the task of building an online assessment program, but they may have Blackboard or other classroom management software product that has test-building capabilities. Often, training is available through the campus ITS department for little or no cost. For our assessment purposes, Blackboard also created a comfortable, familiar atmosphere for students since it is widely used for their UNO classes, making it a familiar meeting ground that students "visit daily" (Karplus, 2006: 7).

The university's Information Technology Services department created a Blackboard organization, titled Criss Library Organization, specifically for our assessment purposes. The questions developed in the Questionmark Perception software were easily rewritten in Blackboard except for the Macromedia Flash question type, which was not available. We composed a pool of questions for the questionnaires and survey, built the pre- and postquestionnaires from the pool, and completed the survey for delivery via Blackboard.

Once the assessment tool was in place, library instructors needed permission from the English 1160/64 faculty to use their students for the study and to gather student rosters for enrollment into the assessment organization. Unfortunately, students cannot be automatically enrolled in Blackboard's Criss Library Organization because the organization is not a credit-producing entity like regularly scheduled classes. So before students can gain access to the organization and its contents (the questionnaires and survey), their username (last name and first initial) has to be manually added to the organization and placed in a group under their English 1160/64 section number and instructor. The graduate assistant (GA), who was hired with the grant money to assist the librarians with the study, developed shortcuts in Blackboard so that we could add students to the organization and then set up the groups. He also developed a system to download the data we would receive from Blackboard into Excel, which would allow us to create charts and graphs.

When all was in place, the organization's administrators (Hillyer and Maring) granted student access, and the Criss Library Organization link became available on the students' Blackboard Welcome page. We asked instructors to have students take the prequestionnaire before the first library instruction session, then take the postquestionnaire and survey within two weeks after the last library instruction session. We noted greater student participation when instructors encouraged students to take the questionnaire or added additional motivations like extra credit.

Pedagogical Impact

Developing the assessment study influenced library instruction in terms of consistency of focus, materials, and methodology. We were forced to think through and build a curriculum focused on the key information literacy concepts important to the English Department, library, and students. As a first step, essential information literacy concepts had to be clearly defined. Librarians and English faculty met several times to select the key concepts to emphasize, and then the library instruction team planned the curriculum. These collaborative decisions provided greater consistency among library instructors, promising that students were being taught the same concepts.

The assessment also encouraged consistent use of materials, specifically existing handouts, developed when the information literacy course was first introduced. Over the years, the handouts were used inconsistently in the first-year library instruction classes, and end-of-session student evaluations reflected that inconsistency. When library instructors did not use or sufficiently promote the handouts, students commented that materials were not helpful or a waste of time. With increased, consistent use of the handouts, students perceived the materials as practical aids for completing their research assignment.

Planning a consistent curriculum also led to the development of several interactive learning exercises. Such learning exercises are time-consuming, which can lead to some information being dropped from the curriculum, but the exercises are well received by the students. We have found in the literature that learning is improved when interactive techniques are used (Gray and Madson, 2007). The literature also suggests that "students of teachers who taught with interactive approaches made twice the average gain in learning—greater than two standard deviations" (Gray and Madson, 2007: 83).

One collaborative learning exercise that we used involved asking the students to list tools and types of sources they used when researching a question. This question led to discussion of different types of sources and the kinds of information within each type. Another successful exercise involved discussion of journals versus magazines. Each student was given an academic journal and a popular magazine. The librarians then asked them to list and contrast the characteristics of each type of periodical, which allowed discussion of the different types of information each contains.

Evaluating Web sites comprised a third collaborative learning exercise. Before the exercise, library instructors explained criteria to consider when evaluating Web sites and how to use the library's databases and catalog to find information about an author or sponsor of a site. We then offered several Web site examples, positive and negative, and offered tips on how to use Google's Advanced Search. To complete the exercise, students searched for Web sites on their subject, evaluated them using the criteria, shared their Web sites by displaying them for the class, and justified their evaluations.

The prequestionnaire also affects student learning and instruction. The preliminary advice from our faculty consultants was to use challenging questions on the test instrument that required critical thinking rather than mere guesswork. In this way, the prequestionnaire raised the bar and acted as a motivator. Our consultants reasoned that if students received a low score on the prequestionnaire it would be easier to capture their attention during the library instruction sessions. In addition to motivating students, the prequestionnaire also has the potential to shape instruction. By reviewing scores on prequestionnaire performance-based questions, librarians will gain insight into what students know (or do not know) before coming to the library. The assessment will allow instructors to tailor sessions based on students' needs.

STUDY SIZE, INITIAL EFFECTS, AND RESULTS

Study Size

Fifteen sections of English 1160/64 classes were included in the assessment study, 293 students. A total of 257 students completed the prequestionnaire, 197 students completed the postquestionnaire, and 115 students took the survey. The analysis of the data was run as a paired sample t-test, which meant that each individual must have both a pre- and postquestionnaire. If one of the students' scores was missing, that student was omitted from the analysis. As such, the sample size was reduced from $n = 293$ to $n = 184$.

In one of our final debriefing sessions, English faculty speculated on reasons for the reduced number of participants in the postquestionnaire and survey: Some instructors devoted class time for students to take the prequestionnaire but did not allot class time for the postquestionnaire. Some classes ended their library sessions right before spring break, so students were only reminded rather than required to take the postquestionnaire. Additionally, several classes were not able to complete their second library instruction class due to inclement weather; most of those students did not complete the postquestionnaire.

Initial Effects and Results

Our initial measure of results focused on the numbers, and indicators were positive. We predicted that students would demonstrate greater knowledge of information literacy skills following library instruction as compared to before instruction, as indicated by higher questionnaire scores. Since pre- and postquestionnaires are equal in difficulty, any change in scores can be viewed as valid (Kaplowitz, 1986). Students achieved significantly higher test scores following instruction (M = 9.89) than before instruction (M = 8.23). The results of a one-tailed paired samples t-test support our prediction ($t(183)$ = –8.085, $p < .001$). Figure 7.1 lists the mean and standard deviation for the pre- and postquestionnaire.

In order to assess the impact of instruction, we compared students' scores who completed the prequestionnaire to students who received library instruction and also completed the postquestionnaire. The results of a one-way analysis of variance (ANOVA) test compared 72 randomly selected students' scores who completed the pre- and postquestionnaire. Students' scores indicated a significant difference between postinstruction (M = 10.05) and preinstruction (M = 7.73) ($F(142)$ = 24.087, $p < .001$).

We also wanted to calculate the precision or consistency displayed by the questionnaires over time. Repeatedly administering a reliable questionnaire to a population will yield similar results across all administrations. It is important to have reliable measures, as reliability allows us to feel more confident in the results. One form of reliability is internal consistency, which shows the degree of relatedness among the questions: the extent to which items assess the same characteristics or quality, in this instance knowledge of information literacy skills. Reliability coefficients range from zero (for a totally unreliable measure) to 1.00 (for a measure that is 100 percent reliable). Thus, a coefficient of 0.2 would suggest a lower level of reliability than a coefficient of 0.8. Our results show the internal consistency of the questionnaires to be .699 (a = .699).

Figure 7.1. Details of the Pre- and Postquestionnaires			
Prequestionnaire Details		**Postquestionnaire Details**	
Points Possible	15	Points Possible	15
Average Score	8.23	Average Score	9.89
Standard Deviation	2.46	Standard Deviation	2.80
High Score	14	High Score	15
Low Score	0	Low Score	0

Where the curriculum incorporated active learning exercises, we also saw questions with the biggest jump in percentage of correct answers. As Figure 7.2 illustrates, questions based on information conveyed using interactive techniques showed greatly improved scores from the pre- to postquestionnaire.

For example, scores on question 3, which asks the student to match the tool to a source, increased from 58 percent to 76 percent. Questions 5, 6, and 7 tested students' knowledge of journals and magazines. Their scores were 16 percent higher from the pre- to the postquestionnaire. After students experienced a learning exercise on using a database, questions 13 and 14 showed an increase of 10 percent and 21 percent respectively. The biggest increase in the number of correct answers was the fill-in-the-blank question about Web evaluation, question 10. In the instruction sessions, students performed an active learning exercise on the Internet and also received a handout regarding Web evaluation. On their postquestionnaires, the number of correct answers on Web evaluation increased 27 percent.

Figure 7.3 is a chart of 29 randomly selected students with their pre- and postquestionnaire scores and the times it took for them to complete the questionnaires.

The upper line indicates the time in minutes it took for each student to take the prequestionnaire. The lower line shows times for the postquestionnaire. The average prequestionnaire score for 29 students is 8.27; the postquestionnaire average is 9.76. Seventeen students scored an 8 or above on the prequestionnaire, and 12 students' scores were below 8. Students with a high prequestionnaire score decreased their average from a 10.3 on the prequestionnaire to a 9.8 on the postquestionnaire. Students who scored low on the prequestionnaire increased from a 6 average score on the prequestionnaire to a 9.5 average score on the postquestionnaire. Ronald Berk found the same results in his investigation.

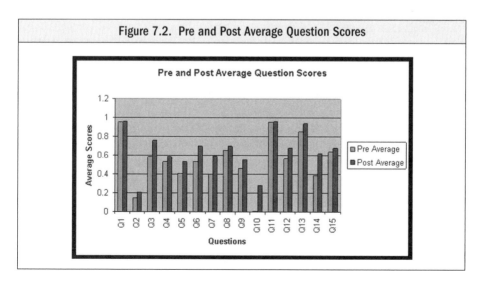

Figure 7.2. Pre and Post Average Question Scores

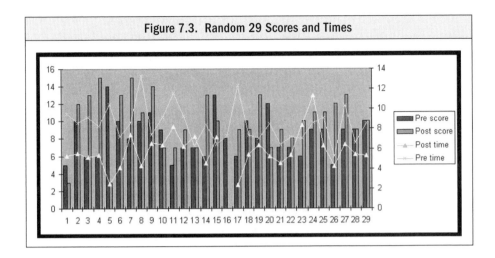

Figure 7.3. Random 29 Scores and Times

Students who scored at the average or above on the prequestionnaire did not have significant improvement in scores on the postquestionnaire, but students with a low prequestionnaire score on average obtained a higher score on the postquestionnaire (Berk, 1988). This change in scores has been named "statistical regression" and is not attributed to the teacher (Berk, 1988: 356). A student with a high prequestionnaire score may not feel the need to improve his or her skills, but a student who scores low on the prequestionnaire is more motivated to gain from the library instruction.

WHAT WE LEARNED FROM PHASE I

Prioritize

The assessment yielded several positive outcomes. First, our library instruction team clarified and focused the purposes of the information literacy sessions for first-year composition students. The planning process in the beginning of the study required the instruction team to think about the curriculum and its implications. Library instructors met and decided which key concepts from the ACRL Information Literacy Competency Standards were important for the students, the English Department, and the information literacy instructors at the library. The five ACRL Standards contain more than 100 outcomes (Neely, 2006). This overwhelming number led us to prioritize and use the most relevant standards and outcomes that fit our program and institution (Neely, 2006).

Less Is More

Although as instructors we want to cover essential material, and all our material seems (at least to us) essential, today's students learn more from interactive exercises focused on a few essential concepts than from comprehensive lectures. The National Survey of Student Engagement (NSSE) Annual Report 2006 emphasizes, "Students learn more when they are intensely involved in their education and are asked to think about and apply what they are learning in different settings" (National Survey of Student Engagement, 2006: 39). In our experience, information literacy concepts that were taught using active learning showed the most improvement in test scores. On the questions where interactive or collaborative exercises were used in the library sessions, there was a significant increase in scores. Figure 7.2 shows the scores for each question for the pre- and postquestionnaire. Some of the biggest jumps in score from the pre- to the postquestionnaire are illustrated in questions 3, 5, 6, 7, 10, 13, and 14. The concepts in those questions were taught using collaborative, active learning exercises.

Reinforce the Basics

When students were asked in the survey what other information would have been helpful, surprisingly we received several requests for a library tour, and several students asked how to find books in the library. In the ideal world, English instructors and librarians would take each class on a walking tour of the library to guarantee such basic questions are answered. However, due to time constraints such an approach is seldom feasible or even desirable since it risks boring a large segment of library-savvy students. Since the English 1160/64 sessions are packed with information and learning exercises, we decided to create a virtual tour of the library with a link added to the library's Web site. This virtual tour will save time for instructors, give students a tour of the library at their convenience, and show students where reference materials, books, and government documents are located.

Use What You Have

Although Blackboard is our university's course management system, we initially considered it as only a backup because we were enamored with the flashy options of the other programs. However, we discovered Blackboard can easily transform its purposes to suit our needs. Unfamiliar with the program's perimeters at the outset, we learned that its boundaries are pliable. Changing some of our questions' formats did not alter their effectiveness, and rewording them slightly to fit into Blackboard's narrower constricts did not change their usefulness in the assessment. For example, we changed our question concerning Library of Congress call numbers from a drag-and-drop format to matching. Other than eliminating the interactive, colorful qualities of this question, Blackboard's format did not detract from the question's impact. The fact that Blackboard did not require us to learn HTML or other programming skills facilitated our assessment's quick implementation. Quick implementation was also achieved thanks to easy access to instruction and help from our ITS department. Instead of dealing with a vendor located states away from our university, we had immediate and timely assistance from professionals who not only understood the program but also our project and its requirements.

One downside of Blackboard that we encountered is its inability to separate the data by course section. Once students have taken the assessment, we can access the pre- and postquestionnaire results of an individual student, and we can access the pre- and postquestionnaire results of the entire organization's members (every student who participated in the assessment). However, we cannot eke out information on a single class's responses; thus, we cannot provide an instructor with just his or her class's results. Although this limitation may be unique to our university, this Blackboard blind spot prevents the assessment from being as useful as it might otherwise be for our English faculty who may want to compare their class's information literacy results with that of other sections or the group as a whole.

The only other Blackboard drawback is its limited reporting capabilities. Blackboard reported on average score, total number of attempts, standard deviation, time, and variance. To learn more from the data, it had to be downloaded in Excel. In Excel, the data were organized into bar graphs to visually display the results to show improvements or changes. Data were also imported into SPSS to be used for calculations that detailed reliability, precision, and statistical significance. While this translation into other programs is not burdensome, it is an additional, necessary step in order to fully understand the data and make it accessible to others.

PHASE II: FUTURE POSSIBILITIES

In the final debriefing session, our five faculty consultants from Education, Psychology, and English offered ideas for future assessments. One idea is to pursue the connection between assessment instrument and student motivation to learn. We may give the prequestionnaire to one-half of the students and the postquestionnaire to everyone. If students score above the average on the postquestionnaire after taking the prequestionnaire, it may indicate that the prequestionnaire acts as a motivator for students. Anecdotally, the library instructors found that many students were surprised they did not do well on the prequestionnaire. They came to the library instruction motivated to learn about the questions that they answered incorrectly on the prequestionnaire.

Another idea for future assessments is to change the timing of the postquestionnaire. In Phase I, the students were asked to complete the postquestionnaire within two weeks of the last library session. Therefore, we cannot say conclusively whether the results reflected student learning or memorization from taking the prequestionnaire. If we vary the timing of taking the postquestionnaire, we may discover a correlating drop in student scores. The times suggested are 24 hours after the last library session, one week after the last session, and one month after the last session.

In phase II, we also intend to eliminate the survey, incorporating its perception-oriented questions into the questionnaires in order to measure the correlation between student perceptions and questionnaire scores. We plan to add these Likert-type questions to the questionnaires:

- Rate your level of library expertise.
- Rate your level of computer expertise.
- I enjoy learning about the library.
- I enjoy English classes.
- I enjoy writing.

Linking these perception questions with questionnaire results will allow us to compare students' attitudes and self-evaluations with their actual performance. Christopher Freeman (2004) noted in his study of student perceptions and library instruction that "students have a very positive view of their own abilities to make use of the library in general," but their confidence level drops when they must tell "the difference between a scholarly and popular journals or identify a citation to a book versus one from a journal" (44). In Phase I, because students completed the survey separately from the questionnaire, perceptions could not be linked to scores. The next time this assessment is offered, the Likert questions will be on the pre- and postquestionnaire.

Another question that will help us interpret scores is, "Have you had library instruction before?" Other studies have found that students with previous library instruction do not necessarily receive higher scores than students without previous library instruction (Kunkel, 1996). Adding this yes/no survey question to the questionnaires will test the validity of this premise by duplicating, or failing to duplicate, these results.

We may also vary the wording of some questions to avoid unintentional bias. For example, in response to the question "My overall impression of the library instruction was favorable," over 80 percent of the students rated the library instruction as favorable (see Figure 7.4).

Interpreting these results, one faculty consultant said students from the Midwest tend to regard instruction and teachers positively. To gain a truer picture of actual student perceptions, we plan to reword some of the questionnaires, asking half of the students if their overall impression of the library instruction was not favorable.

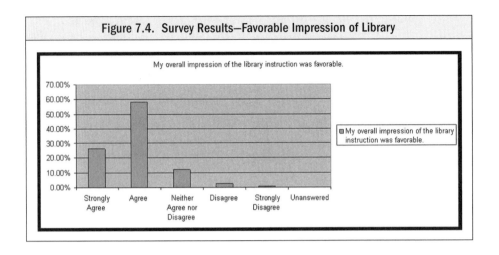

Figure 7.4. Survey Results—Favorable Impression of Library

Beyond the Data

Initially, the multilayered complexities of assessment can seem daunting. Accreditation agencies and state legislatures "require evidence of quality measured in outcomes" (Iannuzzi, 1999: 304), "libraries struggle with the assessment issue" and wonder what methods and tools can effectively measure their "slice" of the information literacy responsibility (Iannuzzi, 1999: 304), and the information literacy standards themselves prove "quite formidable" (Gregory, 2007: 28). Meanwhile, students need simple, direct ways to gain transferable information literacy skills that will extend to lifelong learning, and libraries must find a way to gauge student progress along that path. If information literacy is truly the "key competency for the 21st century" (no pressure there) (Bundy, 1999: 1), then finding ways to motivate students to gain information literacy skills and finding ways to measure those skills are well worth libraries' and universities' time and resources.

Our recent foray into the assessment arena confirmed the value of assessment, even in "small bytes," to answer critical questions about student perceptions and learning. Although our project, typically enough, took extensive effort and planning, that advance planning allowed us to maintain perspective, navigate obstacles, and alter the plan—even while it was already in motion.

The assessment benefited from both campus-wide and internal support. Our bank of faculty consultants gave sage advice at the outset: Define exactly what you want to learn; build a solid instrument; keep it simple and manageable. Their varied expertise as well as their disciplinary distance from our own project helped us to anticipate, even avoid, some problems and to deal with the problems that did arise, recasting them as new opportunities. We also benefited from having a well-established collaborative relationship with our partners in the English department, and a solid information literacy curriculum already in place. The assessment only verified the strength of that framework.

Blackboard also played a critical role in our ability to develop this assessment and to complete it in the time frame we had hoped. Without our immediate access to testing and survey training, ITS's support and expertise, and Blackboard's adaptability, we would still be planning our assessment instead of writing about it. Blackboard's additional benefits include ease of modification and ease of translation from rough data to meaningful reports. Although Blackboard was not our first choice, in the final analysis, it proved a valuable tool with unexpected benefits.

Ultimately, our three questions about the impact of library instruction and student learning have begun to be answered, but they have also opened the door to myriad new questions and ideas for future assessments. We did not find out everything we want to know, but through the process, we continue to gain insights that will benefit our instruction and our students. Assessment is complex, it often does not go as planned, and it is time and labor intensive. But its rewards justify its sacrifices. For those viewing the complex layers of assessment and hesitating on the brink, we leave you with two words of advice: Just start.

REFERENCES

ACRL Task Force on Information Literacy Competency Standards. 2000. "Information Literacy Competency Standards for Higher Education: The Final Version, Approved January 2000." *College and Research Libraries News* 61, no. 3 (March): 207–215.
Barclay, Donald. 1993. "Evaluating Library Instruction: Doing the Best You Can With What You Have." *Reference and User Services Quarterly* 33, no. 2 (Winter): 195–201.
Berk, Ronald A. 1988. "Fifty Reasons Why Student Achievement Gain Does Not Mean Teacher Effectiveness." *Journal of Personnel Evaluation in Education* 1 (July): 356–363.
Blixrud, Julia C. 2003. "Project SAILS: Standardized Assessment of Information Literacy Skills." *ARL* 230/231 (October/December): 18–19.
Bundy, Alan L. 1999. "Information Literacy: The Key Competency for the 21st Century" [Computer File]. *IATUL Proceedings*. Available: http://vnweb.hwwilsonweb.com/hww/jumpstart.jhtml?recid=0bc05f7a67b1790e50c64c5d6b9bbacc1000c48008d808608f254f47652787c76d07f46dd881e191&fmt=H. Accessed July 16, 2008.
Carter, Elizabeth W. 2002. "Doing the Best You Can With What You Have: Lessons Learned from Outcomes Assessment." *The Journal of Academic Librarianship* 1: 36–41.
Ferguson, Jessame E., Teresa Y. Neely, and Kathryn Sullivan. 2005. "A Baseline Information Literacy Assessment of Biology Students." *Reference & User Services Quarterly* 46, no. 2 (April): 61–71.
Fowler, Rena, John Berens, and Paul Duby. 1990. "Northern Michigan University Olson Library Assessment of Library Skills and Traits of Entering and Lower Level English Students." *ERIC* (Fall): ED339370.
Franklin, Godfrey, and Ronald Toifel. 1994. "The Effects of BI on Library Knowledge and Skills among Education Students." *Research Strategies* 12, no. 4 (Fall): 224–237.

Freeman, Christopher A. 2004. "The Relationship of Undergraduate Students' Self-assessment of Library Skills to their Opinion of Library Instruction: A Self-reporting Survey." *Southeast Library* 3: 39–46.

Gray, Tara, and Laura Madson. 2007. "Ten Easy Ways to Engage Your Students." *College Teaching* 55, no. 2: 83–87.

Gregory, Gwen M. 2007. "Raising the Bar for Information Literacy." *Information Today* 24, no. 2 (February): 28.

Gullikson, Shelley. 2006. "Faculty Perceptions of ACRL's Information Literacy Competency Standards for Higher Education." *The Journal of Academic Librarianship* 32, no. 6: 583–592.

Iannuzzi, Patricia. 1999. "We are Teaching, but are They Learning: Accountability, Productivity, and Assessment." *The Journal of Academic Librarianship* 4: 304–305.

Kaplowitz, Joan. 1986. "A Pre- and Post-test Evaluation of the English 3-library Instruction Program at UCLA." *Research Strategies* 4 (Winter): 11–17.

Karplus, Susan S. 2006. "Integrating Academic Library Resources and Learning Management Systems: The Library Blackboard Site." *Education Libraries* 29, no. 1 (Summer): 5–11.

Krentz, Roger F., and Donald E. Gerlach. 1989. "Library Literacy of Incoming College Freshman." *ERIC*: ED346866.

Kunkel, Lilith R., Susan Weaver, and Kim N. Cook. 1996. "What Do They Know? An Assessment of Undergraduate Library Skills." *The Journal of Academic Librarianship* 22: 430–434.

National Survey of Student Engagement (NSSE). 2006. "Engaged Learning: Fostering Success for all Students Annual Report 2006." Available: http://nsse.iub.edu/NSSE_2006_Annual_Report/docs/NSSE_2006_Annual_Report.pdf.

Neely, Teresa Y. 2006. *Information Literacy Assessment Standards-Based Tools and Assignments.* Chicago: American Library Association.

O'Hanlon, Nancy. 2007. "Information Literacy in the University Curriculum: Challenges for Outcomes Assessment." *portal: Libraries and the Academy* 7, no. 2: 169–189.

Owusu-Ansah, Edward K. 2004. "Information Literacy and Higher Education: Placing the Academic Library in the Center of a Comprehensive Solution." *The Journal of Academic Librarianship* 30, no.1: 3–16.

Rockman, Ilene F. 2002. "Strengthening Connections Between Information Literacy, General Education, and Assessment Efforts." *Library Trends* 2: 185–198.

Rockman, Ilene F., and Gordon W. Smith. 2005. "Information and Communication Technology Literacy: New Assessments for Higher Education." *C&RL News* 66, no. 8: 587–589.

Senn Breivik, Patricia. 2000. "Information Literacy and Lifelong Learning: The Magical Partnership." Keynote address, International Lifelong Learning Conference. Available: http://lifelonglearning.cqu.edu.au/2000/keynote/Breivik.doc. Accessed May 31, 2007.

Warner, Dorothy Anne. 2003. "Programmatic Assessment: Turning Process into Practice by Teaching for Learning." *The Journal of Academic Librarianship* 3: 169–176.

Appendix 7.1. Pre- and Postquestionnaire

Question 1. Multiple Choice

Not giving proper acknowledgment for another writer's words or ideas is known as _____.

Correct   answers

✔   Plagiarism

    Originalism

    Citation

    Referencing

    Unanswered

Question 2. Multiple Answer

From the list below, select all that represent a characteristic of a primary source. (Check all that apply.)

Correct   answers

✔   An eyewitness account of the event

    The first book written on the event

    The most important journal article written on the event

    A biography of someone involved in the event

    A newspaper article written a year after the event

✔   Field research, artwork, letters

Question 3. Matching

Match the information source (first column) to the best access tool (second column).

Books

Correct   answers

    Search engine

✔   Catalog

    Index (electronic or print)

    Unanswered

Articles (from magazines, journals, and newspapers)

Correct   answers

    Search engine

    Catalog

✔   Index (electronic or print)

    Unanswered

Web sites

Correct   answers

✔   Search engine

    Catalog

    Index (electronic or print)

    Unanswered

(Continued)

Appendix 7.1.   Pre- and Postquestionnaire (Continued)

Question 4. Matching

Pretend you are looking for four books on the shelves in the library. On the end of each shelf is a list of the range of call numbers contained on that shelf. Match each book's call number with the shelf where you would find it.

Z473.K74K7

Correct   answers
        Z473.T − Z1005.2
  ✔ UA853.K − Z473.5
        S441.R3 − SB407.G
        RJ499.T8 − S441.R3
        Unanswered

S605.5D87 2005

Correct   answers
        Z473.T − Z1005.2
        UA853.K − Z473.5
  ✔ S441.R3 − SB407.G
        RJ499.T8 − S441.R3
        Unanswered

Z711.4.I57 1996

Correct   answers
  ✔ Z473.T − Z1005.2
        UA853.K − Z473.5
        S441.R3 − SB407.G
        RJ499.T8 − S441.R3
        Unanswered

S441.E15

Correct   answers
        Z473.T − Z1005.2
        UA853.K − Z473.5
        S441.R3 − SB407.G
  ✔ RJ499.T8 − S441.R3
        Unanswered

Question 5. Multiple Answer

From the list below, select the characteristics of a scholarly journal. (Check all that apply.)

Correct   answers
  ✔ Contains advanced vocabulary
  ✔ Indicates source of information
        Contains a variety of advertisements, classified ads, photos, and coupons
  ✔ Written by person who did the research
        Contains articles that are not always footnoted
  ✔ Contains articles that are peer reviewed by scholars in the field.

Question 6. Multiple Answer

From the list below, select the characteristics of magazines. (Check all that apply.)

Correct   answers
  ✔ Purchased at a newsstand, bookstore, or grocery store
  ✔ Often written from a particular political, economic, or social point of view
  ✔ May be dedicated to a particular industry or occupation
        Often have the same depth of information as a scholarly journal
        Contains articles that are peer reviewed by scholars in the field
        Contains articles that are always footnoted

(Continued)

Appendix 7.1. Pre- and Postquestionnaire *(Continued)*

Question 7. Multiple Choice

Which of the sources listed below would lead you to a journal article?

Correct   answers

✔   Ecology: Vol. 75, No. 7, pp. 1861–1876. Beyond Global Warming: Ecology and Global Change

www.epa.gov/globalwarming

Global warming: the science of climate change by Francis Drake, Publisher: London: Arnold; New York: Co-published in the United States of America by Oxford University Press, 2000.

Copyright 2006 The New York Times Company The New York Times September 24, 2006 Sunday Late Edition—Final SECTION: Section 4; Column 1; Week in Review Desk; The Basics; Pg. 2 LENGTH: 277 words HEADLINE: An Entrepreneur Sees Green BYLINE: By HEATHER TIMMONS

Unanswered

Question 8. Multiple Answer

From the list below, select all of the accurate descriptions of the World Wide Web. (Check all that apply.)

Correct   answers

        Always provides authoritative and accurate information

✔   Offers some daily updated sites

✔   Presents a variety of information

        Is edited by a WWW Editorial Board

✔   Provides different types of information including current, historical, research, secondary, or primary

        Contains only .com and .org websites

        All of the statements are true

Question 9. Multiple Answer

When researching a topic, why would you consult a book? (Check all that apply.)

Correct   answers

✔   For background information

        For very current, up-to-date information

✔   For understanding the complexity of the topic

✔   For facts and statistics

        All statements are true

(Continued)

Appendix 7.1. Pre- and Postquestionnaire *(Continued)*

Question 10. Fill in Multiple Blanks

When you are using the Web for your research, it is particularly important that you evaluate the quality of Web sites. List four words describing what you need to consider when evaluating the reliability of a Web site. [answer1], [answer2], [answer3], [answer4]

Category	Attempt count	Attempt count as Percentage of total
Total attempts	257	100%
Unanswered attempts	25	9.728%
Correct answer	3	1.167%

Question 11. Hot Spot

From the catalog record shown below, use your mouse to click on the call number.

Question 12. Hot Spot

From the catalog record shown below, use your mouse to click on the publisher.

Question 13. Hot Spot

Below is a search result from the database EBSCO–Academic Search Premier.

Question 14. Hot Spot

Below is a search result from the database EBSCO–Academic Search Premier.

Question 15. Hot Spot

Below is a search result from the database EBSCO–Academic Search Premier.

Appendix 7.2. Preview Assessment Student Survey

Preview Assessment: Criss Library Assessment Student Survey

Question 1

Rate your level of computer experience.

1. Expert   2. Competent   3. Neither novice   4. Advanced   5. Beginner   6. Novice
                            nor expert   beginner

Question 2

You understood the instructions for taking the online assessment test.

1. Strongly agree   2. Agree   3. Neither agree   4. Disagree   5. Strongly disagree
                                nor disagree

Question 3

You understood the purpose of the online assessment questionnaire.

1. Strongly agree   2. Agree   3. Neither agree   4. Disagree   5. Strongly disagree
                                nor disagree

Question 4

The library instruction was organized and presented clearly.

1. Strongly agree   2. Agree   3. Neither agree   4. Disagree   5. Strongly disagree
                                nor disagree

Question 5

My overall impression of the library instruction was favorable.

1. Strongly agree   2. Agree   3. Neither agree   4. Disagree   5. Strongly disagree
                                nor disagree

Question 6

The library instruction contributed to the completion of class assignments.

1. Strongly agree   2. Agree   3. Neither agree   4. Disagree   5. Strongly disagree
                                nor disagree

Question 7

The handouts were helpful during library instruction.

1. Strongly agree   2. Agree   3. Neither agree   4. Disagree   5. Strongly disagree
                                nor disagree

Question 8

The handouts were helpful while completing my assignment.

1. Strongly agree   2. Agree   3. Neither agree   4. Disagree   5. Strongly disagree
                                nor disagree

(Continued)

Appendix 7.2. Preview Assessment Student Survey *(Continued)*

Preview Assessment: Criss Library Assessment Student Survey

Question 9

What did you find most useful about the library instruction?

Question 10

What other information would have been helpful to complete your assignment?

Question 11

List suggestions to improve the online assessment questions.

Chapter 8

A Constructivist Approach to Instructional Technology and Assessment in ESL Course Design

Penny Bealle and Kathleen Cash-McConnell

INTRODUCTION

English as a second language (ESL) college students need academic discourse skills for the academic rigor required in content courses. This chapter will examine an instructional collaboration between Penny Bealle, a library professor, and Kathleen Cash-McConnell, an English as a second language professor. The authors teach at Suffolk County Community College (SCCC). The collaboration facilitates the acquisition of structured academic discourse for oral and written tasks. This discourse focuses on the grammar and vocabulary germane to interpretation of the statistical and graphic data that students encounter in content readings and online research. Familiarity with academic discourse ensures student success in subsequent lecture courses such as Introduction to Sociology, Marketing, or Health Concepts.

The collaboration discussed in this chapter emphasizes the pedagogical value of infusing information literacy (IL) and technology instruction into ESL016: ESL College Listening/Speaking Skills II, a three-credit advanced speaking and listening course. By incorporating techniques learned from IL and technology instruction into their assignments, students demonstrate competency with several intertwined components of academic discourse. Especially important are critical thinking strategies, IL competency standards, and the targeted language germane to many academic disciplines. Competency with essential aspects of academic discourse is critical because successful completion of ESL016 provides students with one of the prerequisites to enroll in content courses. These students gain facility with the required learning outcomes through a series of library and computer workshops. During the four IL workshops, cotaught by Bealle and Cash-McConnell, students engage in hands-on research using specified library databases and library-recommended Web sites, select appropriate information resources, prepare MLA style bibliographic citations, and write an evaluation of an online information resource. During the numerous computer workshops taught by Cash-McConnell, she and the class use hardware including camcorders, electronic whiteboards, and digital projectors, as well as software applications such as Microsoft (MS) Word, Excel, and PowerPoint. Through the workshops, students incrementally acquire the skills to complete the final project, a demographic study in which they synthesize information into digital presentations that are projected onto an interactive whiteboard and orally delivered to the class. While not cutting-edge, the technology helps ESL students cross the threshold into the academic community. Their technological competency, coupled with their acquisition of IL skills, give students the confidence to use their oral and digital presentation skills in subsequent content courses and to enroll in online classes. Rather than sheltering these students in the ESL department, our collaboration ensures that they are fully integrated into the college; they learn that library and academic computing services are readily available and develop the competency to navigate these important components of the academic setting.

A unique feature of this case study is that technology is not only used by the students as a means of increasing their technological competency but is also used to motivate students and assess learning outcomes. Their presentations are videotaped at three stages during the semester. The students are aware that they will be videotaped; this motivates them to prepare all three oral presentations with impressive seriousness. The recordings provide valuable opportunities for student engagement in self- and peer assessment as well as feedback from the professor.

RELATED LITERATURE

IL and Technology Instruction for ESL Students

Recent publications stress that college-level IL instruction most effectively improves learning outcomes when it is closely linked to course objectives and assignments. Numerous authors emphasize that the ideal undergraduate IL program is systematically integrated throughout the curriculum and that assignment-related IL instruction cultivates engaged learners because it occurs at the point of need (Jacobson and Xu, 2004: 12–14; Rockman, 2004: 16–17). While this approach is also applicable to the ESL population, publications focusing on course-integrated IL instruction for ESL students are less common. Two publications' literature reviews inventory many of the library services and programs that academic libraries have offered ESL students over the last 25 years including: library instruction in the native language, cultural roadmaps to help librarians understand international patrons, and methods of bibliographic instruction, including those with course-integrated library instruction (Conteh-Morgan, 2001: 30; DiMartino and Zoe, 2000: 19–22, 26–27, 37–38). In addition to these studies, some recent publications add to our understanding of library instruction for ESL students. Karen Bordonaro (2006a,b) does not examine course-integrated IL instruction for ESL students, but her study does demonstrate that ESL students recognize the college library as an excellent environment for self-directed language improvement (Bordonaro, 2006a: 518). Miriam Laskin (2002) describes a three workshop IL program offered by library faculty for a freshman orientation course at a community college with a large ESL population. The workshops that "support the academic readiness skills required by a bilingual, urban student body" are not integrated into the regular course meetings, but are required for passing the course (41). Miriam Conteh-Morgan (2001) advocates a model in which ESL faculty, who have been mentored by library faculty, provide course-integrated IL instruction for ESL students. The advantages of this approach include the ability for ESL faculty to reach more ESL students than library faculty can and the ability to provide hands-on and sustained learning in the "low-anxiety environment" cultivated by the ESL professor (30–31). Conteh-Morgan (2002, 2003) is not alone in advocating that classroom faculty rather than library faculty provide substantive IL instruction. Although this approach is not widely recorded in literature regarding IL instruction for ESL students, a publication coauthored by Grace Peña Delgado, a history professor, and Susan Luévano, a library faculty member, documents a similar model. Peña Delgado and Luévano (2007), who teach students in Chicano and Latino studies rather than strictly ESL students, were awarded a grant which provided the resources to train classroom faculty in teaching IL skills (98–99).

Although Bealle and Cash-McConnell have not formally trained classroom faculty to teach IL skills, like Peña Delgado and Luévano they have shared their commitment to promoting classroom and library faculty IL collaborations by leading a grant-funded professional development workshop for classroom and library faculty at their institution. The workshop series motivated many SCCC classroom faculty to collaborate with library faculty and infuse IL instruction into their courses. Bealle and Cash-McConnell firmly believe, as ACRL (Association of College and Research Libraries) best practices indicate and as Ilene Rockman and associates (2004) state, "Information Literacy is no longer just a library issue" (1).

In addition to infusing IL into ESL016, Bealle and Cash-McConnell also incorporate technology skills into the course because technology competency meshes inextricably with IL to enable students to successfully navigate future content courses. As Trudi Jacobson and Thomas Mackey (2007) state in the introduction to the chapter on technology and IL collaborations, in their book *Information Literacy Collaborations That Work*, effective use of technology can improve student learning in many ways, including: incorporating "opportunities for collaborative problem solving among" classmates; incorporating "video and interactive technologies as a means to advance writing, research and presentation skills;" and increasing students' confidence about seeking assistance from library faculty or academic computing personnel (192). Marjorie Ginsberg and Nancy Weiner (2007), in a chapter titled "Writing in the Guise of a Persona: Combining Basic Reading, Library Research, and Video Performance" from the same book, recognize many of the same benefits that we realize from infusing IL and technology instruction in our collaboration. Like the basic reading students described by Ginsberg and Weiner, our ESL students are developing the skill sets that they require to succeed in college-level content courses. In addition, Ginsberg and Weiner note that their basic reading students are motivated to do their very best because they know that their oral presentations will be videotaped (205). Our students are similarly motivated by the knowledge that several presentations will be taped during the semester for self- and peer evaluation, plus assessment by Cash-McConnell.

Constructivism

Cash-McConnell's design of this course's progressive problem-solving tasks, in addition to its infused IL and technology competency components, is informed by a constructivist philosophy and a "reflective practice" (Kaufman, 2004: 311). The pedagogy is based on the cognitive development and sociocultural theories of Piaget and Vygotsky, whose premises are seminal to constructivism (Kaufman, 2004: 304). The professor presents himself or herself not as a conveyor of knowledge, but as a facilitator in a learner-centered environment focusing on the cognitive and social processes of learning. He or she structures the learning environment to maximize student engagement. Students work primarily in groups, interacting with peers to complete an inquiry-oriented task. This pedagogy is particularly emphasized in Jacqueline and Martin Brooks's (1993) book *In Search of Understanding: The Case for Constructivist Classrooms*; students "search for meaning, appreciate uncertainty, and inquire responsibly" ("Constructivism in the Classroom," 1994: 6). While Brooks focused on K–12, Cash-McConnell applies the pedagogy to the postsecondary level. The class is student-centered, and learners are actively engaged in monitoring their progress through the cycle of scaffolded tasks. Small groups of peers work together to explore the questions presented by both the classroom and library faculty.

Guided by the standards of TESOL (Teachers of English to Speakers of Other Languages, 2003) and constructivist pedagogy, ESL016's dynamic process is designed to enable the following learner transformations to occur:

1. Learners actively engage in meaningful activities to support concept acquisition. They are invited to solve a purposefully ambiguous but relevant problem in a demographic study, using raw census data and primary sources along with interactive technologies.
2. Cash-McConnell models and coaches participation in the scaffolded activities, which are broken into comprehensible units, preparing learners to become self-directed. She uses cognitive terms—*classify, analyze, hypothesize, predict*, and *create* to frame tasks. The stage of "external scaffolding" (Kaufman, 2004: 304) begins here and continues into the third step, sustaining students' acquisition of knowledge.
3. The class members engage in self-directed and independent learning both alone and in groups, with coaching as needed by Bealle and Cash-McConnell. Classmates work together to sort through information, prioritize key points, and make connections to their research. The professors encourage dialogue, scaffold discourse with open-ended questions, and seek elaboration of initial responses where suppositions are valued, yet challenged.
4. Students independently work through their process of reflection, inquiry, problem solving and task performance. At this stage, "internal scaffolding" (Kaufman, 2004: 310) launches students toward a construction of deeper levels of understanding and awareness of their metacognitive strategies ("Constructivism in the Classroom," 1994: 6; Reza-Hernandez, 2004: 309; Brooks, 2006).

While integration of the constructivist process is common in mathematics and science, it has basically been ignored in the literature on language education (Kaufman, 2004: 310). Yet, academic language as a tool for communication is essential to the establishment of the constructivist learning classroom. As advocates of learning strategy instruction have pointed out, cognitive and metacognitive strategies complement an academic orientation; such strategies help learners satisfy their immediate needs while developing knowledge and skills. Moreover, ESL students' real-life interests can be targeted in inquiry-based courses, maintaining their engagement in their process of language learning (McDonough and Chaikitmongkol, 2007: 124). Over the past two decades, a paradigm shift has occurred in language pedagogy with the emergence of content-based language learning. This shift has altered the tradition of teaching a language in isolation to its incorporation in the context of a discipline both here and abroad (Kaufman, 2004: 309).

In ESL016, Cash-McConnell incorporates problem-based tasks to engage student investigation of a relevant demographic topic on urban growth in the United States. These tasks are conducted in the classroom, computer lab, library, and in online dialogue with her. A major learning objective is to prompt understanding and usage of the targeted strings of academic discourse in group discussion, graphic interpretations, written summaries, and oral presentations. Students, preparing for their own careers and mobility, and curious about cities in other regions of the United States, are a captive audience for the theme. Bealle and Cash-McConnell work in tandem integrating the three learning domains of Bloom's Taxonomy, the cognitive, affective, and psychomotor, to help students work through the tasks to construct knowledge about the cities.

This demographic theme lends itself well to our role of scaffolding thoughtful, open-ended questions to guide learners in their inquiry, as recommended by TESOL in 2002. Suggestions for a contextualized, constructivist pedagogy are implicit in TESOL standards, sanctioning use of linguistic scaffolding to boost learning (Kaufman, 2004: 313).

Of further relevance to ESL learners is engagement with the interactive technology that is most obviously available to them on campus: personal computers with Microsoft software applications and Internet access. Many arrive with educational experiences grounded in the industrial age, dominated by traditional print and analog educational media. In stark contrast, the classroom, library, and academic computing center can all function as dynamic "micro-socioconstructivist" settings, creating communities of learners in electronic learning environments. Here students work through an understanding of direct manipulation of graphical user interfaces in a highly interactive computer system to access library databases, create graphics for an electronic slide presentation, and communicate with Cash-McConnell as they exchange documents via e-mail. As Michael Spring notes in his article "Interactive Systems," the human-computer interaction is defined in terms of the "gulfs of execution and evaluation" (Spring, 2002: 111). To fill the gulf, the learner must create a plan to reach his or her goal; the plan involves executing a series of actions on the computer system. The actions' results "must be perceived, interpreted, and evaluated by the user" (Spring, 2002: 111). In the ESL settings, learners' perceptions, interpretations and evaluations are likewise developed as they work together with interactive computer tools and develop their critical thinking strategies.

Throughout the inquiry process in our class settings, learners acquire the chunks of memory for both the psychomotor skills on the computer and scaffolded language tasks. Learner motivation grows as they gain facility with the tools and academic language. Of immediate relevance here is Marshall McLuhan's concept of media as *hot* or *cool* with this reflection: "Learning is cool as a measure of the individual's involvement in the medium" (McLuhan, 1964: 23). A learner's "hot mindlessness" of Web surfing contrasts sharply with his or her cool absorption in inquiry-based learning. Interactivity is key in this pedagogical challenge, for the cool medium is one in which a "little is given and so much has to be filled in" (McLuhan, 1964: 23). This is the essence of ESL016's micro-socioconstructivist learning environment. We provide a stimulating, and, yes, "cool" interactive experience for students to tackle the demographic topic with critical IL and technology capabilities to complete the tasks.

ESL AND IL AT SUFFOLK COUNTY COMMUNITY COLLEGE

Suffolk County is a large and diverse county that is served by Suffolk County Community College, an open-admission, three-campus, nonresidential college with approximately 20,000 students. SCCC offers associate degrees, applied associates degrees, and certificates in wide-ranging curricula that include credit and noncredit ESL courses. The Eastern Campus, where we teach, is in Riverhead, NY, and serves the eastern end of Suffolk County, a large geographical area that is about 60 miles long by 20 miles wide, including both vast rural and densely suburban areas. Our campus is the smallest of the three with about 3,000 full- and part-time students.

The instructional collaboration discussed in this chapter involves the ESL016 course. Consistent with national trends, the ESL population at the Eastern Campus has risen since the courses were first offered. In fall 1993 the seat enrollment was 31; in fall 2007 seat enrollment reached 116, a nearly fourfold increase. Student language groups over this period experienced a significant shift in representation. In 1993 Spanish speakers comprised the majority at 60 percent of the population. An additional 30 percent spoke Polish, and the remaining 10 percent spoke a variety of tongues: Malay, Turkish, Dutch, French, and Portuguese. Over time the diversity of the learners grew exponentially. By 2006, only 40 percent of the students were Spanish speakers. The proportion of Polish speakers had dropped to 20 percent. Another 40 percent spoke languages as diverse as Chinese, Arabic, Urdu, Georgian, Ewe, and Brazilian Portuguese. A number of these students spoke between 3 and 5 languages and dialects. The ESL016 students enrolled in 2003–2007 represented 5 continents and 30 countries of origin.

The current ESL population comprises nonnative English speakers who include not only international students but also "generation 1.5" students educated in the United States. The latter sector shows gaps in their academic English proficiency and frequently needs developmental courses. The collaborative instructional process discussed here prompts students' engagement in academic discourse so that they may be more comfortable and successful in future content classes.

SCCC currently lacks a college-wide incremental IL plan, but does have some effective IL initiatives. A cornerstone of the library instruction program is the one-session class attended by all sections of the freshman orientation course, a requirement for all full-time SCCC students. While there are no other college-wide requirements for library instruction, many classroom faculty include it in their courses. In addition, "information management," which includes information and computer literacy, is mandated as a State University of New York (SUNY) General Education infused competency. At the Eastern Campus our professional library personnel (comprised of two full-time and several part-time library faculty and one head librarian) teach about 200 library instructional sessions per academic year. Library instruction consists of numerous single session meetings, either as general overviews, which are required for all freshman orientation classes, or subject-specific classes for a range of courses including English, history, and psychology. From the time Bealle joined the library faculty at the Eastern Campus in 2003, she has cultivated infused library instruction collaborations. These have consisted of two or more library instruction sessions per course, with numerous classroom faculty members, including Cash-McConnell.

Library faculty and administrators are capitalizing on the momentum from the 2007 Middle States Commission on Higher Education (MSCHE) reaccreditation visit to promote IL at SCCC. Most notably, the SCCC libraries as a department will undergo a library program review in the 2007–2008 academic year. While the SCCC libraries routinely participate in departmental program reviews to evaluate how effectively the libraries support academic programs throughout the college, this will be the first time that the libraries are reviewed as a separate department. In this context, the Information Literacy Committee has adopted the ACRL information literacy assessment standards as a framework for a review of the library instruction program. As part of this initiative, the IL committee is currently evaluating assessment instruments such as the James Madison University Information Literacy Test to determine if an existing instrument is appropriate for evaluating the IL outcome behaviors of our students. With the absence of a systematic IL plan noted in our 2007 MSCHE's self-study, it is apparent that we will want to provide evidence of improvement for future reaccreditation visits. Recognizing that MSCHE values library and classroom faculty collaborations as evidence of integrating IL into the curriculum, collaborations such as ours are taken seriously at SCCC as exemplary models for other courses and departments.

ALIGNING ESL016 OBJECTIVES WITH STUDENT LEARNING NEEDS

Students enrolled in ESL016 have a wide range of educational backgrounds from having completed a General Equivalency Diploma for high school (GED) to completion of a bachelor's degree in another country. They have usually had a course in conversational English, but not one focused on academic English.

Neither the noncredit ESL nor the Communications Departments at SCCC has intensive instruction to prepare this population for the creation and delivery of an academic presentation.

In spring 2003, during conversations with faculty in sociology and accounting, Cash-McConnell learned that students exiting the ESL program were having difficulty with a SUNY General Education task of interpreting quantitative information in graphs and charts. Their limited academic vocabulary frustrated their ability to accurately describe and interpret quantitative information, a core component of social science and natural science curricula. Additionally, a grasp of information and computer literacy was erratic across this population. With these apparent gaps in experience for the advanced ESL student, Cash-McConnell redesigned the ESL016 course that summer with financial support from a Title III grant, "Demographically Speaking: An Interactive Approach to Teacher and Student Assessment of Academic Discourse." She chose the linguistic domain of demography, for it involves interpretive data analyses of race, ethnic group, religion, language, and socioeconomic status. In the current syllabus, students learn the basic research skills to locate the demographic information of a United States city.

Cash-McConnell's learning outcomes now include the use of contextualized and targeted grammar and discourse focusing on quantitative information. She prepares ESL students to read, interpret, write, and vocalize such discourse by modeling statements like the following for her students:

In the graph of population growth in Las Vegas between 1990 and 2000, the trend reveals that the population has doubled and continues to accelerate. This growth is due to the migration of workers seeking employment in the tourism and construction industries.

The demography research project culminates at the end of the semester when each student presents information on a city in a ten-minute PowerPoint show. A learner's project is not a conversational travel log but rather an analysis of why that city is economically thriving or floundering.

The revision of the course in summer 2003 included adding IL and technological competency instruction. To finesse the ten minute PowerPoint presentation, students must evaluate and synthesize information from numerous information sources. Multiple library workshops ensure that they begin to acquire effective online search techniques as they interpret and synthesize current demographic information. The course scaffolds tasks via the demographic research project on a city, whose data prompts analysis and discussion of population trends. Students learn to create their own charts and graphs in MS Excel and import them into their PowerPoint slide show. Over the semester, classmates form a supportive learning community as they enthusiastically discuss data on each others' cities. For example, student KK used the table in Figure 8.1 to help her peers visualize

Figure 8.1. KK's Table: Oklahoma City Educational Attainment in Population 25 Years and Over, 1990–2000 (Fall 2006)

Education	1990 (%)	2000 (%)
Less than 9th grade	6.77	4.91
Some high school, no diploma	13.99	11.45
High school graduate	27.55	27.76
Some college, no degree	25.01	26.11
Associate degree	5.06	5.32
Bachelor's degree	14.34	16.05
Graduate or professional degree	7.28	8.40

Figure 8.2. PK's Table: Cost of Housing in Orlando, Florida (Fall 2006)

	2004	2005	2006 (q2)*
Median Home Price, Orlando, FL	$169,600	$243,600	$271,700
U.S. National Average	$184,000	$219,000	$227,500
*q2 – Second Quarter			

how the educational attainment of Oklahoma City's population over two census periods affected the preparedness of its labor force for the job market. A different student, PK, provoked discussion of not only the trend in median housing costs over a three-year period in Orlando, Florida, but also its affordability for its burgeoning population (see Figure 8.2).

INFORMATION LITERACY: AN INCREMENTAL PROCESS

When Cash-McConnell began incorporating fundamentals of research and technology literacy into the course in fall 2003, the IL component involved only one library visit. This schedule of one library instruction session was based on the most common model at the Eastern Campus Library at the time. During this fall 2003 class, the library faculty member explained the features of many sources of demographic information, including the homepage for the U.S. Census Bureau at www.census.gov, with the expectation that the students would explore the resources and identify relevant data for their projects outside of class meetings. Three concerns became evident. First, these resources were too complex as a starting point for a developmental course in which students need to further their English and academic proficiency. Second, information needs for the assignment would be best approached on an incremental basis. Third, the library presentation should not exceed 20 minutes in order to allow for a substantial amount of hands-on research during the class meeting. From this genesis, our collaboration and infused IL model developed.

Bealle and Cash-McConnell began conferring after the initial library visit in fall 2003 and began coteaching four library sessions per semester in fall 2004. When they initially discussed learning objectives, they recognized the compatibility of their approaches and goals. Cash-McConnell knew that the students needed to develop facility with IL and technology skills as well as targeted language focusing on quantitative terms to acquire enough academic discourse to move on to content courses. Clearly IL instruction could help facilitate these outcome behaviors. As we formulated new course objectives, we referred to the ACRL Information Literacy Competency Standards for Higher Education (Association of College and Research Libraries, 2000). In order to provide a constructivist learning environment, which would nurture the outcomes linked to the five ACRL information literacy competency standards, we designed the course to embrace these best practices in the academic library profession: First, library instruction is most meaningful when it is infused by linking it closely to class assignments. Second, it is most practical when it is incremental. Third, it has lifelong relevance when students can confidently apply these strategies toward future information needs in academic, professional, and personal realms. In addition to these broad constructs, we targeted specific outcome behaviors for students and defined the parameters of the research tasks. These behaviors are linked to the five ACRL information literacy competency standards as indicated in parentheses in the following discussion of the incremental process.

The ESL016 class is introduced to the assigned demographic topic for their culminating research projects by the fourth week of the semester. In preparation for this project the students have already had cumulative lessons on quantitative terms and demographic phrases. These lessons are presented in context through reading, discussion, and dictation. Once the demographic research project is underway, two key questions guide the students: (1) "Why has a particular city experienced a dramatic shift in population?" and (2) "What does this shift mean for the city's infrastructure, industries, and labor force?" In preparation for the scaffolded inquiry-based tasks, Cash-McConnell engages the class in a discussion by applying similar questions to a specific city, such as Orlando:

- What kind of educational attainment shift did Orlando experience between the 1990 and 2000 census?
- Interpret what this shift means for the preparedness of some of Orlando's population to enter low-skilled jobs and others to enter professional positions.
- Summarize how the preparedness of Orlando's population for the low-skilled and professional labor force is similar/different than those of cities that your peers are researching.

Cash-McConnell explains to the students that they will learn to research and interpret the answers to these questions with the assistance of a series of library and computer workshops (ACRL Standard One).

The approach to the culminating project is inquiry-oriented, with enough ambiguity to establish a dynamic constructivist process of discovery. Each learner ultimately selects his or her "own" city to research from a list of cities in the various census regions of the United States provided by Cash-McConnell. The cities may include Las Vegas, San Antonio, Denver, Atlanta, Detroit, and Boston. Some of these are purposefully included to reveal negative population growth over time, adding interest to group interpretations of the data.

Having selected their cities and gained familiarity with quantitative terms and demographic phrases, the students are ready for the first library visit. In the first IL workshop, using the SCCC library Web page as a starting point, they learn that library databases are appropriate sources for college research, an important lesson in today's quantity-rich but quality-poor information landscape. To explore their cities, we initially direct them to the World Almanac in the Facts.com library database. It exposes them to a well-organized factual database that includes demographic and numerical terms integral to the targeted discourse. Moreover, this site is understandable to those having limited academic English proficiency or limited exposure to IL skills. With the experience of a structured library database under their belt, learners are better equipped to handle data from the U.S. Census Bureau and other sources (ACRL Standards One and Two).

During the second library workshop, we introduce discreet information from the U.S. Census Bureau and other sources of statistical information produced by the federal government. MapStats: United States at www.fedstats.gov provides data such as population diversity, educational attainment, major employment sectors, and crime rate (ACRL Standards One and Two).

This structured approach lends real meaning to the facile statement that "I'll go to the Internet (or to Google) for my information." Students are often surprised to learn about the varying reliability of Googled sites. They notice these differences when they visit links to their cities' chamber of commerce sites. When they visit a discreet Web site such as www.census.gov they discover that they must determine how it is structured in order to access the appropriate information. Students also realize that the library reference team can provide meaningful direction for their inquiry. From this second workshop they acquire an important survival tool that can greatly assist them in future content classes: knowing where to start rather than wandering aimlessly through Google search results when seeking credible information and scholarly articles for future content classes (ACRL Standards Two and Three).

During the third library class, we provide guidance in three areas. The first task is framed as follows by Cash-McConnell: "Identify an issue of environmental concern for your selected city (or its county), using these two Web sites: (1) Scorecard: The Pollution Information Site and (2) Environmental Protection Agency: Envirofacts Data Warehouse. With the coaching of the librarian, students evaluate the two Web sites, discussing ease of access as well as the authority and currency of the information. Then they distinguish and generate a list of the local industries that are major contributors to that area's reported poundage of air, ground, and water pollutants. Next, Cash-McConnell expands the critical thinking with this step: "Identify which major businesses in your city are at the top of the watchdog list." Students realize that the big business employers of their cities—for example, marinas and utility companies—may be the major contributors to a city's pollution. This is an "aha!" moment as they reflect and predict an ethical challenge for any city's growth (ACRL Standards Three and Four).

The second task requires learners to use a chamber of commerce site. They are directed to follow educational links for a city's local community college(s) to identify popular associate degree career majors. With an introductory lecture, Cash-McConnell explains the difference between an associate degree designed for transfer and one for immediate employment and models an analytic construct of how a community college best serves the workforce needs of the region. For example, SCCC offers degrees in culinary arts, interior design assistant, and nursing (RN or LPN), all of which include internships and the opportunity for immediate job placement upon graduation. The professor fosters dialogue on the demographic factors that give rise to expanding both entry and professional level employment opportunities for these and other careers in eastern Suffolk County. This coaching helps learners work through the next step, which is framed in this way: "Identify and hypothesize how five career majors at the local community college may address demographic issues and supply a trained workforce in the city you selected" (ACRL Standard Four).

For the third task, we provide instruction and workshop time to discuss academic integrity and how to cite sources in MLA style. Students learn how to prepare bibliographic citations for the final slide of their presentation. Since library sessions have been increased from one to four, the quality of the citations has shown a marked improvement. An understanding of academic integrity is evident in both their citations and their presentations (ACRL Standard Five).

Collaboration with the SCCC reference librarians has been crucial to the students' projects and also beneficial to Cash-McConnell, who had no previous training in how to locate current demographic data on the students' cities. She has learned the same techniques required of students and is prepared to provide guidance to them as their projects evolve.

The searching and evaluating requires the learners to apply critical thinking strategies to select appropriate information and determine how to incorporate it into their projects. The scaffolded dialogues that Cash-McConnell fosters in the classroom help them reconsider some of their premises for why population shifts have occurred in their selected cities and what those shifts mean for city infrastructure. Critical reflection is paramount in each step of the information competency and classroom process. The course provides the opportunity for students, who are simultaneously in ESL Composition II, with the opportunity to hone their skills in determining such constructs as the main idea and supporting details of their arguments. It also fully supports the demands in the advanced reading and grammar classes, which focus on various clause structures and their underlying meanings in text (ACRL Standard Four).

TECHNOLOGICAL COMPETENCY: AN INCREMENTAL PROCESS

Interspersed with the library workshops are multiple sessions in technology instruction, ensuring that students acquire the competencies to successfully complete the semester-long project. The students are empowered by gaining facility with MS Excel and PowerPoint to present demographic information. The learners transfer their research to an electronic slide show format with the assistance of peer tutors and professional assistants who demonstrate this process. They bond as a socioconstructive learning community through the discussion and refinement of the manipulation of the computer tools. Although the technology literacy of each student varies, they all learn how to e-mail documents and correct comments inserted by the professor as well as attempt to present a substantive and well-paced slide show. They stay connected to the project and reinforce a sense of learning community with intermittent e-mail messages to the class. They learn from seeing others' performances. Students also raise or readjust their own expectations of themselves in line with the rubrics that assess the scaffolded skills throughout the semester (ACRL Standard Four).

The students' three major oral performances are videotaped with a digital camcorder as they build their projects in increments. Cash-McConnell subsequently transfers each videotaped performance to a compact disk (CD-ROM). Students can easily view these recordings on a computer and use the rubric "Student Self-scoring Rubric for Oral Presentations: Delivery Criteria" to assess team and individual performances (Figure 8.3). When the professor critiques the recording, she uses a similar rubric to comment on student progress in the acquisition and use of academic discourse. She also adds captions to particular frame images on the CD-ROM, highlighting a student's mastery or errors in usage of the strings of targeted discourse. The captions help students see and hear where their errors tend to occur. The three videos of increasingly difficult tasks provide immediate feedback to the students (ACRL Standards Three and Four).

Figure 8.3. EF06: ESL College Listening/Speaking II Student Self-scoring Rubric for Oral Presentations: Delivery Criteria

Student Self-scoring Rubric for Oral Presentations:
Delivery Criteria

View your videotaped presentation and self-score yourself on this rubric. I will also score your performance. We will then meet to discuss your progress in this class.

	1 Weak	2 Fair	3 Adequate	4 Very good	5 Excellent
Use of the time allotted for speaking	1	2	3	4	5
Begins speech effectively	1	2	3	4	5
Key ideas are clear	1	2	3	4	5
Clear support for key ideas	1	2	3	4	5
Use of appropriate vocabulary to describe graphs/tables	1	2	3	4	5
Explanation of the subjects of the tables/graphs	1	2	3	4	5
Explanations of axis/column details of the graphs/tables	1	2	3	4	5
Pronunciation of numerical terms	1	2	3	4	5
Use of transition terms and coordinating conjunctions	1	2	3	4	5
Word order of phrases/clauses of grammar strings	1	2	3	4	5
Implications of the findings of the research	1	2	3	4	5
Concludes speech effectively	1	2	3	4	5
Cites a few sources orally	1	2	3	4	5
Overall organization of the presentation	1	2	3	4	5
Innovative and creative in approach	1	2		4	5
Eye contact	1	2	3	4	
Use of gestures	1	2	3	4	5
Rapport with audience	1	2	3	4	5
Evidence of risk-taking	1	2	3	4	5

Overall Evaluation: 1   2   3   4   5   Length of presentation: ____ minutes

The class sees a dramatic difference between the first and third tapings of their work. Recordings are timed for the third, seventh, and thirteenth weeks of the 14-week course. In the initial six weeks, they work on their first two projects with different partners: a team project on Pittman's 1986 narrative *A Grain of Rice* is a five-minute dramatized performance that includes quantitative expressions. It is followed by a seven-minute academic explanation of a data table based on the dramatic growth of selected cities in the latest census period; students use an overhead projector for the presentation on the demographic data, so the focus is on delivery, not technology (ACRL Standards Three and Four).

Between the seventh and thirteenth week, students prepare for the final individual project: an analysis of population shift in one city, requiring a ten-minute academic presentation with electronic slide support. The final videotaping records each student's 12-slide digital presentation. Student presentations integrate use of IL and critical thinking strategies as well as competency with MS Excel, Word, PowerPoint, and SMART Board tools. To reach this point, Cash-McConnell and more tech-savvy student peers use the SMART Board to explain how to create, incorporate, and enhance charts and images. The class begins this component by using MS Excel to input data for tables and graphs and to analyze data regarding ethnicity, educational attainment, and employment sectors. During this stage, they use MS Word to type data interpretations, noting the implications for their cities' infrastructures. As part of the assessment process, students e-mail both Excel and Word attachments to Cash-McConnell. The professor responds using the MS Word features to insert comments and track changes, and returns attachments to them to edit and resubmit electronically. They gradually master how to locate, save, and cite downloadable maps and photographs for use in the slide shows. More advanced students take on a leadership role in tutoring their peers in the software skills, and may even incorporate sound effects in PowerPoint. By the time all of the students give their digital presentations, peer rapport with the class is maximized, for they have been learning how to use the touch features of the SMART Board and have become accustomed to being on camera (ACRL Standards Three and Four).

Students' PowerPoint slides and video recordings of their presentations indicate to Cash-McConnell whether they have attained step four of the constructivist model, the level of internal scaffolding, as they interpret knowledge of their cities. Students cannot merely read the hard data they have collected; they must use the targeted academic discourse in their presentations. By using logical strings of grammar with academic terminology embedded, the students demonstrate their ability to convey the trends made apparent by data analysis. For example, ER, in referring to her data on Boston's vehicles per household, explained to the class that whereas some households have three vehicles, others have none (Figure 8.4). She clearly connected this data with Boston's existing option of mass transit and future

Figure 8.4. ER's Slide: Boston's Traffic Congestion —Vehicles per Household (Spring 2004)	
Boston's Traffic	
• 1 vehicle	105,300
• 2 vehicles	43,250
• 3 vehicles	10,962
• No vehicles	76,194

implications for the city's infrastructure if vehicles per household were to increase. Another student, CR, highlighted the environmental challenges facing Las Vegas (Figure 8.5). Her elaborations on the impact of population

Figure 8.5. CR's Slide: Las Vegas's Environmental Challenges (Fall 2004)
Las Vegas's Challenges
• New energy sources
• Solar supply
• Water plan

growth in that desert location were well developed in her discussion of the need for conservation of natural resources and alternative energy sources.

BENCHMARKS OF STUDENT PROGRESS

Bealle and Cash-McConnell use various instruments to assess outcome behaviors and student perceptions regarding the acquisition of targeted outcome behaviors. Cash-McConnell uses rubrics to assess the following: aural comprehension and oral explanations of data, usage and accuracy of the targeted academic language, critical thinking strategies, and technological competency. One rubric is a "Student Self-scoring Survey of the Learning Process" distributed at closure of the course (Figure 8.6a). In addition, student perceptions of their learning are appraised using narrative surveys. Cash-McConnell also creates an electronic portfolio of students' work. This archive is useful for analysis of learner growth both within a semester and to compare classes over time.

Acquisition of IL competency skills is assessed with three additional instruments. First, pre- and posttests consisting of multiple choice questions are evaluated. Second, anecdotal data is collected during the last class meeting as a library faculty member leads an informal discussion to determine student impressions of what they gained from the library instruction sessions. Third, a written evaluation of an Internet source that students used for their demographic project is completed by each participant during the final class meeting (Figure 8.6b). The results of the spring 2007 "Student Self-scoring Survey of the Learning Process" strongly suggest that the participants recognize that they have acquired a more complex range of capabilities to use library resources, apply technical skills, handle the targeted academic discourse, and create organized electronic presentations.

Over the semester, students valued their own critiques of video-recorded performances as a self-assessment tool with comments such as, "When I was reviewing the film I was correcting myself" (DS: May 9, 2007). They closely analyzed their CD-ROMs, noting errors as well as improvements in gestures, use of note cards, pronunciation, grammar structures, speech organization, use of digital technology, and a sense of confidence. For example, "I felt really confident when I was talking about the majors offered by the community college supporting the

Figure 8.6a. EF06: ESL College Listening/Speaking II Student Self-scoring Survey of the Learning Process					
Student Self-scoring Survey of Learning Process					
Circle the number that best represents your reaction to the following:	1 Not at all	2 Poorly	3 Adequately	4 Well	5 Extremely well
a. I am now able to give an interesting oral presentation, using academic English, such as quantitative information.	1	2	3	4	5
b. When I reviewed the videos of my presentations, they helped me understand my performance's strengths and weaknesses.	1	2	3	4	5
c. Our discussions of table/graph interpretations have helped me understand the academic vocabulary, numerical terms, and grammar in this course.	1	2	3	4	5
d. Preparing my presentations of the table/graph interpretations has helped me practice saying and writing academic vocabulary, grammar, and numerical terms.	1	2	3	4	5
e. Put an (x) beside the skills you can now comfortably do. _____ Take dictation of academic sentences _____ Take dictation of numbers and quantities _____ Search on the Internet for a city's business information _____ Search on the Internet for environmental challenges facing a city _____ Explain, with supporting details, why a population rose or fell over time					

top job activities because I deeply researched this topic and I was impressed how perfectly those two aspects matched" (ES: May 9, 2007). Furthermore, they supported the learning community with whom they had bonded by expressing wonder at and appreciation of the creativity of others' slide shows and oral performances.

Students also reflected on growth they had made in other language areas. They reported significant improvement in: ability to locate key information, acquisition of contextual vocabulary, reading speed as a result of the extensive online searches, and organizational writing skills to prepare their presentations.

Student comments demonstrate the value of the technology instruction in the course. Learners shared that their technical competencies expanded as a result of the integrated instruction, whether they were novices or more experienced. The mastery of the basics of PowerPoint was a strong motivator and a reward in itself for the novices as reflected in statements such as, "Now I know how to use PowerPoint and coordinate information from Internet or another source" (BB:

Figure 8.6b. Responses to Student Self-scoring Survey of the Learning Process (Spring 2007)					
Student Self-scoring Survey of Learning Process					
Survey Question	1 Not at all	2 Poorly	3 Adequately	4 Well	5 Extremely well
a			2	11	1
b				8	6
c			1	8	5
d			1	6	7

Responses to item "e"
13   Take dictation of academic sentences
14   Take dictation of numbers and quantities
14   Search on the Internet for a city's business information
14   Search on the Internet for environmental challenges facing a city
14   Explain, with supporting details, why a population rose or fell over time

Note: The enrollment was 15, the seat maximum; 14 students completed the survey (*n* = 14).

May 9, 2007). The more tech-savvy students delighted in using their expertise to peer tutor in segments of the Excel and PowerPoint lessons. For example, a student who helped teach a mini-lesson wrote on the survey: "I [previously] got a lot of experience with all the computer software used in this semester [MS Word, PowerPoint, Excel]. But the experience of teaching and helping a whole class was unique. Thank you!" (MR: May 9, 2007).

Participants' statements also demonstrate that the infused IL instruction nurtured substantive improvements in fundamental research. They were amazed at the amount of reliable information they could find on the library databases and felt they could recognize reliable Web sites. In the end of semester surveys, they commented that whereas with a Google search they spend significant time muttering, "Next, next, next . . . " to themselves as they link to one Web site after another, on the library databases they more quickly find relevant, authoritative information. One student commented, "The library database saves us time because in Google or Yahoo they gave us so many Web sites, and not all of them are necessary" (SP: May 11, 2005). In the written evaluations of a Web source (Figure 8.7) participants demonstrated an understanding of applying evaluative criteria such as currency and the author's credibility to determine if the information was reliable and relevant enough to use in their research project. They reported increased confidence, for they had successfully worked through the ambiguities of their tasks to make sense of their research questions. This student comment sums up the McLuhan type of *cool* energy that propelled participants in the IL

Figure 8.7. EF06: ESL College Listening/Speaking II Evaluate Information from a WWW Source

Evaluate Information from a WWW Source

Select an information source that you used for your research project. The source can be from a library database (e.g., Facts.com, World Almanac; Custom Newspapers), a library-recommended WWW source (e.g., MapStats: United States; U.S. Census Bureau; American Factfinder), or another WWW source.

Name of WWW source: _____

URL of WWW source: _____

In a paragraph explain why this WWW source is useful and reliable for your research project. Another way of saying this is: Why would you recommend this source for a student working on this project?

You will essentially be answering the questions that you should ask yourself when you are deciding if an information source is appropriate for your college research project.

- Why is this source credible? Who is the author?
- Is it accurate and objective? How does it help you understand your subject?

Is the information current enough for your needs?

---

process: "I think it was cool to do this research because now I can talk to people about different cities in the United States" (AS: May 9, 2007). Gratifying to Cash-McConnell and the library faculty is the extent to which the students realize that the reference librarian is a valuable resource for their research needs. In written surveys and oral briefings students note that they are comfortable asking a librarian for assistance. On our small campus, the reference librarians are familiar with the demographics project and regularly field questions from the class members.

Learners' written reflections on their own progress closely match the outcomes that Cash-McConnell had hoped for in the course. Her paradigm, based on constructivist pedagogy, successfully fosters the intentional integration of academic discourse communication skills with critical evaluation strategies and technical competencies. This model has resulted in positive outcomes for the ESL learners consistent not only with Cash-McConnell's aspirations and the TESOL standards for her field but also with the performance indicators of the ACRL information literacy competency standards, and those of our institution's accrediting agency the Middle States Commission on Higher Education (MSCHE).

Through the realization of the final project, the ESL students demonstrate proficiency in the IL and technological competency skills required by the MSCHE in Standard 11, Educational Offerings, and Standard 12, General Education (Middle States Commission on Higher Education, 2006). They use technologies such as library databases, USB drives, and spreadsheet software "to identify, retrieve, and apply relevant information" (Standard 11, p. 42). In addition, through our constructivist approach, they demonstrate facility with "oral and written communication . . . quantitative reasoning, critical analysis . . . and technological competency" (Standard 12, p. 47). These competencies are demonstrated in crucial outcome behaviors, including: the recognition that library databases are often more appropriate sources for college than Googled Web sites, the ability to cite their sources in a consistent style and articulate the importance of documenting sources, and the incorporation of information and quantitative content from their research as well as targeted language into their digital presentations. Our assessment indicates that when library instruction is increased from one to four class sessions per semester, improvement in culminating projects is significant.

Students also gradually learn to trust their own voices for their presentations. The course provides intense practice in numerous synonym structures to express a message. However, those who attempt to memorize statements verbatim from a Web site do not succeed; the idioms and style are cumbersome for them, resulting in stage fright and poor performance. Such an experience provides the teachable moment for the class to realize that rephrasing is essential. Speaking in one's own voice is a critical step to establishing identity within the academic environment. As one student remarked, "The course helped me to better understand academic English because I mostly listen only to 'regular' English at work" (PK: December 13, 2006).

CONCLUSION

Over a semester, the ESL students' experiences with an incremental approach to IL yield lasting results. They demonstrate a strong grasp of critical thinking strategies and usage of targeted discourse. The class also forms a learning community that challenges its members to raise their performance to higher levels (Babbitt, 2006). Students become more comfortable with using the "semantically dense sentences" germane to a discussion of a demographic issue (McCarthy, 2006: 2). The course's emphasis on technological competency reinforces the constructivist process as students construct knowledge in their projects (Kern, 2006: 200). Their fluency with the technology also gives them the confidence to use their digital presentation skills in subsequent content courses and to enroll in online classes. These ESL students have begun an identification with and socialization into the academic milieu.

CURRENT CHALLENGES AND FUTURE DIRECTIONS

The results of our collaboration have been gratifying, and we have enjoyed sharing them with our SCCC colleagues and in presentations at professional conferences. Wider dissemination of this model is highly desirable. Nevertheless, the time-intensive nature of the collaboration presents obstacles. Particularly difficult to replicate is the time and dedication required to videotape the students throughout the semester. While we fully intend to continue with ESL016 as a pedagogical showcase, which is dependent on the extraordinary commitment of professors such as Cash-McConnell, we are also working to develop modified versions that may be embraced by a wider teaching audience or perhaps supported by campus technology partnerships. In this regard, we have experienced some notable successes.

Another challenge for the collaboration has been the scheduled time for the class at the Eastern Campus. During the initial semesters when this course was a daytime offering, Bealle provided the infused library instruction. More recently, it has been an evening class, testing the transferability of the collaboration. An experienced part-time librarian, April Brazill, has been providing this infused instruction. Meanwhile, Bealle and Cash-McConnell have frequently conferred to refine the plans for the instructional sequence upon which Brazill has based her lessons.

An important milestone in the evolution of the course has been the grant-funded Faculty Development Workshop titled "Information Literacy Prepares Developmental Studies Students for Academic Success." Bealle and Cash-McConnell featured their collaboration when they led this workshop during the 2006–2007 academic year. This program was presented over four nonconsecutive days on all three campuses. It heightened interest for infused IL and techno-logical competency instruction in other SCCC courses. As a result, aspects of our collaboration have been adapted by numerous colleagues who participated in these discussions.

To date, with focus on the IL component, Bealle and Cash-McConnell have incorporated a less ambitious collaboration into an additional ESL course, ESL College Reading II. In addition, an ESL colleague who attended our faculty devel-opment workshop now infuses IL instruction into ESL College Composition II. Several faculty from other disciplines have also incorporated an IL component consisting of two or three hands-on IL instructional sessions. One professor of developmental reading has integrated the IL and computer instructional com-ponents into her class, but has not ventured into the videotaping component.

If there is a drawback to our approach it is that the whole package is extremely time intensive for both the library and classroom faculty members. It may be prohibitive for classroom faculty to incorporate technology as extensively as in this case study without substantial campus technology support. Indeed, if the Eastern Campus Library at SCCC were to remain as intensively involved with Cash-McConnell's classes as it currently is, then it would not be practical from a people-hour perspective to replicate this model for an ever-increasing number of courses without a corresponding increase in the number of library faculty.

Despite these concerns, the pedagogical value of our process makes it a model worth aspiring to. Students gain academic confidence by having structured contact with library resources and library faculty as well as with academic computing resources and professionals. Clearly, this is vital for all students, not just ESL learners, whose first impulse in today's complex information landscape may be to Google their way through their research assignments. An additional challenge, of course, is how to provide such a pedagogically sound approach in an era of limited resources.

On a positive note, our collaboration and grant-funded faculty development venture have increased IL visibility and credibility at SCCC. Our recent MSCHE reaccreditation self-study includes the recognition that the college provides many opportunities for IL instruction. Although we do not currently have a college-wide incremental IL program, our collaboration has provided a prototype for one course with the goal that it could be refined and more widely applied. Our current goal is expansion of this prototype within the ESL curriculum at the Eastern Campus, and eventually as an institution-wide component in the ESL program.

Like any successful endeavor, this collaboration has experienced many transformations (and will surely experience many more). These transformations indicate the extent to which the course has become embedded into the fabric of ESL and IL instruction at the Eastern Campus, and is gaining visibility on the other SCCC campuses.

ACKNOWLEDGMENTS

The authors gratefully acknowledge the support and assistance of the SCCC Eastern Campus Library reference team, especially Mary Ann Miller, Jay Schwartz, and April Brazill, and the Educational Technology Unit staff, particularly Edward Hassildine and Grzegorz Fabiszewski. In addition, we wish to recognize the conscientious efforts of the ESL016 students and the inspiration of former colleagues at SUNY Stony Brook, Jacqueline Grennon Brooks and Dorit Kaufman, who promote reflective practice and a constructivist pedagogy. Without the dedicated and enthusiastic participation of all involved our collaboration would not be possible.

REFERENCES

Association of College and Research Libraries (ACRL). 2000. *Information Literacy Competency Standards for Higher Education*. Chicago: ACRL. Available: www.ala.org/ala/acrl/acrl standards/informationliteracycompetency.htm.
Babbitt, Marcia. 2006. "Strength in Community: Effectiveness of Community in Building College Success." In Marilyn Spaventa (Ed.), *Perspectives on Community College ESL, Volume 1: Pedagogy, Programs, Curricula, and Assessment* (pp. 61–67). Alexandria, VA: TESOL Publications.

Bordonaro, Karen. 2006a. "Language Learning in the Library: An Exploratory Study of ESL Students." *Journal of Academic Librarianship* 32, no. 5 (September): 518–526.

Bordonaro, Karen. 2006b. "We All Have an Accent: Welcoming International Students to the Library." *Feliciter* 52, no. 6: 240–241.

Brooks, Jacqueline Grennon. 2006. "Learning Among the Mandates." *The Constructivist* 17, no. 1 (Fall). Available: www.odu.edu/educ/act/journal/vol17no1/brooks.pdf.

Brooks, Jacqueline Grennon, and Martin G. Brooks. 1993. *In Search of Understanding: The Case for Constructivist Classrooms*. Alexandria, VA: Association for Supervision and Curriculum Development.

"Constructivism in the Classroom." 1994. *NAECS/SDE. Newsletters* (National Association of Early Childhood Specialists in State Departments of Education) 1, no. 3 (Summer). Available: http://naecs.crc.uiuc.edu/newsletter/volume1/number3.html.

Conteh-Morgan, Miriam E. 2001. "Empowering ESL Students: A New Model for Information Literacy Instruction." *Research Strategies* 18, no. 1: 29–38.

Conteh-Morgan, Miriam E. 2002. "Connecting the Dots: Limited English Proficiency, Second Language Learning Theories, and Information Literacy Instruction." *The Journal of Academic Librarianship* 28, no. 4: 191–196.

Conteh-Morgan, Miriam E. 2003. "Journey with New Maps: Adjusting Mental Models and Rethinking Instruction to Language Minority Students." In Hugh Thompson (Ed.), *Learning to Make a Difference: Proceedings of the Eleventh National ACRL Conference*, April 10–13, Charlotte, North Carolina (pp. 257–266). Chicago: ACRL.

DiMartino, Diane, and Lucinda R. Zoe. 2000. "International Students and the Library: New Tools, New Users, and New Instruction." In Trudi E. Jacobson and Helene C. Williams (Eds.), *Teaching the New Library to Today's Users* (pp. 17–24). New York: Neal-Schuman.

Ginsberg, Marjorie, and Nancy J. Weiner. 2007. "Writing in the Guise of a Persona: Combining Basic Reading, Library Research, and Video Performance." In Trudi E. Jacobson and Thomas P. Mackey (Eds.), *Information Literacy Collaborations that Work* (pp. 205–219). New York: Neal-Schuman.

Jacobson, Trudi E., and Thomas P. Mackey (Eds.). 2007. *Information Literacy Collaborations that Work*. New York: Neal-Schuman.

Jacobson, Trudi E., and Lijuan Xu. 2004. *Motivating Students in Information Literacy Classes*. New York: Neal-Schuman.

Kaufman, Dorit. 2004. "Constructivist Issues in Language Learning and Teaching." *Annual Review of Applied Linguistics* 24 (January): 303–319.

Kern, Richard. 2006. "Perspectives on Technology in Learning and Teaching Languages." *TESOL Quarterly* 40, no.1 (March): 183–210.

Laskin, Miriam. 2002. "Bilingual Information Literacy and Academic Readiness: Reading, Writing and Retention." *Academic Exchange Quarterly* 6, no. 4 (Winter): 41–46.

McCarthy, Michael. 2006. *Explorations in Corpus Linguistics*. Cambridge: Cambridge University Press.

McDonough, Kim, and Wanpen Chaikitmongkol. 2007. "Teachers' and Learners' Reactions to a Task-Based EFL Course in Thailand." *TESOL Quarterly* 41, no. 1 (March): 107–132.

McLuhan, Marshall. 1964. *Understanding the Media*. Cambridge, MA: MIT Press.

Middle States Commission on Higher Education (MSCHE). 2006. *Characteristics of Excellence in Higher Education: Eligibility Requirements and Standards for Accreditation.* Philadelphia: MSCHE.

Peña Delgado, Grace, and Susan Luévano. 2007. "Semillas de Cambio: The Teaching of Information Competency in Chicano and Latino Studies." In Trudi E. Jacobson and Thomas P. Mackey (Eds.), *Information Literacy Collaborations that Work* (pp. 95–108). New York: Neal-Schuman.

Pittman, Helena Clare. 1986. *A Grain of Rice.* New York: Bantam Skylark.

Reza-Hernandez, Laura. 2004. Book Review: *Schooling for Life: Reclaiming the Essence of Learning* by Jacqueline Grennon Brooks. *Teachers College Record* 106, no. 2 (February): 308–310.

Rockman, Ilene F., and Associates. 2004. *Integrating Information Literacy into the Higher Education Curriculum: Practical Models for Transformation.* San Francisco: John Wiley & Sons.

Spring, Michael B. 2002. "Interactive Systems." In Roger R. Flynn (Ed.), *Computer Sciences,* Vol. 1: *Foundations: Ideas and People.* (pp. 109–115). New York: Macmillan. Reference USA. Available: *Gale Virtual Reference Library,* Thomson Gale, SCCC, http://lib1.lib .sunysuffolk.edu:2053/gvrl.

Teachers of English to Speakers of Other Languages (TESOL). 2003. *TESOL/NCATE Program Standards. Standards for the Accreditation of Initial Programs in P-12 ESL Teacher Education.* Alexandria, VA: TESOL.

About the Editors and Contributors

Thomas P. Mackey, PhD, is Associate Dean at Empire State College, SUNY, at the Center for Distance Learning in Saratoga Springs, New York. Previously, he was the Associate Dean of Continuing Studies for the Sage Colleges in Albany, New York. Tom developed and taught his course on social and community informatics, discussed in the first chapter of this book, while he was a faculty member in Information Studies at the University at Albany, SUNY. His teaching and research interests involve information literacy, teaching with technology, Web-based multimedia, and social informatics. In 2007 he published a co-edited book with Trudi E. Jacobson for Neal-Schuman Publishers titled *Information Literacy Collaborations That Work*. He has published articles in such journals as *Computers & Education, The Journal of General Education, College Teaching, The Journal of Information Science,* and *The Journal of Education for Library and Information Science.* Tom worked with the Middle States Commission on Higher Education (MSCHE) as a member of the Advisory Panel on Information Literacy, which led to the publication of a guidebook on information literacy titled *Developing Research & Communication Skills: Guidelines for Information Literacy in the Curriculum* (2003). He may be contacted by e-mail at Tom.Mackey@esc.edu.

Trudi E. Jacobson, MLS, MA, is Head of User Education Programs at the State University of New York at Albany. She coordinates and teaches in the undergraduate Information Literacy course program. Her professional interests include the use of critical thinking and active learning activities in the classroom. She is the coauthor, with Lijuan Xu, of *Motivating Students in Information Literacy Classes* (Neal-Schuman, 2004), coeditor of *Information Literacy Collaborations that Work* (Neal-Schuman, 2007, with Thomas Mackey), *Teaching the New Library to Today's Users* (Neal-Schuman, 2000), and *Teaching Information Literacy Concepts: Activities and Frameworks from the Field* (Library Instruction Publications, 2001). She is the editor of *Critical Thinking and the Web: Teaching Users to Evaluate Internet Resources* (Library Instruction Publications, 2000). She has published articles in a number of journals, including *The Journal of General Education, College & Research Libraries, portal, Journal of Academic Librarianship, Research Strategies, College Teaching,* and *The Teaching Professor.* She is the editor of *Public Services Quarterly.* She may be contacted by e-mail at tjacobson@uamail.albany.edu.

✍️

Penny Bealle, MLS, PhD, is Associate Professor of Library Services and coordinates library instruction at the Eastern Campus of Suffolk County Community College. Prior to joining the library faculty at Suffolk she was the Collection Development Librarian at Adelphi University. She holds an MLS from Queens College (2000) and a PhD in Art History from Cornell University (1990). At Suffolk, she promotes infused library instruction as a means to enhance student outcome behaviors for critical thinking and synthesis skills. She may be reached by e-mail at beallep@sunysuffolk.edu.

Laura E. Briggs, BSc, MSc, MLIS, has a BSc in chemistry from the University of Waterloo (UW) and a MSc in inorganic chemistry from the University of Western Ontario. After earning her MLIS degree from Western, she returned to UW to haunt her former professors by becoming the chemistry librarian. In 2003, she jumped at the opportunity to work with UW's Centre for Learning and Teaching Through Technology (LT3), which she did until May, 2007, when she returned full time to the library. The position at LT3 allowed her to cajole faculty members (such as her coauthor James Skidmore) into making the library's resources an integral part of their courses.

Keith Butler, PhD, is Associate Dean of Extended Learning at California State University–San Marcos (CSUSM). His responsibilities include financial and business affairs, ongoing programs, marketing, and communications, biotechnology programs, and community linkage assistance. Prior to his current position Keith was the Director of Operations for the College of Business Administration at CSUSM as well as the Director of the Senior Experience program. Keith Butler received a PhD in Educational Leadership and Higher Education from the University of Nebraska–Lincoln and may be reached at kbutler@csusm.edu.

Kathleen Cash-McConnell, MA, MSEd, is a professor in the English as a Second Language Department (EF) at Suffolk County Community College's Eastern Campus in Riverhead. She is also the campus coordinator for placement and advising of ESL students at that campus. Her current focus is in integrating information literacy with computer assisted learning modules and teaching an advanced EF course online. She holds masters degrees in TESOL (teaching of English to speakers of other languages) from SUNY Stony Brook (1992) and in developmental reading from Long Island University (1984). Kathleen may be reached by e-mail at mcconnk@sunysuffolk.edu.

Jean Chow, RN, PhD, is an assistant professor with nurse midwifery and acupuncture clinical skills at the University of Calgary. She teaches in the Faculty of Nursing in the undergraduate and graduate programs. She completed her PhD in the Health Sciences Center at the University of Colorado. Her doctoral work focused on health promotion and the health messages in teen magazines. Her teaching incorporates inquiry learning and technology as a tool to facilitate student-centered goals. Jean may be contacted by e-mail at j.chow@ucalgary.ca.

Abby Clobridge, MS, is currently Digital Initiatives Group Leader at Bucknell University in Lewisburg, Pennsylvania. She was responsible for creating the foundation for Bucknell's Digital Library Program and coordinates day-to-day work related to building digital image collections. Prior to working at Bucknell, she worked as a news researcher at CNN. Her graduate degree is in library science from Florida State University, and her bachelor's degree is from Tufts University. Abby may be reached via e-mail at abby.clobridge@bucknell.edu.

Claudette Cloutier, MLIS, is Associate Librarian at the University of Calgary, responsible for library instruction in geology, geophysics, the natural sciences and northern studies. One of her interests is how students in the sciences incorporate information seeking into their coursework and into their professional careers. She may be reached by e-mail at claudette.cloutier@ucalgary.ca.

David Del Testa, PhD, is currently an assistant professor of history at Bucknell University in Lewisburg, Pennsylvania. His primary research concerns the radicalization of Vietnamese railroad workers during the 1920s and 1930s in French colonial Indochina and the impact of those radical workers on the anticolonial movements of the 1930s and 1940s. He primarily teaches courses in Modern Europe, Modern Southeast Asia, cross-cultural encounters, and on methods. He received his PhD from the University of California–Davis. David may be reached via e-mail at DeTham1913@yahoo.com.

Regina Eisenbach, PhD, is Associate Dean of the College of Business at California State University–San Marcos. Her responsibilities include serving as director of the Undergraduate Program which includes supervising college student advising services in addition to working with faculty on all curricular issues. She is also an associate professor of management. Her research has included topics such as power and influence strategies of leaders and followers, the nature of mentoring relationships, and pedagogical techniques designed to enhance adult learning.

Regina received her PhD from the University of Miami and may be reached by e-mail at regina@csusm.edu.

Ann Manning Fiegen, MLS, is Associate Librarian at California State University–San Marcos. She is liaison to College of Business Administration and to the department of economics in the College of Arts and Sciences. She has responsibilities for instruction, reference, and collection development. Her current publications and research are in the area of information literacy instruction for business in academic libraries. She is an active member of the American Libraries Association, where she has consulted with a team on information literacy for the Association of College and Research Libraries and served in various capacities within the Business Reference and Services Section of the Reference and User Services Association. Ann received her MLS from the University of Arizona. She may be reached by e-mail at afiegen@csusm.edu.

Cindy Graham, PhD, is currently Assistant Director of the Natural Sciences Program and holds a joint appointment between the Natural Sciences Program and the Department of Biological Sciences at the University of Calgary. She received her PhD from the University of Calgary in 2001 in the area of plant hormone physiology. Her current interests focus on building an authentic learning community within the Natural Sciences Program and improving students' abilities to communicate scientific information to both academic and nonacademic audiences. She may be contacted by e-mail at cmgraham@ucalgary.ca.

K. Alix Hayden, MLIS, PhD, has more than 14 years experience as a librarian in academic libraries and is currently the Librarian for Education, Nursing, and Kinesiology at the University of Calgary. She received her MLIS and MSc from the University of Alberta and completed her PhD in 2003 from the University of Calgary. Her doctoral work, supported by a three-year SSHRC Doctoral Fellowship, investigated undergraduate students' lived experience of information seeking. Her current research interests focus on establishing communities of practice among academic and school librarians. She may be reached by e-mail at ahayden@ucalgary.ca.

Nora Hillyer, MLS, is Reference Librarian and Subject Specialist at the University of Nebraska–Omaha Criss Library. Her subject specialties include information technology, engineering, math, physics, and all of the physical sciences. Nora teaches information literacy and her current research interest is in assessment of library instruction. Nora may be contacted via e-mail at nhillyer@mail.unomaha.edu.

Marvel Maring, MLIS, MFA, received her MLIS and MFA in book arts in 2003 from the University of Alabama in Tuscaloosa. She joined the staff at the Dr. C. C. and Mabel L. Criss Library in 2004 and is the Fine Arts and Humanities Reference

Librarian. She serves as the library liaison and subject specialist for the departments of English, Foreign Languages, Theatre, Music, Art, and Art History. Her research interests include public programming, information literacy, and assessment. Marvel may be reached by e-mail at mmaring@mail.unomaha.edu.

Jean E. McLaughlin, MSLIS, is Honors College/Assessment Librarian at the State University of New York at Albany. She earned her MS in library and information science from Drexel University and has worked in health sciences and academic libraries. In addition to library positions, she worked in electronic publishing in health care information systems development. She may be reached by e-mail at JMcLaughlin@uamail.albany.edu.

Christopher P. Motz, BEd, BA, MA, is a newly appointed instructor at Carleton University in Ottawa. A former public school teacher, he returned to the university environment to pursue his interests in psychology and teaching at the postsecondary level. His academic interests include the scholarship of teaching and learning at the postsecondary level and the psychology of academic success, but his main love is jazz music. He may be contacted via e-mail at Chris_Motz@carleton.ca.

Timothy A. Pychyl, BSc, BEd, MA, PhD, is an associate professor of psychology at Carleton University, Ottawa, Canada. His research interest in procrastination complements his passion for teaching, with a clear focus on students and their learning. An early adopter of technology for teaching and learning, Dr. Pychyl has been recognized as a 3M National Teaching Fellow, and he was the inaugural recipient of the University Medal for Distinguished Teaching. When not engaged in teaching or research, he enjoys home life with his children Laurel and Alex, running his sled dogs, and tending horses with his wife Beth. Contact Tim through his Web site www.procrastination.ca.

Flavia Renon, BSc, BA, BEd, MLIS, is currently a reference/instruction librarian at Carleton University, Ottawa, Canada. She taught high school for over ten years before joining the ranks at Carleton University. Her areas of interest include the transition from high school to university, library/community partnerships, and graduate students and information literacy. She may be contacted by e-mail at flavia_renon@carleton.ca.

Dorianne Richards, MA, is a lecturer in the English Department at University of Nebraska–Omaha and recently accepted the position of Writing Center Director. She became part of the U.N.O. faculty upon completing her MA in English there in 1995. Her primary assignment has been to teach English 116, Argument and Research, the second course in a two-semester English sequence for undergraduates. Dori's areas of interest include using technology to teach composition, collaborative pedagogy for the undergraduate classroom, digital portfolios, and visual rhetoric. Dori may be reached by e-mail at drichards@mail.unomaha.edu.

Shauna Rutherford, MLIS, is Information Literacy Coordinator at the University of Calgary. Finding effective and innovative means of teaching students how to find and use information has been the focus of Shauna's career since she began working at the U of C in 1997. Since that time she has worked with professors and students in the faculties of Communication & Culture, Social Sciences, Environmental Design, and Social Work. She may be reached by e-mail at srutherf@ucalgary.ca.

James M. Skidmore, PhD, is Associate Professor of German Studies at the University of Waterloo. A child of the Canadian prairies, he studied French and German at the University of Saskatchewan and acquired a PhD in German at Princeton University. When he is not dispensing indispensable wisdom about all things German, he sits in his luxuriously appointed office where his coauthor Laura Briggs cajoles him into integrating library instruction into courses on German culture. James takes great interest in the use of course management systems for the organization and enhancement of student learning. Learn more about James at www.arts.uwaterloo.ca/~skidmore.

Index